THE GALILEO CONNECTION

Resolving Conflicts between Science & the Bible

CHARLES E. HUMMEL

INTERVARSITY PRESS
DOWNERS GROVE, ILLINOIS 60515

InterVarsity Press is the book-publishing division of Inter-Varsity Christian Fellowship, a student movement active on campus at hundreds of universities, colleges and schools of nursing. For information about local and regional activities, write IVCF, 233 Langdon St., Madison, WI 53703.

Distributed in Canada through InterVarsity Press, 860 Denison St., Unit 3, Markham, Ontario L3R 4H1, Canada.

Quotations from the Bible, unless otherwise noted, are taken from the Holy Bible, New International Version. Copyright © 1973, 1978, International Bible Society. Used by permission of Zondervan Bible Publishers.

Figures 1, 4 and 5 are adapted from Galileo, Science and the Church (Ann Arbor, Mich.: University of Michigan Press, 1971), © Jerome Langford, and used by permission.

Figures 2 and 3 are from Thomas S. Kuhn, The Copernican Revolution, published by Harvard University Press, 1957, and reprinted by permission.

Permissions for the portraits at the beginnings of chapters have been granted as follows:
Aristotle, Copernicus, Kepler, Galileo (p. 9), Newton, Darwin, Maxwell and Pascal: courtesy Burndy Library.
Galileo (p. 81): Smithsonian Institute Libraries.
Augustine, Bellarmine and Calvin: Historical Pictures Service, Chicago.
Gray: Collections of the Library of Congress.
Lewis: Bettmann Archive/BBC Hulton.

Cover: Guy Wolek

ISBN 0-87784-500-X

Printed in the United States of America

Library of Congress Cataloguing in Publication Data
Hummel, Charles E.
  The Galileo connection.

  Bibliography: p.
    1. Science, Renaissance.   2. Bible and science.
  3. Science—Philosophy.   4. Galilei, Galileo,
  1564-1642.   I. Title.
  Q125.2.H86   1986   509'.032   85-24057
  ISBN 0-87784-500-X

17   16   15   14   13   12   11   10   9   8   7   6   5   4   3   2   1
99   98   97   96   95   94   93   92   91   90   89   88   87   86

To
Bernard Ramm
and
Richard Bube, Frank Cassel,
Walter Hearn, Jim Neidhardt

Preface

Since the time of Galileo, science has replaced theology on the throne of Western thought. It has won this position through many conflicts in which biblical Christianity found itself on the defensive. Often failure to define terms and identify basic issues has sparked unnecessary controversy.

My suggestions for resolving conflicts between science and the Bible are meant to be a constructive way forward and not a final solution—a foundation rather than a completed structure. I have had two primary goals: (1) to whet the appetite of general readers with little if any scientific background and (2) to provide an up-to-date introduction to the history and philosophy of science and its relationship to the biblical perspective on the natural world.

I want to express my profound gratitude to the scholars who have devoted their lives to research and writing in this crucial arena. I am indebted to many theologians and scientists among my friends who took time to critique this manuscript and offer suggestions for improvement.

Above all I want this book to deepen our understanding of the creative and redemptive activity of the living God: the Maker of heaven and earth, the Lord and Judge of history.

Preface

Prolog
THE TRIAL

*The Bible tells us
how to go to Heaven,
not how
the heavens go.*
GALILEO GALILEI

ON JUNE 22, 1633, THE LONG TRIAL FINALLY ENDED. THE LAST session took place in Santa Maria Sopra Minerva, a Dominican convent in the center of Rome, built on the ruins of an ancient temple dedicated to the goddess of wisdom. The defendant, dressed in the white robe of a penitent, was led in. Shaking beneath the folds of his loose-fitting robe, Galileo Galilei knelt before the ten judges of the Inquisition to hear his sentence.

The clouds of that judicial storm had begun to gather early in 1632 when Galileo published his *Dialogue on the Two Principal World Systems*. Written in Italian rather than the Latin customarily used by scholars, it covered a wide range of topics in astronomy and physics. The book took the form of a conversation among three characters: Salviati, Simplicius and Sagredo. Salviati, advocating the Copernican theory of astronomy, was speaking for Galileo himself. Simplicius, the Aristotelian, resembled the obstinate university professors who had opposed Galileo over the years. The two advocates vied with each other to win the neutral Sagredo to their cause. Using that standard literary form of the day, an author could discuss hypothetically a controversial or even heretical doctrine without being held responsible for teaching it himself.

The *Dialogue* was a masterpiece of scientific writing easily understood by literate citizens. Public response was so enthusiastic that the first edition sold as fast as it came from the printer. Within a few months, however, a strong reaction began to brew in high places. Galileo had enemies in Rome who convinced Pope Urban VIII that he had been ridiculed by having his words put into the mouth of the foolish Simplicius. In August 1632, that simmering opposition boiled into ecclesiastical action. The Pope ordered the Florentine publisher to suspend all sales of the *Dialogue* and appointed a special committee to examine the book. Their report stated that Galileo had presented the Copernican teaching as fact rather than hypothesis. The *Dialogue* in its current form was unacceptable to the church; publication was to be suspended, pending correction.

Summoned to Rome
On October 1, the Inquisitor of Florence served Galileo with a summons from the Holy Office to appear in Rome within thirty days. Galileo was being called to account for promoting the doctrine that the earth is not stationary but moves around the sun. Since he had done everything required to obtain official approval before publication, the Inquisition's action took Galileo by surprise. Appalled at the sudden turn of events, he immediately went to bed in a state of shock.

Galileo was by then sixty-nine and in failing health. He suffered from arthritis and a double hernia, which required an iron truss. Further, the plague was raging unchecked. Galileo's physician ordered complete rest and warned against his taking such a journey of more than two hundred miles in winter weather. A medical certificate was sent to the Vatican with a request that the old scientist be spared the rigors of that trip. But the Holy Office demanded that Galileo come to Rome without undue delay.

The Grand Duke of Florence reluctantly advised him to go, providing a litter to minimize the pain of the journey. On January 23, 1633, Galileo set out for Rome. Three weeks later he arrived at the Villa Medici, where the Florentine ambassador, Francesco Niccolini, provided him with a comfortable apartment and servants for the next two months. Such a concession was unprecedented; all others called before the Tribunal, whether prelate or noble, had been placed in custody on their arrival in Rome.[1]

As the initial shock of his summons wore off, Galileo recovered some of his fighting spirit. The old warrior resolved to have it out with the authorities in a debate, confident of his position and power to persuade. Both Galileo and his influential friends believed that his case would gradually be allowed to die. To their dismay, the Holy Office sent notice on April 8 that Galileo would go on trial.

Four days later a hearing took place before the Commissary-General, Vincenzo Maculano, a Dominican friar. The questioning focused on certain events of 1616, when Galileo had gone to Rome to discuss his views with Cardinal Bellarmine. After an initial period of questioning about those discussions, the inquisitors revealed the contents of an injunction reportedly given to Galileo at that time:

> Galileo was by the said Commissary [Cardinal Bellarmine] commanded and enjoined, in the name of his Holiness the Pope and the whole Congregation of the Holy Office, to relinquish altogether said opinion that the Sun is the center of the world and immovable and that the Earth moves: nor further to hold, teach or defend it in any way whatsoever, verbally or in writing; otherwise proceedings would be taken against him in the Holy Office; which injunction the said Galileo acquiesced in and promised to obey.[2]

Galileo was shocked. He declared that he had never received that formal injunction and certainly not the words "in any way whatsoever, verbally or in writing." As proof of his assertion, he produced the notification Cardinal Bellarmine had actually given him, in the form of a *precetto,* a personal prohibition, not an official injunction. It concluded with the words, "It is set forth that the doctrine attributed to Copernicus is contrary to the Holy Scriptures and therefore cannot be defended or held."[3] Galileo remembered nothing about a charge not to teach or discuss it "in any way whatsoever."

Now it was the judges' turn to be perplexed. Faced with a document that contradicted the report in the Vatican archives, they could not consult Bellarmine because he had died a decade earlier. The court decided to consider that problem later and to proceed with the questioning. The judges now focused on a more recent issue, the newly published *Dialogue*. When pressed about his views, Galileo responded, "I have neither maintained nor defended in that book the opinion that the Earth moves and that the Sun is stationary but have rather demonstrated the opposite of the Copernican opinion and shown that the arguments of Copernicus are weak and inconclusive."[4]

But Galileo went too far in his disclaimer. Although the Copernican in the *Dialogue* did not finally win the day, he so undermined his opponent's view that by no stretch of the imagination could the Aristotelian's reply be thought convincing. Galileo had kept the letter of the law but not the spirit. Like many prisoners under questioning, he protested too much—to his own undoing. His claim that he had demonstrated the opposite of the Copernican doctrine sounded like an attempt to fool the judges.

Five days after that hearing an official report conveyed the court's conclusion: Galileo had indeed maintained and defended the Copernican view. Further, there was a "vehement suspicion" that he still held it. The report cited a long list of passages in the *Dialogue* that left no doubt. Galileo had successfully countered the charge based on the reported injunction of 1616, but now his overly pious comments about conforming became a noose around his neck.

After two more interrogations during April and May, the case was sent up to higher authorities for a final decision. By that time Galileo had confessed his error, promised to correct it in the future and made a plea for mercy because of his poor health. Everything seemed to point to a mild sentence. But conflicting forces in a complex political struggle (described in chapter 5) brought about a crisis that overruled the Commissary's lenient recommendation.

On the morning of June 21, 1633, Galileo appeared in court for a final hearing. It had been decided that he should recant. He was questioned once again about his conviction concerning the systems of Ptolemy and Copernicus. In reply Galileo said, "I do not hold and have not held this opinion of Copernicus since the command was intimated to me that I must abandon it; for the rest, I am here in your hands—do with me as you please."[5] He was then held in custody overnight pending his appearance for sentencing.

Now, in the large hall of the Dominican convent, the final hour had arrived. The sentence declared the errors in the *Dialogue,* which would be banned by public edict. Galileo was pronounced "vehemently suspected of heresy" and given the following punishment: "We condemn you to the formal prison of this Holy Office during our pleasure, and by way of salutary penance we enjoin that for three years to come you repeat once a week the seven penitential Psalms. Reserving to ourselves liberty to moderate, commute, or take off, in whole or in part, the aforesaid penalties and penance."[6]

On June 30, Galileo was released in the custody of a friend, Archbishop Ascanio Piccolomini, to recover from his ordeal. After five months Pope Urban VIII allowed him to return to Florence. By December the old scientist was back home on his small farm of Arcetri, a few miles from that city. There, under house arrest for the remaining eight years of his life, Galileo continued his scientific investigations and writing.

Science versus Religion?

Over the centuries Galileo's condemnation by the Catholic church has loomed large in controversies between science and religion. His trial has been held up as the prime example of Christianity's hostility to free inquiry and to scientific progress. For example, one biography of Galileo concludes with this assessment:

> Galileo does stand as a classic example of the evils of a totalitarian regime. He was persecuted and prosecuted by men who . . . were afraid of the power of independent thought. Galileo queried the Scriptures, he made his own interpretation, and so cut right across the religious authority of the Church. . . . All they could see was a man who could disrupt their system, and they took the one course they could: they stifled the dissension at its source.[7]

But was the conflict so clear-cut? Whose system did Galileo set out to disrupt, the religious authority of Rome or the scientific authority of Aristotle? How did an academic conflict originating within the university become a theological issue for the church? And what forces of power politics—ambition, envy, prejudice, rancor, special interests—propelled the conflict to its disturbing conclusion?

Some of the questions raised by that seventeenth-century trial are still relevant to contemporary controversies between science and Christianity. For example, the creation-evolution issue is again prominent in American classrooms and courts. In the 1925 Scopes trial, a high-school teacher was prosecuted for breaking a Tennessee law against teaching evolution. After a sensational trial, public concern turned to other issues and eventually the law was repealed. The evolution-creation controversy seemed a thing of the past. Then, in 1969, the California State Board of Education was petitioned to recognize "creationism" as a scientifically valid doctrine deserving equal status with other scientific explanations of origins. Local school boards, state boards of education, and state legislatures across the country were soon under pressure to mandate the teaching of "scientific creationism" in public schools.

In 1980 Arkansas passed legislation to require equal time for teaching "creation-science" whenever evolution was taught. That law was immediately challenged in court by a variety of opponents, and two years later it was overturned. By now the fully revived controversy over various views of biblical creation and biological evolution has produced hundreds of articles and dozens of books.

By learning from the past we hope to avoid repeating its errors. For any intelligent discussion of these issues, we need to clear up two major areas of misunderstanding. The first concerns the nature of modern science and the status of its laws. Through the influence of naturalism, a philosophy that considers the natural world to be the whole of reality, the scientific method has come to be widely accepted as the only valid approach to understanding reality. Scientists are thought to be objective in their search for facts, as opposed to others (especially theologians) who are considered biased by their faith.

But is that a true picture? Each year Dr. Paul Earl, a biology professor at Nassau College on Long Island, New York, asks that question as he orients his classes. He tells his students that no scholars are completely objective, not even scientists. Like all others, they bring a certain point of view and their own set of values to their subject. Because authors seldom reveal their presuppositions at the outset of their books, Earl teaches his classes how to discover a book's biases and evaluate its conclusions accordingly. The students react with surprise; halfway through college, they have never before heard a scientist admit any kind of subjective bias. Professor Earl, who is a Christian, also shows his students the limitations of science and the provisional nature of its theories.

A second area of misunderstanding has to do with proper interpretation of the Bible. Many think that one can prove almost anything from Scripture. They point to a bewildering spectrum of popular doctrines that seem to support that view. Yet the biblical texts cannot legitimately be made to teach whatever a person wants to find. As with any other kind of literature, the meaning is best determined by recognized rules of interpretation respecting the author's purpose, historical context, literary forms and usage of words.

This book tries to clear up both misunderstandings by exploring the nature, purpose and limitations of the scientific and biblical views of nature, and the relationship of those views to each other. The initial approach is historical, an attempt to understand how the scientific method developed during the sixteenth and seventeenth centuries. We will focus not only on revolutionary scientific ideas but also on the lives of those who played major roles in the revolution. Science developed through the work of many individuals with their personal motivations, religious convictions and quirks of personality. They were influenced by the cultural constraints, economic conditions and political pressures of their times.

Historians of science have sometimes selected an important law of contemporary science and then traced its origin back to the scientific revolution. That method can ignore the breakdown of once-accepted and useful theories, bypassing the intellectual wanderings of scientists along meandering routes to occasional dead ends. Historians who know what they are looking for could search in the most likely areas and produce a success story unblemished by failures. In contrast to such a *linear* view of history stands the *contextual* view which aims at better understanding of the thought processes of the same scientists: "On this second view, history of science must not only account for present theories in the light of past developments, it must also assess old theories in terms of the conceptual framework of the scientists who held them, and judge them against the background of the world picture of their age."[8]

In this book the historical chapters take the contextual approach a step further, examining the total life of four prominent scientists:

Nicholas Copernicus, Johannes Kepler, Galileo Galilei and Isaac Newton. We will view each one in the context of his family background, cultural and political milieu, religious commitment and the personal as well as the scientific problems he faced. In our brief acquaintance we will try to understand each scientist's circumstances, to walk in his shoes. What was his attitude toward Christianity? What influence did Christian commitment have on his scientific work? And how did he relate his discoveries to the biblical view of nature?

The Scientific Revolution

When does a political revolution begin? We usually think of an overt military action: Julius Caesar crossing the Rubicon, leading his army toward Rome; citizens storming the Bastille in Paris; the shots exchanged at Lexington and Concord. Revolutions actually begin, however, in the minds of people who have grown restive under an old regime. Dissatisfaction with the status quo creates cracks in the system. A desire for change gradually permeates the thought of a growing number of people until some outstanding figure rises to lead them. Suddenly thought becomes action, the momentum increases, and open conflict flares between new and old authorities. The palace is stormed and finally falls in a decisive battle. Yet even after the new regime takes control, dissident elements remain active for a time throughout the realm.

Revolution—whether political, social or religious—requires both process and crisis.[9] Such a pattern of continuity and discontinuity, lasting one hundred fifty years, was characteristic of the scientific revolution. The late medieval and early Renaissance period was a time of ferment in many dimensions of life and thought. Aristotle's philosophy, which had dominated Western science for more than fifteen hundred years, was being questioned. A significant salvo against his system of thought was fired by Copernicus in 1543 with the publication of *On the Revolutions of the Heavenly Spheres*. Its immediate impact was slight, but that work, like a delayed-action bomb, eventually blew apart the traditional cosmology.

The next shots also came on the celestial front. Johannes Kepler reaffirmed the Copernican system in his *New Astronomy* of 1609, showing that the planetary orbits were ellipses and not the perfect circles taught by Aristotle. Meanwhile Galileo was attacking traditional science on the terrestrial front of physics; he also supported Copernicus with telescopic discoveries and polemic writing. A final barrage came in 1687, when Newton published *Mathematical Principles of Natural Philosophy,* containing his laws of universal gravitation and motion.

The discoveries of these four men in astronomy and physics, and especially their method of investigation, established a new kind of science on a foundation of mathematics and experimentation. This approach to the natural world led to the development of modern chemistry in the eighteenth century, geology and biology in the nineteenth, and a second revolution in astronomy and physics in the twentieth.

Of the four scientists, Galileo occupies the center of our stage for several reasons. It was he who waged an unrelenting attack against the contemporary followers of Aristotle for almost fifty years. When Galileo's scientific opponents turned the controversy into a religious issue, he replied by differentiating between the scientific and biblical views of nature.[10] Since his subsequent trial has been widely misrepresented and used as a weapon against the church, the facts need to be known. Galileo was both a pioneering scientist and a practicing Christian. His experience can point the way for those in current conflicts who wish to maintain the integrity of both science and the Bible.

Through the scientific revolution science won an important role in the development of Western society. It has been a leading influence in shaping our values. Thomas Kuhn observes that "contemporary Western civilization is more dependent both for its everyday philosophy and for its bread and butter, upon scientific concepts than any past civilization has been."[11] At the same time, the discoveries of science have made possible a technology able to destroy the earth's environment as well as human life. Science has become a valuable but dangerous tool that needs ethical guidelines for constructive use. It is urgent that we understand the value and limitations of science in order to enhance its partnership with Christianity.

A Personal Journey

This book is a result of my lifelong interest in both the Bible and modern science. While studying chemistry and physics in high school, I eagerly read Christian books on science. The few available volumes attempted to demonstrate the scientific reliability of the Bible and so gain a respectful hearing for its message. Armed with such arguments, I went off to university to study science and convert my skeptical classmates. In many vigorous discussions about miracles, natural laws and evolution—some wins, some losses—I failed to prove the truth of the Bible and thus win my friends to Christ. In fact such discussions rarely moved toward a consideration of the life, death and resurrection of the Savior. Yet it never occurred to me to question the strategy of my campaign for Christianity until my senior year. It was a non-Christian friend who took me to task: "Why are you so desperately concerned to make the Bible scientifically respectable? Isn't Christianity essentially a matter of commitment to Jesus Christ?"

Later, in graduate school, I discovered a more effective approach to present the claims of Christ. It was also more biblical, having been used two thousand years ago by a physician named Luke in writing one of the Gospels. He reported the *historical* reliability of his information about Jesus Christ so that his reader might "know the certainty of the things you have been taught" (Lk 1:4 NIV). I have found that his approach—also used consistently by the apostles in their preaching—brings people to face the Lord who calls for their repentance and faith.

Nevertheless, I continued my interest in the relationship of modern science to biblical teaching. Those questions sowed seeds that flowered many years later on a sabbatical leave as I studied the history and philosophy of science. The consequences of a science-proves-the-Bible approach then became clear. It was unsettling to realize that, contrary to popular opinion, our scientific laws present only a partial view of nature. Further, they are subject to revision and possible rejection. A Bible whose credibility depends on its agreement with "modern" science, therefore, will eventually find its place alongside obsolete scientific theories on a shelf of historical relics.

Continued study led me to appreciate the role of science as one of many different perspectives on the natural world, each with its own value and limitation. I also perceived the purpose of the biblical view in revealing the relationship between God and his world. Such an understanding enables one to relate the two perspectives in a way that does justice to each and to other ways of looking at nature.

The first major section (chapters 1 to 7) of this book describes the emergence of the new science in the sixteenth and seventeenth centuries as it freed itself from the old authority of philosophy and religion. We focus here on the achievements of Copernicus, Kepler, Galileo and Newton in the arenas of astronomy and physics where this development initially took place.

The second section (chapters 8 to 10) presents the biblical view and its way of describing nature. We examine some principles for interpreting the various literary forms of the Bible and applying their teachings to modern life. The relationship of the biblical and scientific views of nature is illustrated in the chapter on miracles and natural law, followed by an exposition of the creation narrative in Genesis 1.

The third section (chapters 11 to 13) applies those insights to the current controversy over "creation-science" and the teaching of evolution. The choice of that subject might seem to be a digression, since the most radical changes in twentieth-century science have occurred not in biology but once again in astronomy and physics. The theories of special and general relativity, an expanding universe, and a new physics at the subatomic level have superseded the more static Newtonian universe characterized by permanence and balance. For the general reader, however, the realm of biology presents the most urgent need to relate the biblical and scientific views, now that the theory of evolution has again sparked such widespread controversy. A clear understanding of the conflict that does justice to both perspectives has immediate implications for classrooms and courts, pulpits and parishes. We sum up with a review of similarities and differences between the biblical and scientific perspectives and suggest a model for relating them.

Take note of what this book does not attempt. It is not a full-fledged theology of nature or philosophy of science. Our biblical perspective on the creation deals only with the way the Bible describes natural events and not with general revelation, which considers what can be known about God from observing his creation (Ps 19:1-4; Rom 1:19-20). Nor does our scientific perspective develop an overall philosophy of science. Yet a clear understanding of these two perspectives, with their value and limitations, makes a contribution to the comprehensive tasks of theology and philosophy. In this respect the following chapters represent a foundation more than a completed structure.

This book is meant to stimulate your thinking, to present the possibility that although Christianity and science are very different responses to nature, they nevertheless share some vital components. For example, both are rooted in faith-commitments to a reality beyond ourselves; both are community activities sharing respected traditions. We should consider them allies rather than enemies.

Religion and science *are* allies in the lives of many who regard science as their Christian vocation. In the Epilog we look at the life of Blaise Pascal, distinguished pioneer of science in whom the biblical and scientific perspectives came together in a beautiful and beneficent way.

I
THE SCIENTIFIC
PERSPECTIVE

1
GREEK SCIENCE: ARISTOTLE & ARCHIMEDES

*It is not the facts
which divide men
but the interpretation
of the facts.*
ARISTOTLE

OR MORE THAN TWO THOUSAND YEARS ANCIENT GREECE HAS CAP-
tured the imagination of the West. Long after Pericles and
Alexander, Greek thought influenced Rome, the Renaissance and the modern world. The Greek influence emanated
mainly from the city of Athens, which defeated the Persians in 479
B.C. and enjoyed a fifty-year Golden Age of cultural vitality unique in
human history. Then after losing a long war against Sparta, its rival
city, Athens entered a period of classical philosophy produced by
Socrates, Plato and Aristotle. Before turning to Aristotle, whose
thought came to dominate Western science for nearly twenty centuries, we will look at some of the early highlights of Greek science.

Early Greek Science

From the dawn of civilization people have tried to understand the natural world. The Babylonians developed an interest in the heavenly bodies and kept accurate records of their astronomical observations. The Egyptians worked out a decimal notation and the basic operations of arithmetic. Such activities were carried on for practical purposes like astrological prediction and land measurements.

The Greeks, however, pursued knowledge for its own sake, becoming the original scientists of ancient Europe. For them science and philosophy were inseparable companions. Greek philosophy covered all areas of thought, including music, ethics and politics; natural philosophy dealt with the natural world of the earth and heavens.

From the outset, Greek philosophy was bound up with mathematics. The earliest Ionian philosopher, Thales of Miletus (ca 640-550 B.C.), was a mixture of practical scientist and philosopher.[1] He is reported to have originated the science of deductive geometry. Thales earned his place as the initiator of Greek philosophy by conceiving the idea of "unity in difference." He held that all things were varying forms of one primary and ultimate element, water. The Milesian school of philosophy was the first to assume that the whole universe was natural; potentially it could be explained by ordinary knowledge and rational inquiry.

The following century produced a dozen able philosophers who wrestled with the problems of knowledge, substance, being and change in a variety of ways. Of particular interest is Pythagoras (ca 530 B.C.), who founded a great religion as well as a scientific tradition.[2] He created a community of men and women that prescribed a simple lifestyle with all possessions held in common, a distinctive costume and rules for daily living. Pythagoras discarded the idea of one single element. He believed that matter was composed of varying combinations of earth, water, air and fire. He considered the earth to be a sphere, resting at the center of a spherical universe, because he believed the sphere to be the perfect shape. He also considered the sun, moon and five known planets to be spheres with uniform circular motions around the earth.

Pythagoras saw order, harmony, balance, proportion and universal law in the world, the key to all of which is mathematics. During the sixteenth century, a "Pythagorean school" in southern Italy re-emphasized the importance and religious significance of numbers in understanding the world. That conviction provided an intellectual climate for the acceptance of the Copernican view of the solar system. The belief that ultimate reality is found in numbers and their relationships still influences modern science.

A Pythagorean named Philolaus (ca 450 B.C.) taught that the earth moved around the center of the universe like any other planet. That center was not the sun but a "central fire" which could not be seen. Philolaus's system, the earliest to have a revolving earth, was later noted by Copernicus when he searched among ancient philosophers for an alternative to Aristotle and Ptolemy.

Aristotle (384-322 B.C.)

Aristotle was born in 384 B.C. in Thrace.[5] His father became the personal physician of King Amyntas II of Macedon, grandfather of Alexander the Great. The family moved to the Macedonian capital and participated in court affairs. Both of Aristotle's parents died when he was a boy. In 367 B.C., around the age of seventeen, he went to Athens to complete his education. There he entered Plato's Academy and soon earned praise as "the mind of the school."

Aristotle remained at the Academy for twenty years. There he began his original studies in zoology which later earned him a high reputation. Not having strong family ties, he spent much of his time with other teachers, including the orator Demosthenes.

When Plato died in 347 B.C., Aristotle left Athens and stayed away for a period of twelve years. His reasons may have been both professional and political. The new head of the Academy, Plato's nephew Speusippus, reportedly overemphasized the mathematical side of his uncle's teaching. A more compelling pressure might have been the new anti-Macedonian mood in Athens.

This middle period of Aristotle's career took him first to a court on the far side of the Aegean, where the ruler Hermeias, a fellow alumnus, founded a branch of the Academy. Aristotle married Hermeias's niece Pythias and settled down in a Platonic environment with other distinguished graduates from Athens. In 344 B.C. Aristotle moved to the Aegean island Lesbos to be near Theophrastus, another Academy scholar whose work on plants made him the father of modern botany. The two became lifelong friends.

In 343 B.C. Aristotle moved again, this time back to Macedon as tutor to King Philip's young son Alexander. Three years later that formal relationship ended as Alexander became regent in the absence of his father on a military campaign. Aristotle probably remained in Macedon for another five years, possibly as an informal adviser to Alexander, who became king in 336 B.C. when Philip was assassinated.

The final period of Aristotle's career began in 335 B.C. when he returned to Athens, now under Macedonian rule. He established his own school on the grounds of the Lyceum, a place already popular with sophists and scholars. Among the buildings was a covered courtyard (*peripatos,* a walking place) where it was possible to carry on a discussion while strolling. From that habit the students became known as Peripatetics.

Aristotle built up a natural history museum and a collection of manuscripts and maps that became the prototype of the modern university library. Everything he prepared for public reading in Plato's style has been lost, except for fragments and later reports. Most of the surviving documents, a collection of which was edited in the first century, are more like notes produced in the course of Aristotle's teaching and study. The research program undertaken by Aristotle and his colleagues far surpassed any earlier achievements. Its scale was the result of his insistence on reviewing the data and the common opinions in order to discover the problems and begin to resolve them.[4] This research produced histories of speculative thought, study of the social sciences and work in the natural sciences. Aristotle became the greatest collector and organizer of knowledge in the ancient world.

Aristotle taught in Athens for only twelve years. During that time his wife Pythias died and he remarried. In 323 B.C. Alexander the Great, king of Macedon and conqueror of Greece, friend of Aristotle and patron of the Lyceum, died of malaria in Babylon. An outbreak of anti-Macedonian feeling spawned a movement to expel Aristotle. Faced with the charge of impiety and the prospect of an unjust trial like that of Socrates, he refused to allow Athens to "sin twice against philosophy" and left the city. The philosopher traveled to Chalcis, where he died a few months later.

Aristotle's character can be seen by his will. It made financial provision for his wife Herpyllis, including a dowry in case she should remarry. It provided for his two children, one by each wife, and bequeathed his library to Theophrastus, his friend and favorite pupil, who had directed the Lyceum after Aristotle left Athens. It also made good provision for his slaves. Aristotle showed understanding in his dealings with people as well as in his scientific pursuits.

Aristotle's Universe

Aristotle believed that the universe is finite and spherical, with the stationary earth at its center. The simplest entities in nature are the four elements of which the world is composed, earth, water, air and fire, each of which is an ideal substance. At the center of the universe is a motionless sphere composed of *earth*, forming the dry land. Over this is a layer of *water*, comprising the ocean; next comes the atmosphere of *air*; then comes an outer coating of *fire* extending as far as the moon. Objects in our world are composed of two or more of these elements. For example, paper consists of fire and earth; during combustion the *fire* is released as flames and the *earth* remains as ash.

Observation of his earthly surroundings showed Aristotle that terrestrial bodies are changeable and destructible—they are born and they die. He also noted that the natural motion of objects on earth is up or down. Since air and fire are light, they move upward; because earth and water are heavy, they move downward. Aristotle concluded that "natural" motion is innate, leading each body to seek its own resting place. He also noted another kind of motion which he called "violent." When a heavy object like a projectile is thrown upward, the motion is contrary to its natural downward tendency and so needs a force to sustain it. When that force ceases to operate, the projectile descends, seeking its natural place at the center of the earth.

Aristotle concluded that the composition of celestial bodies differs generically from the four terrestrial elements. They are composed of a fifth element, *aether*, not subject to change or decay and far superior to the elements of our world. Further, the natural motion of the celestial bodies is circular, the perfect form with no beginning, end or limit. Therefore the *aether* must be eternal as well as immutable and indestructible.

Within his concept of the universe Aristotle saw all bodies arranged in an orderly hierarchy of perfection, from formless matter at the center to matterless form at the periphery. On earth the degrees of perfection range from the lowest inanimate objects up through plants, animals and human beings. The living beings have their particular kind of soul: vegetative, sensitive and rational. The highest matter in the heavens has the perfect form not found on earth. Beyond the outer sphere of the stars is the most perfect being with form and no matter.

Clearly such a cosmology calls for two different systems of dynamics. Everything below the moon is governed by terrestrial physics; motion elsewhere in the universe is controlled by celestial mechanics. The first system is easier to explain. Since terrestrial bodies rise from or fall toward the center of the earth (also the center of the universe), the earth must be resting in its natural place. It has no need of moving, no place to go. Aristotle remarks: "This view is further supported by the contributions of mathematicians to astronomy, since the observations made as the shapes change, by which the order of the stars is determined, are fully accounted for on the hypothesis that the earth is at the center."[5]

Although not an astronomer, Aristotle was interested in formulating an explanation for celestial motion. He accepted the theory of concentric spheres proposed by another Academy alumnus, Eudoxus of Cnidus (ca 401-355 B.C.): The earth is the center of the universe. The sun, moon and planets are embedded in their own transparent, crystalline spheres which carry them around the earth. (To account for the celestial observations, each has its own major sphere with a nest of helping spheres.) The "fixed" stars, which do not move with respect to one another, are all attached to a single outer sphere that also revolves around the earth. Enclosing the whole universe is the sphere of the *Prime Motion,* from which all motion in the universe ultimately comes. That primary sphere is turned by the *First Unmoved Mover.* Thus the universe consists of a nest of concentric spheres, one within another, with the earth as a common center (figure 1).

Although short-lived as an astronomical device, this system of concentric spheres was significant in the development of astronomical thought. During the brief time when it seemed to be the most promising explanation of planetary motion, Aristotle incorporated the spheres in the most comprehensive, detailed and influential cosmology of the ancient world. His model was generally accepted in West-

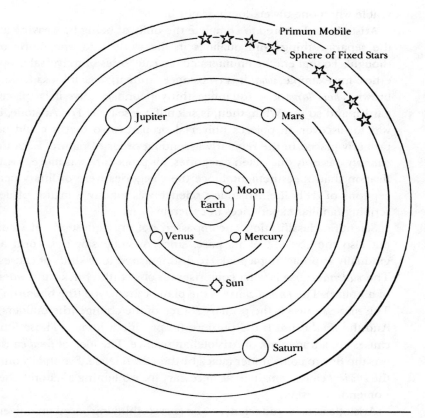

Figure 1. The Aristotelian Universe

ern thought until the early seventeenth century.

Aristotle's doctrine of the two different realms also persisted for many centuries. The sharp distinction between the incorruptible heavens and our corruptible earth took firm hold on people's minds. In fact it was not completely abandoned until after the time of Newton.

Aristotle's Science

Unlike many earlier philosophers, Aristotle carefully argued his points on the basis of scientific principles. He gave specific reasons, for example, for believing that the earth is a sphere: its curved shadow on the face of the moon in eclipse; the sight of stars not previously visible when one travels south or north.

Aristotle endeavored to complete the unity of being by weaving all the separate things and qualities in the world into one fabric of thought. To that end he enumerated ten categories of universal properties: for example, *what* it is (substance: animal); *how* it looks (color: brown); *how large* it is (quantity: thirty pounds); *where* it is (place: earth); and so on. What, then, is scientific research? For Aristotle, it was to discover an object's universal properties so that it could be properly placed in the regularly ascending order of nature. Because *quantity* was only one of ten categories, his procedure was more classification than measurement. Since the categories were ordinary perceptions of daily life, Aristotle's science was mainly a matter of describing familiar experiences in concrete form.

Scientific classification encompassed not only questions of value but also the concept of purpose, since Aristotle saw the world as gradually approaching a goal. He distinguished four kinds of causes: The *material* cause is what comprises an object (the bricks and wood of a house). The *formal* cause is the plan or archetype (the blueprint). The *efficient* cause is the primary source of the change (the builders). And the *final* cause is the purpose (to provide a home). Those four causes are a trademark of Aristotelian science. The idea of *final* cause was the first to come under attack by the new science. Eventually only the *efficient* cause remained as necessary for explaining a natural phenomenon or event.

Aristotle considered science to be correct thinking based on universal principles. Human knowledge (1) begins with sense perceptions (observed data) and (2) proceeds inductively to universal principles. Science then (3) consists of logical reasoning which derives particulars from those universals. In other words, the work of observation and induction is simply a necessary preliminary to the "true" science, which is *deduction from first principles by reasoning*. It is not surprising that Aristotle is known as the founder of logic, which rests on definition and syllogism (the process of proof).

What, then, is the task of the scientist according to Aristotle? Mainly to range over the physical world and put things in their proper place within the system Aristotle developed; that is, to discover the qualities of things in order to classify them. Since through action and reaction the world, governed by a regular process, is becoming a unity and moving toward an end, the scientist is concerned with the final cause or purpose of phenomena as well as their efficient cause or mechanism. Because Aristotle developed so comprehensive a philosophical system into which everything must fit, it became impossible to challenge one feature without weakening the entire framework.

Eventually the scientific revolution of the sixteenth and seventeenth centuries challenged not only Aristotle's astronomy but also his scientific method. Copernicus's sun-centered solar system, Kepler's elliptical planetary orbits, Galileo's physics and Newton's universal gravitation rearranged the heavens and unified nature. In the process they introduced a significantly different concept of science.

Nevertheless, Aristotle's influence on Western civilization has persisted in many concepts that continue to determine the structure of our thinking, expressing and even inquiring. Our philosophy and science still use as conceptual tools a number of words he coined and defined: for example, *category, matter* and *form, universal* and *individual, genus* and *species, property.*

More important for science, however, was Aristotle's approach to nature, which was forgotten by the later Aristotelians who bitterly opposed Galileo. "It is through observation, *aporia* [Greek for "doubt"], reasoned and cautious argument, that he thought our statements should fit the phenomena."[6]

Archimedes (287-212 B.C.)

The influence of Archimedes on Galileo warrants a review of that Greek philosopher's achievements in mathematics and mechanics. His name appears more than a hundred times in Galileo's writings.

Archimedes was born into an aristocratic family at Syracuse in Sicily around 287 B.C. His father was the astronomer Phidas, possibly a kinsman of King Hieron II, ruler of Syracuse. Archimedes studied in Alexandria, Egypt, where he played an important role in the development of Euclidean mathematics as it became a science of its own. For the rest of his life he exchanged ideas with the scholars he had met in Alexandria.

Archimedes returned to Syracuse and there continued his research and composed most of his works. His main interest lay in mathematics, especially geometry. Like later mathematicians such as Newton and Gauss, Archimedes united theory and application. More than any other Greek, he demonstrated the modern scientific combination of mathematics and experimental inquiry applied to a specific problem. He set forth a hypothesis, deduced the logical consequences and then tested it by observation and experiment. The two best-known examples concerned floating bodies and levers. "Archimedes' principle" states that a body immersed in a liquid is buoyed up by a force equal to the weight of the liquid displaced. Although the lever had been used from time immemorial, Archimedes worked out its theoretical principle. He exclaimed, "Give me a place to stand on and I will move the earth."[7] Archimedes ranks with Newton as a founder of mathematical physics.

His reputation in antiquity was also founded on his mechanical inventions. One of those was the water snail, a screwlike device to raise water for irrigation, which he invented in Egypt. He also devised an endless screw and compound pulley to launch a ship. Plutarch reports that when Hieron asked Archimedes to show how a great weight could be moved by a small force, the philosopher chose a three-masted merchantman that had been dragged ashore by the great labor of many men. After putting aboard the customary freight and many passengers, he seated himself at some distance and easily moved the ship with his system of pulleys.

For his work in astronomy Archimedes built an instrument to measure the angles of the rising sun and to estimate accurately the length of the year. He also constructed a model planetarium of spheres— with the relative positions of the sun, moon, planets and stars—to illustrate the Eudoxian system of the universe.

Nevertheless, like other Greek natural philosophers, Archimedes looked down on technology. Practical applications of science were acceptable only for agricultural and military projects.[8] In the latter he excelled with an array of fabulous ballistic weapons used against the Romans. In 215 B.C. the Roman general Marcellus moved against Syracuse after it made an alliance with Carthage. Attacking the city by land and sea, he was repulsed by a variety of weapons effective against his ships and his soldiers who tried to scale the walls. Marcellus then besieged Syracuse for three years while he conquered most of Sicily. He was finally able to exploit a weakness in the defenses and capture the city. During the ensuing battle Archimedes was killed by a Roman soldier.

Greek Astronomy

After the death of Alexander the Great, his empire was divided into three separate kingdoms, one of which was Egypt. There Ptolemy Soter, a son of Macedonian parents who had served under Alexander, founded a dynasty. As Ptolemy I he made the new city of Alexandria his capital. He founded a magnificent library and museum, whose first director was Demetrius of Phalerum, a pupil of Aristotle and former governor of Athens. Ptolemy had an ingenious method for increasing acquisitions to his library: every foreign ship coming into port was required to leave copies of its books before departure. About a hundred scholars, including Euclid the famous geometrician, came from all over the Mediterranean area. Teaching took second place to research as Alexandria became the new center of Greek science. Astronomy and mathematics prospered for several centuries, culminating in the work of Claudius Ptolemy. Later, Alexandria also became a center of Christian influence in the Roman world (chapter 8).

Greek astronomy had a considerable history before it became associated with the name of Ptolemy the astronomer (not to be confused with Ptolemy the ruler). Heraclides of Pontus (ca 350 B.C.), a contemporary of Aristotle, had made steps toward a heliocentric idea of the solar system. He held that the earth rotates on its axis. Heraclides also taught that while the sun and major planets revolve around the earth, Venus and Mercury revolve around the sun as it moves. His model was a forerunner of the one adopted by Tycho Brahe (chapter 3).

Aristarchus of Samos (ca 310-230 B.C.) came on the scene about seventy-five years later.[9] He looked at the problems of the solar system geometrically and did some original measuring to determine the distances and sizes of the sun and moon. But most significant was his view of the universe: the center is the sun, around which the earth and other planets revolve. The outermost sphere of the stars is stationary; it appears to move because the earth rotates daily.

Several factors worked against acceptance of Aristarchus's theory. First, the idea that the earth moved violated common sense; anyone could plainly see that it was the sun which moved. Second was the absence of any stellar parallax (not observed until 1838). Third, the climate of scientific thought was against such a novel and far-reaching idea. It would have played havoc with the logical system of crystalline spheres taught by Plato, Eudoxus and Aristotle. Finally, Aristarchus neither worked out his theory in detail nor made use of it to calculate planetary tables. That task was carried out with increasing accuracy by the Alexandrian astronomers, using the more complex but traditionally acceptable model—which soon left Aristarchus's idea in the dust.

Eudoxus's model of homocentric spheres had been designed to account for the "wanderings" of the planets—their apparent *retrograde* motions.[10] A planet can seem to stop its movement eastward across the sky and move back westward (in retrograde motion) for a time before resuming its eastward journey. (We now know that the apparent retrogression of Mars, for example, is caused by the earth's faster movement. When the earth passes Mars, Mars appears to stop and then move in the opposite direction.) To solve the problem, Eudoxus assigned each planet a set of spheres. The outer one, carrying the planet like a marble on a rotating beachball, was moved by the next inner sphere, and so on. For Mars an adjustment of the velocity and tilt of the four spheres could account for most of the planet's apparent motions. All told, twenty-seven spheres were needed to account for the variations of the planetary motions. In spite of its general success, however, the system had several weaknesses. Because all the spheres were homocentric with the earth as their center, there was no way for the planets to approach the earth or recede and thus account for changes in their brightness.

Hipparchus of Rhodes (ca 190-120 B.C.) made a contribution toward the solution of that problem.[11] We know nothing of his life, and his only two writings to survive are insignificant. Yet the astronomer Ptolemy had the highest respect for his work. Hipparchus was the first to determine the true length of the year and the *precession,* or gradual moving forward on the calendar, of the semiannual *equinoxes.*[12] He also invented many astronomical instruments. Hipparchus prepared a detailed catalog with the measured positions of 850 stars. He also specified their brightness with six ranges of intensity, introducing a method fundamentally the same as the one used today. His catalog, modified by Ptolemy, was the one later used by Copernicus.

Although Hipparchus is known mainly for his observational work, he gave some thought to the solar and lunar orbits. He represented the motion of the sun, for example, by a circle not centered exactly on the earth. That circular orbit, eccentric with respect to the earth

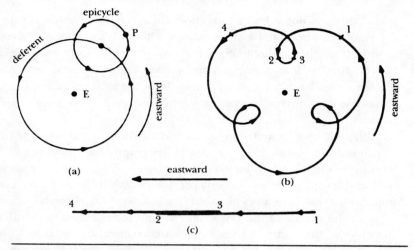

Figure 2. The Basic Epicycle-Deferent System
(a) A typical deferent and epicycle; (b) the looped motion that they generate in the plane of the ecliptic; (c) a portion (1-2-3-4) of the motion in (b) seen by an observer on the central earth, E, as retrograde.

and later called a *deferent,* allowed the sun to move with uniform speed and still appear from the earth to spend more time in the summer quadrant than in the winter one. The model preserved the perfect, uniform, circular motion of a heavenly body required by Aristotle's philosophy. Still, Hipparchus failed to build a geometric model to predict the retrograde motion of Mars and its faster movement in the half of the sky toward Capricorn.

Apollonius of Perga (ca 200 B.C.) made an additional step toward the solution of the problem.[13] He placed a secondary circle on the larger one—an *epicycle* on the deferent (figure 2). The planet on the rim of the epicycle now traced out a looped path moving toward and away from the center of the deferent. But the question remained: Could this model represent the apparently irregular motion of Mars while still retaining the required uniform motions for the epicycle and deferent? By the time of Ptolemy's work around A.D. 135, the accurate representation of Mars's orbit was the greatest unresolved problem in astronomy.

Ptolemy (A.D. 100-170)

Claudius Ptolemaeus worked in Alexandria between A.D. 127 and

151.[14] By then Rome had gained political ascendancy and was ruled by Hadrian, who had a love of culture. Although the library at Alexandria flourished, scholarship lapsed into a reminiscent mood, like the empire itself, as it assessed and consolidated past achievements. Ptolemy's work was affected by that outlook, but Ptolemy was a Greek; his books demonstrate the probing, inquiring spirit of his great predecessors.

Although he also wrote on optics and astrology, Ptolemy made his greatest contribution in the fields of geography and astronomy. A treatise in eight sections covered the known world; it was more accurate and comprehensive than any previous atlas. His map of the heavens, on the main contours of Aristotle's, had a spherical earth immovable in the center of the universe. Ptolemy considered the possible rotation of the earth, but the best available measurements did not support such a motion. He realized that the astronomical phenomena would look the same whether the earth spun or the stars moved. But he rejected the earth's rotation for physical reasons: objects would fly off the earth; birds would be left behind.

Even though he agreed with Aristotle that the earth was the center of the universe, as an astronomer Ptolemy was concerned to account for the motions of the heavenly bodies in the best possible manner. He inherited the problem of Mars along with the works of Euclid, the observations organized by Hipparchus and a great amount of astronomical data from the Babylonians.

Ptolemy's goal was the calculation of planetary positions at any time—past, present or future.[15] Using a theorem from Apollonius, he could calculate the size of the epicycle with respect to the deferent to reproduce the average retrograde loop (figure 2). Yet the observations still caused two problems. The loops themselves varied in size from one retrogression to another. Further, Mars appeared to move 40 per cent faster on one side of its orbit than the other. Ptolemy wondered how he could produce the necessary variations in the loops and in the speed of the center of the epicycle.

After experimenting with several possibilities, he finally solved the problem by adding an *equant*, a circle with an equalizing point. In figure 3 the geometric center of the deferent is the earth, from which the equant point is displaced. The rate of rotation of the deferent is required to be uniform, not with respect to the earth, but with respect

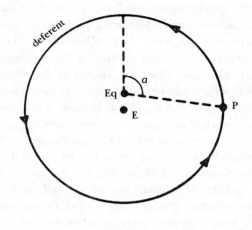

Figure 3. The Equant
The planet, P, moves on its earth-centered deferent at an irregular rate, yet in uniform motion with respect to the equant point, Eq, as the angular motion, a, remains constant.

to the equant point. Although the planet moves at an irregular rate with *nonuniform circular* motion, it has *uniform angular* motion (equal angular movement in equal times). In that way the philosophical principle of uniformity is preserved from the equant viewing point, although not along the deferent itself. Ptolemy's achievement is remarkable in view of the rough and incomplete observations available to him. Only for Mars are the effects readily seen; hence that planet played a key role in his discovery, just as it did almost fifteen hundred years later in Kepler's calculations.

Ptolemy discarded Aristotle's spheres and developed a system with the above-noted devices to explain the apparent motions in the heavens. Ptolemy could "save the appearances" (phenomena) by mathematically accounting for the celestial observations. In modern terms, he "formulated a theory to fit the data." His geometric devices did not necessarily correspond to the reality they represented. That became the crux of the later conflict over Copernicus's heliocentric theory: was it to be taken simply as a better mathematical tool or as a representation of reality?

Because Ptolemy's system displaced that of his predecessors, so that all his successors (including Copernicus) used his model, it became known as "Ptolemaic astronomy." He was the first astronomer to put together the deferent-epicycle-equant model to account for the apparent motions of the sun, moon and each of the five known planets.

Ptolemy presented his work in thirteen "books" entitled *Great System of Astronomy*, which later became known as *The Greatest*. The Arabic translation *Al-majisti* was changed centuries later to *Almagest*. Written in Alexandria around A.D. 150, it is indeed the greatest surviving astronomical work of antiquity, a remarkable synthesis of a treatise on theoretical astronomy and a practical handbook.

Even though Ptolemy's goal was achieved within the now-discarded earth-centered cosmology of his day, the *Almagest* is still honored as a timeless classic. "More than any other book, it demonstrated that natural phenomena, complex in their appearance, could be described by relatively simple underlying regularities in a mathematical fashion that allowed for specific predictions."[16] Such interaction between theory and observation continues to lie at the heart of the scientific method.

For the next fourteen centuries the *Almagest* was considered authoritative. Although they had to make adjustments from time to time, astronomers seldom if ever looked for fundamental modifications of Ptolemy's technique. His complicated geocentric model of the universe persisted until a Polish astronomer became exasperated with what he called "a monster"—and decided to try a radically different approach to the motion of the sun and its planets.

2
COPERNICUS:
SUN &
EARTH

The universe has been
wrought for us
by a supremely good
and orderly Creator.
NICHOLAS COPERNICUS

POLAND HAS LONG SUFFERED THE RAVAGES OF INVADING ARMIES. For a thousand years the land was periodically partitioned and ruled by foreign powers. In the fourteenth century Poland was reunited under King Casmir the Great, whose reign initiated a new period of prosperity. Cracow became his capital and a leading cultural center of Europe. In 1364 Casmir founded the University of Cracow, which he celebrated at an international congress.

Following Casmir's death, Grand Duke Jagellon of Lithuania founded one of the most fruitful dynasties in Polish history. It dominated eastern Europe and in 1410 defeated the powerful Teutonic Knights, a German military religious order. Under the Jagellons Poland entered a brilliant Renaissance period in which architecture, art and literature flourished. The University of Cracow became a famous educational center; during the fifteenth century it enrolled 18,338 students.[1]

Emigration from western Europe was encouraged. Into the Polish lands swarmed farmers, tradespeople, merchants, miners, adventurers and drifters eager to carve out new lives. They formed a prosperous middle class, filling the social gulf between nobility and serfs. Among them was the Kopernik family, a branch of which settled in Cracow.[2] There in 1448 a Niklas Kopernik was a merchant and dealer in copper. Ten years later he migrated northward to Torun on the Vistula, where he became prosperous and was appointed a magistrate for life. Soon after his arrival Kopernik helped to lead an uprising against the Teutonic Order, which still had control of that city. After thirteen years of hostilities, the Knights were defeated and Torun came under the rule of Poland.

Early Years

In 1463 Kopernik married Barbara Watzenrode, daughter of a wealthy merchant from an established German family. They had four children: Barbara, Katherina, Andreas and Nicholas, who was born on February 19, 1473.[3] Nothing is known about the first ten years of Nicholas's life. We can imagine that in his father's home he probably had contact with other leading families of Torun as they discussed art, literature, music, commerce—perhaps even science.

Often present at family gatherings was a man who figured prominently in Polish history and in Copernicus's career. Lucas Watzenrode, Barbara's brother, was a canon (staff clergyman) at the cathedral of Frombork (Frauenberg), the northernmost Catholic diocese in Poland. In 1483, when the elder Kopernik suddenly died, Watzenrode took responsibility for the four children.[4] In 1489 he became bishop of Varmia (Ermland), one of the four districts into which the church had divided the country for administrative purposes.

At the age of fifteen Nicholas entered the cathedral school of Wloclawek, thirty miles south of Torun, which offered excellent preparation for university study. The faculty were humanistic in their reaction to medieval religious authority and open to the revival of classical learning then radiating from Italy. One of the teachers was Nicholas

Wodka (a word for Russian liquor), who was evidently a teetotaler since he assumed the name Abstemius. An expert in building sundials, he may have stimulated young Copernicus's interest in the path of the sun.

In 1491 Bishop Watzenrode arranged for his two nephews to enter the flourishing University of Cracow from which he himself had graduated. There they could receive an excellent education in the standard medieval curriculum and also move in high cultural and social circles. Copernicus studied and wrote in Latin, spoke German and had a basic knowledge of Polish.

By the time Copernicus enrolled in the arts faculty of Cracow, the university had become an important center of mathematical and astronomical study abreast of developments elsewhere in Europe. Around 1430 Professor Sedziwoj had revised the *Alfonsine Tables* (celestial calculations based on the Ptolemaic system), of which Copernicus bought his own printed copy. The university encouraged an attitude of philosophical questioning. Although the arts curriculum continued to appear Aristotelian, its content was designed to oppose ancient authority. Both the course content and intellectual climate of Cracow were conducive to provoking the critical questions that eventually led Copernicus to his conceptual breakthrough.

Like many of his classmates, he did not complete his degree but returned home after three years. In 1495, eager to provide for his nephew's future, the bishop arranged for Copernicus to be elected one of the sixteen canons of the cathedral chapter responsible for the administration of the diocese. Each canon received for life an equal share of the ample income derived from the peasants working the chapter farmlands. But his election was disputed, and Copernicus decided to continue his studies pending a final decision.

Like many other bright students of the time, Copernicus made his way to Italy. In 1496 he enrolled in canon law at the University of Bologna, where his uncle had earned a doctorate in the same subject. A year later Copernicus received the welcome word that his election as canon was confirmed. He continued in that position for the rest of his life, though he never went on to become a priest (as erroneously reported by Galileo and later legend).

Although Copernicus studied law, his first love was astronomy. He became a friend of Domenico Maria de Novara, professor of astronomy at Bologna, a confirmed Neoplatonist who searched for simple geometric and arithmetic regularities in nature. Novara criticized Ptolemy's planetary theory on the ground that no system so complex could represent the true mathematical order of nature. Copernicus lived in Novara's home for a time and assisted him in measuring the positions of stars. Often the two would discuss ways in which the problems of Ptolemy's theory could be corrected. Copernicus's earliest recorded observation occurred on March 9, 1497, when he watched the moon approach eclipse at 11 P.M.

We do not know exactly when Copernicus developed his radically new heliocentric view. He may have begun to think along those lines as an undergraduate at Cracow or during his graduate studies in Italy. At any rate, he began to wonder whether alternatives to the Ptolemaic system had been expressed in antiquity. He decided to learn Greek so that he could read important scientific sources not yet translated into Latin.

At the end of classes in September 1500, Copernicus visited Rome, where he stayed during the Jubilee Year proclaimed by Pope Alexander VI. On November 6, Copernicus was able to observe an eclipse of the moon. On Easter Sunday he and his brother Andreas joined an estimated two hundred thousand pilgrims to receive the pontiff's blessing, probably as canonical representatives from the diocese of Varmia.

In July 1501 Copernicus arrived home to appear in person before the cathedral chapter and to be officially installed as a canon. Although his allotted period of three years was more than used up, he requested permission for an additional two years of study, with a stipend. His request was granted, mainly because trained physicians were scarce and he promised to study medicine to increase his usefulness. Copernicus also had another motive. In those days the study of medicine was related to astrology, with parts of the body linked to signs of the zodiac. That would give him a good excuse to continue his planetary observations. He needed both the intellectual stimulus of the Italian universities and their clear southern skies to sharpen his astronomical skills.

Copernicus chose Padua, the most famous university of the time, where the brilliant anatomist Vesalius published his great book *Fabrica* ("On the Fabric of the Human Body") in 1543. But because of the heavy expense of getting a doctoral degree at Padua, Copernicus interrupted his studies and went to the University of Ferrara. There, on May 21, 1503, he finally received a degree in canon law.

Shortly before Copernicus arrived in Ferrara, the Arab astonomer al-Farghani's *Elements of Astronomy* had been published. A book that aided the revival of science in Europe, it became available to Copernicus at Ferrara if he had not read it before.

Copernicus returned to Padua for additional study of medicine, although he did not plan to obtain a degree since the course required three full years. In autumn 1503 he left Italy for the last time, after seven years of study that had given him the most complete education available at the time. At age thirty Copernicus was grounded in the classics, law, theology, mathematics, metaphysics, languages—and astronomy.

Canon and Astronomer

Shortly after his nephew's return to Frombork, Bishop Watzenrode arranged for him to become his personal physician and administrative aide. At his uncle's side at Lidzbark (Heilsberg) for the next five years, Copernicus functioned as traveling companion, private secretary, counselor and diplomatic representative. During those years Lucas Watzenrode, a wily politician, walked a tightrope to maintain his independence between two ambitious and mutually hostile neighbors, Poland and the Teutonic Knights.

Copernicus managed to continue his astronomical observations and discussions with Cracow mathematicians. Watzenrode wanted his nephew to succeed him as bishop of Varmia, but Copernicus knew he could not pursue astronomy while handling the responsibilities of that office. Declining the opportunity, he left for the quieter scene of Frombork where, except for special assignments, he spent the rest of his life. In March 1512, Lucas Watzenrode, well into his sixties and worn down by years of strain, suddenly became ill and died. Copernicus was then freer for a time to pursue less demanding duties and devote more attention to astronomy.

As a canon Copernicus was entitled to living quarters within the fortress walls surrounding Frombork Cathedral. Although canons had specific ecclesiastical duties, they usually avoided taking holy orders. Many were noblemen who lived well, traveled abroad, owned estates and played politics. Each canon oversaw considerable property in the diocese, for which he had to collect taxes, hold court, mete out justice and protect his peasants in time of war.

By 1514 Copernicus had written an initial outline of his new astronomy, known generally by its abbreviated title *Commentariolus* ("Brief Treatise").[5] Following the example of the Italian Pythagorean school, he anonymously circulated a few manuscript copies among some of his trusted friends. His treatise criticized the traditional geocentric system of Aristotle and Ptolemy: "The center of the Earth is not the center of the universe."[6]

The *Brief Treatise* opens with a complaint against the equant. Then comes a list of seven assumptions, of which the two most important are the third and seventh:

3. All the spheres surround the Sun as though it were in the middle of all of them, and therefore the Sun is near the middle of the universe.

7. What appears as the direct and retrograde movements arises not from the planets themselves, but from the Earth. This motion alone therefore suffices to explain many apparent irregularities in the heavens.[7]

Copernicus also states that the distance from the sun to the earth is insignificant compared to that of the fixed stars (figure 4).

Seven short chapters describe the sequence of the celestial spheres, deal with the earth's motions, describe the mechanism of planetary motion and give data for the dimensions of the circles and epicycles. The treatise tells little about how Copernicus arrived at his new concept. He states that for the sake of brevity he omitted the mathematical demonstrations planned for a larger book. We do not know exactly what he had in mind. But by the time he acquired a copy of the *Almagest* (first printed in 1515), Copernicus realized that for his new system to rival Ptolemy's he would have to present it in a work of comparable structure and magnitude.

In November 1516 Copernicus was given a three-year appointment as administrator of chapter holdings in Olsztyn and Mingajny. Shortly after that term expired, the Teutonic Order invaded Varmia and sacked the town of Frombork. The small province became a cruel battleground on which the antagonists took turns pillaging and slaughtering the peasants loyal to the other side. All but three of the

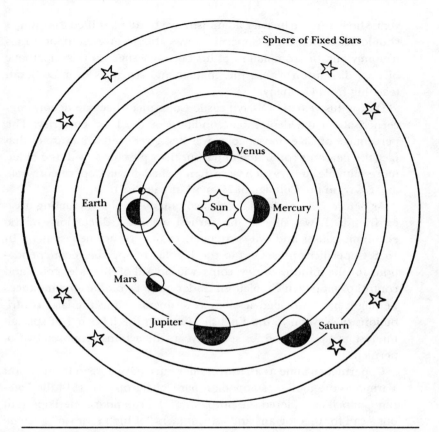

Figure 4. The Copernican Universe

canons fled the country to sit out the war in easy exile. In November 1520, soon after Copernicus began a second term as administrator at Olsztyn, the castle was besieged. With the assistance of another canon he successfully led its defense. After peace was restored in 1521, Copernicus was made commissioner of Varmia with responsibility for rehabilitating the towns and farms. Yet in the midst of such disruptions the astronomer continued to make his celestial observations and calculations.

In 1523 Copernicus was appointed administrator-general of the diocese during a six-month interim between bishops. Then in 1525 he served as chancellor of the cathedral chapter. During the following years, however, the heavier administrative burdens shifted to younger shoulders. Increasingly Copernicus was able to give attention to astronomy and the completion of his book—despite an unsympathetic bishop, dissension within the chapter and struggles over Lutheran teaching from Germany.

During his years at Olsztyn castle Copernicus became deeply concerned about the deplorable condition of the local currency. The percentage of silver in the coins was being reduced. Unaware of that fact, the peasants continued to pay for their purchases with the older, more valuable coins, which were then melted down. Copernicus wrote an "Essay on the Coinage of Money" in Latin in 1517.[8]

As before, he circulated the essay in manuscript form among trusted friends. It was one of the earliest empirical discussions of the economic causes and evil consequences of currency debasement. In 1528 Copernicus presented to the legislature specific recommendations for the minting of new coins, withdrawal of the older coins and control of money in circulation. Under more favorable circumstances he might have provided services as distinguished as the later contributions of Newton to the English Mint. But the lobbying of special-interest groups delayed for several years the actions proposed by Copernicus.

Copernicus's fame as an astronomer must have spread from distant Varmia to the more cosmopolitan parts of Europe. In 1514 the Lateran Council considered the problem of the calendar. The Pope sent out a call for theologians and astronomers "of high renown" to come to Rome and rectify the old Julian calendar.[9] Copernicus was among those who wrote their opinions. Many years later, in the preface to *De Revolutionibus* ("On the Revolutions"), he referred to the calendar problem and pointed out that it could not be solved until the lengths of the year and month, and the motions of the sun and moon, were first precisely measured. His improved tables paved the way for the calendar reform eventually introduced by Pope Gregory XIII in 1582.

The Final Years

Little is known of Copernicus's last fifteen years before his death in 1543. He continued his efficient administration of church estates, practiced medicine, observed the heavens and continued work on his book. Yet he became increasingly lonely and isolated. Around 1512 his brother Andreas had contracted leprosy, then prevalent in Prussia, a disease beyond the reach of Copernicus's medical skills. The other canons, fearing that the dread disease might spread, sent the helpless patient on his way to find a cure. Andreas died abroad, probably in Rome, in 1518. As years went by, Copernicus witnessed the death of lifelong friends.

Another cause of isolation was the rapid growth of the Reformation and its influence in Poland. Although the country remained strongly Catholic, Martin Luther's teachings began to find favor. Copernicus and his respected friend Tiedemann Giese, later bishop of Varmia, were open to some of the new ideas. Copernicus did not leave a written record of his views, but he authorized Giese to quote him in a polemical book supportive of a mediating position he hoped would avoid disruption in the church.

The bishop of Varmia at the time, Maurice Ferber, was adamant against Lutheranism. Although Copernicus's tolerant attitude was known, he survived largely because he was greatly respected as a physician. Ferber himself, suffering from colic and gout, constantly summoned his moderate canon for treatment. But within the chapter the astronomer felt increasingly isolated from fellow canons who opposed any challenge to established beliefs.

During the 1530s Copernicus continued to work out mathematical support for the axioms of his *Brief Treatise*. For a number of reasons he kept putting off publication of his views. He knew that the manuscript still had many numerical inconsistencies. He had not fully explored the potential offered by the heliocentric model. Further, even though Pope Clement VII expressed interest in knowing more about his views, Copernicus feared that people would ridicule a theory that contradicted everyday experience. Far from academic centers, he also lacked opportunities to discuss his work with technically trained colleagues. In addition, he had no ready access to a major international center of printing that could profitably publish so large and technical a book.

The solution to several of those problems arrived in the person of a young mathematician from Germany in the spring of 1539. Georg Joachim Rheticus had been appointed professor of mathematics at the Lutheran University of Wittenberg at the age of twenty-two. Interested in the new cosmology, he became Copernicus's first and only disciple. A strong friendship developed as the eager pupil began two years of study with the old astronomer. Impressed with the manuscript, Rheticus received Copernicus's permission to publish a brief summary entitled *Narratio Prima* ("First Account"). It appeared in Danzig in 1540 as the earliest printed account of the Copernican system.

That small book awakened interest in the new astronomy and prodded Copernicus to publish the complete book. Unable to continue making changes because of failing health, he had to take that long-delayed step. Rheticus returned to Wittenberg, where in 1542 he published the two noncontroversial chapters on trigonometry. He made arrangements to have the entire book published in Nuremberg by his friend Johannes Petreius, who specialized in scientific works. Nuremberg, a kind of "German Athens," was then in full flower as a center of culture and trade.

While printing was in progress Rheticus accepted an appointment at the University of Leipzig in November 1542. Unable to continue guiding Copernicus's book through the press, Rheticus turned the task over to a well-known Lutheran clergyman, Andreas Osiander, who was recognized for competence in mathematics and astronomy. Osiander had exchanged letters with Copernicus in 1540 about a number of problems. Copernicus had inquired about the potential reception of a book presenting the motions of the earth and the possible outrage of those loyal to Aristotle and Ptolemy.

In April 1541 Osiander suggested a way out of the difficulty. He believed that astronomy had one aim, to provide hypotheses (theories) that compute and predict the positions of the planets, but do not represent their true motions. So he wrote to Copernicus, "I have always believed that hypotheses are not articles of faith, but the bases of computation; so that, even if they be false, it is of no consequence, provided that they exactly reproduce the phenomena of the motions."[10] He counseled Copernicus to make such a statement in order to appease the Aristotelian philosophers and theologians whose opposition he feared. Copernicus rejected the suggestion because he was firmly convinced that his principles were true as well as useful: he was talking about the actual physical world.

Ironically, the final editing of *On the Revolutions* was turned over to Osiander, who decided to follow his own advice. He added an introductory letter *Ad Lectorem* ("To the Reader") in which he expressed his views on the aim and nature of scientific theories at variance with Copernicus's claims for his own theory. The letter states, "Nor is it necessary that these hypotheses should be true, nor indeed even probable, but it is sufficient if they merely produce calculations which agree with the observations. . . . Let no one expect from astronomy, as far as hypotheses are concerned, anything certain, since it cannot produce any such thing."[11]

Osiander has been widely condemned for inserting an anonymous "preface," purporting to be the author's, which hindered the acceptance and use of this work. Yet contemporary commentators who rejected (or praised) it did not cite the letter as their reason for doing so. A good case can be made for Osiander's intention to protect Copernicus's book from possible adverse criticism.[12] The author of *To the Reader* remained generally unknown for many decades until Kepler discovered a note attributing it to Osiander.

Early in 1543 *De Revolutionibus Orbium Coelestium* ("On the Revolutions of the Heavenly Spheres") came from the printer. Written in Latin and about four hundred pages long, the first edition probably had fewer than five hundred copies. The title page carried an advertisement that could match a modern dust-jacket blurb:

> You have in this newly created and published book, diligent reader, the motions of the fixed stars and planets restored from both the old and new observations, and furthermore, furnished with new and wonderful hypotheses. You also have the most convenient tables from which you can with the greatest of ease calculate their positions for any time.
>
> Therefore, buy, read, and profit.[13]

In order to understand the book's significance, we need to review the state of astronomy inherited by Copernicus.

From Ptolemy to Copernicus

Astronomy had fallen into decline during the centuries following Ptolemy's *Almagest*. Although some Islamic astronomers criticized the work, no one had systematically recalculated all the parameters or adjusted the models to make them more accurate. Part of the reason was a dearth of suitable observations. From the death of Ptolemy A.D. 170 to the birth of Copernicus in 1473, only a dozen records with accurate planetary positions existed in the West.

In the interval between Hipparchus and Ptolemy, calculations based on different calendars had led to the difference of a full day in the length of the year. After Ptolemy, the problem continued, and it gradually became evident that his value for the precession of the equinox was significantly in error. Yet no one challenged Ptolemy's observations, lest the foundation of astronomy be undermined. Instead, Islamic astronomers invented an ingenious system called *trepidation*. It introduced a variable precession in such a way as to preserve the values between the times of Hipparchus and Ptolemy, yet give a faster rate in the following centuries. That device was incorporated into astronomical calculations before A.D. 1000.

In the thirteenth century the astronomers of King Alfonso X of Spain prepared new and handier tables for determining planetary positions. Contrary to the idea sometimes set forth today that the *Alfonsine Tables* were burdened with a complex system of "epicycles on epicycles" calling for reform, they served their purpose well. Except for adding the table of trepidation, the meager systematic observations of the Middle Ages provided no basis for making the planetary models more complicated. It is true that in the eastern Islamic world astronomers began to experiment with new models using one or more additional epicycles. But the purpose of those *epicyclets* was not to provide more accuracy; they were designed to replace the equant in order to preserve the philosophical requirement of uniform circular motion, and to construct a strictly mechanical model of the planetary system.

Criticism of Ptolemy's system increased during the Middle Ages because of its failure to provide a philosophically acceptable model. It needed modification to reconcile it with Aristotle's picture of physical reality—the nests of concentric crystalline spheres that moved the planets in their orbits. Primarily for that reason Islamic astronomers of the thirteenth century explored the epicyclet alternatives to Ptolemy's equant. Actually, the resulting tables looked the same as before.

The philosophical attack on the Ptolemaic system filtered into the Latin West. At the end of the fifteenth century, when Copernicus was a student, that criticism was helping to shape astronomical thinking. By then the temporary fix provided by the trepidation was also becoming inadequate to account for the observations. So on both counts some kind of reform was called for. Yet neither criticism of the equant nor failure of the trepidation required a solution so radical as introducing an entirely new cosmology. At that point astronomy was hardly in the state of crisis commonly pictured by modern scholars.[14]

De Revolutionibus

After nearly thirty years of labor Copernicus gave permission for the publication of his manuscript. Knowing that his work would spark controversy, he boldly dedicated it to the scholarly Pope Paul III.

> I can reckon easily enough, Most Holy Father, that as soon as certain people learn that in these books of mine which I have written about the revolutions of the spheres of the world I attribute certain motions to the terrestrial globe, they will immediately shout to have me and my opinion hooted off the stage. . . . And in order that the unlearned as well as the learned might see that I was not seeking to flee from the judgment of any man, I preferred to dedicate these results of my nocturnal study to Your Holiness rather than to anyone else; because, even in this remote corner of the earth where I live, you are held to be most eminent both in the dignity of your order and in your love of letters and even of mathematics.[15]

Copernicus explained that his long-time reluctance to publish his work had been overcome by the persuasion of friends, including Bishop Giese and Cardinal Schönberg.

In proposing the controversial axiom that the earth revolves around the sun, Copernicus made no claim to originality. He reported that he had searched the ancient Greek philosophers to see if any taught that idea. He found references to Hicetus of Syracuse and Philolaus the Pythagorean believing in the earth's revolution; also Heraclides of Pontus and Ecphantus the Pythagorean recognizing its rotation. (Although Aristarchus was the first ancient philosopher to propose the heliocentric idea, there is no evidence that Copernicus was indebted to him. "As far as we can tell both the idea and its justification were found independently by Copernicus.")[16]

Unlike Ptolemy, who could assume his readers' acceptance of a geocentric framework, Copernicus found it necessary to argue strongly for his novel sun-centered system. He proclaimed the obvious uniqueness of the sun, sang of the now-harmonious arrangement of the planets and eloquently described their relationship. Nevertheless,

Copernicus's cosmological arguments comprise a very small part of the work, most of which is a technical treatise.

On the Revolutions has six books, each divided into several chapters. Book 1 gives the clearest overall picture of Copernicus's sun-centered "universe." He presents arguments for the threefold motion of the earth (rotation, revolution and precession), an explanation of the apparent retrogression of the planets, a sketch of the heliocentric solar system and an explanation of the seasons. The book concludes with elementary plane and spherical trigonometry.

Book 2 deals with spherical astronomy and problems connected with the rising and setting of the sun. Copernicus explains the "armillary sphere," an ancient instrument with metal rings representing the celestial equator. Included also is a catalog listing about a thousand stars and their locations, using observations recorded by Ptolemy and others (many of them inaccurate), made over the centuries. Copernicus was never known as a great astronomical observer; he was primarily a mathematician and original thinker who reinterpreted the old data with a new celestial configuration.

Book 3 deals with the length of the year and the orbit of the earth. It explains the tables in such a way that it doesn't matter whether the earth or sun is in motion. Copernicus also raises a question that had bothered him all his life: Is the center of the universe inside or beyond the sun? His calculations were complicated by holding the traditional assumption that the planets move in circles, rather than the ellipses later demonstrated by Kepler.

Book 4 presents the theory of the moon's motion and its eclipses; it also determines the distances of the moon and sun. Book 5, the longest, investigates the longitudinal motions of the five planets and the sizes of their orbits compared to the earth's. Finally, book 6 considers the motions of the planets in latitude.

Copernicus anticipated criticism on theological grounds as well as the verdict of common sense:

> But if perchance there are certain "idle talkers" who take it upon themselves to pronounce judgment, although wholly ignorant of mathematics, and if by shamelessly distorting the sense of some passage of Holy Writ to suit their purpose, they dare to reprehend and to attack my work; they worry me so little that I shall even scorn their judgments as foolhardy. . . . Mathematics is written for math-

ematicians; and among them, if I am not mistaken, my labours will
be seen to contribute something to the ecclesiastical common-
wealth, the principate of which Your Holiness now holds.[17]
"Mathematics is written for mathematicians." That key phrase conveys
two essentials: this is a technical writing for professionals; it deals with
mathematical astronomy. Others before him had taught the earth's
motion; Copernicus was the first to build a complete mathematical
system on that concept.

Because *On the Revolutions* was published within the Lutheran
sphere, relatively few copies initially went as far as Italy, other Catholic countries and England. A second edition published in Basel in
1566 was well distributed in those countries. By the end of the century
Copernicus's views were readily available. Nevertheless, the heliocentric cosmology was rarely taught openly and then usually as a hypothesis—just as Osiander's introduction declared.

Contribution to Astronomy

Copernicus reaffirmed that the goal of astronomy was to explain the
movements of the heavenly bodies on the basis of *uniform circular
motion*. He could thus accept the deferent, epicycle and even epicyclet.
But he had a strong antipathy toward the equant because it violated
this principle with its *nonuniform motion*. His sun-centered system sat-
isfied the requirement that everything should move uniformly about
its own proper center as the law of absolute motion required. Rheticus
made the difference clear: "Only on the basis of this theory was it
possible to make all the circles of the Universe revolve uniformly and
regularly about their own centers, and not about other centers—
which is the essential property of circular motion."[18] Removal of the
sun from the category of planets was one of Copernicus's most influential contributions to the progress of astronomy.

In addition to preserving uniform circular motion, the new system
correlated the distance of the planets from the sun with the times of
their revolution around it. The order now became Mercury, Venus,
Earth, Mars, Jupiter and Saturn. That model showed why the first two
never appear far away from the sun, while the last three seem to roam
far and wide in the sky. The distances of the planets from the "center
of the universe" could be calculated with respect to the "common
measure" of the earth-sun radius—a kind of celestial yardstick.

Further, Copernicus's new system was not only mathematically elegant but physically possible. He insisted that it was not just a device to "save the phenomena" (correlate the data) but also a description of the way the universe really works.

Finally, Copernicus made a significant step toward an understanding of gravity. "Having planetized the earth and raised it out of the universe's center to the third circum-solar orbit, Copernicus could not regard his new planet as the collection depot for all the heavy bodies on the move in the universe."[19] He put forward a revised concept of gravity: heavy objects everywhere tend toward their own center. Whereas Aristotle's universe had only one center of gravity (the earth), from Copernicus the physical world acquired many centers, paving the way toward the universal gravitation of Newton.

Copernicus's system did not, as commonly thought, provide more accurate predictions of planetary positions. The use of modern, refined planetary theory and computers has made it possible to calculate with precision where the planets really were in the sixteenth century. Such calculations show that the errors in prediction based on the Copernican *Prutenic Tables* are about the same as those of the Ptolemaic *Alfonsine Tables*.

Many historical accounts emphasize not the accuracy but the simplicity of the new system in contrast to the horrendous scheme of epicycles-upon-epicycles supposedly developed by pre-Copernican astronomers. It is true that Copernicus closed his *Brief Treatise* with the claim that thirty-four circles now sufficed to describe the entire structure of the universe, in contrast to the eighty supposedly needed by the Ptolemaic system. But during the following years Copernicus refined his theory with the addition of more elaborate devices. As a result, a comparison between the classical Ptolemaic and new Copernican systems shows the *latter* to be slightly more complicated. (The 80-versus-34 myth is based on the prevalent assumption that the Ptolemaic system was repeatedly patched up over the following centuries. Yet recent calculations show that the thirteenth-century *Alfonsine Tables* were based on Ptolemy's original system.)[20]

In a profound sense, however, Copernicus's system has a simplicity in relating the length of planetary orbits to their distance from the central sun:

In the center of all rests the sun. . . . And so the sun, as if resting

on a kingly throne, governs the family of stars which wheel around.
. . . Therefore in this order, we find that the world has a wonderful
commensurability and that there is a sure bond of harmony for the
movement and magnitude of the orbital circles such as cannot be
found in any other way.[21]

Copernicus's radical cosmology sprang not from new observations but
from insight—a grand aesthetic view of the structure of the universe.
That insight became an achievement, that is, a basis for research,
because he defended it with arguments from technical mathematical
astronomy. Vision coupled with mathematical proficiency initiated a
scientific revolution.

Copernicus marks the starting point of a new astronomical and
cosmological tradition, as well as the culmination of the old. His book
made little immediate impact since it was understood only by astronomers. Most of them appreciated its mathematical usefulness even
though they did not accept its model of the universe. Only Rheticus
saw the theory as more than a set of calculating devices; he alone
recognized its important discovery of the unique relationship between
the distances and periods of the planets. Copernicus's system provided the basis for research and a focal point for controversy in the
studies of Kepler and Galileo in the next century. His work was also
significant for the development of modern scientific method in the
use of mathematics as the key to understanding how the universe
works through the fitting together of theory and facts.

The great astronomer saw no conflict between his Christian faith
and scientific activity. During his forty years as a canon, Copernicus
faithfully served his church with extraordinary commitment and courage. At the same time he studied the world "which has been built for
us by the Best and Most Orderly Workman of all." Copernicus
pursued his science with a sense of "loving duty to seek the truth in
all things, in so far as God has granted that to human reason." He
declared that although his views were "difficult, almost inconceivable,
and quite contrary to the opinion of the multitude, nevertheless in
what follows we will with God's help make them clearer than day—
at least for those who are not ignorant of the art of mathematics."[22]

Copernicus was a churchman, a painter and a poet, a physician,
an economist, a statesman, a soldier, and a scientist! A churchman
by the will of his guardian uncle and by vocation, an economist by

accident, a statesman and soldier by necessity, and a scientist—by the Grace of God and by sheer love of truth for truth's sake.[23]

During 1542 Copernicus was worn down by fevers and saddened over growing strife in the church. He also worried about his book, which was never as complete as he wanted it to be. As winter approached, his friends became increasingly concerned. A letter from Bishop Giese to a mutual friend shows the bishop's esteem for Copernicus: "We are all his debtors on account of his pure soul, his integrity, and his extensive learning . . . a friend who has abundantly earned our love and gratitude."[24]

Early in 1543 Copernicus suffered from hemorrhage, paralysis and stroke. He lived for nearly five more months, then died on May 24, 1543. The complete, printed volume of *On the Revolutions* was given to him on his deathbed. The astronomer was buried in Frombork Cathedral. He bequeathed to the cathedral chapter his library, to friends some textbooks, to his married sister his estate—and to the Western world the beginning of a new scientific era.

3
KEPLER: PLANETARY ORBITS

*O God, I am thinking
thy thoughts
after thee.*
JOHANNES KEPLER

HE SEVENTEENTH CENTURY HAS BEEN CALLED THE CENTURY OF
Genius. Most European countries look back to that period
as a symbol of their brilliance. Philosopher Alfred North
Whitehead observed, "It is one century which consistently,
and throughout the whole range of human activities, provided the
intellectual genius adequate for the greatness of its occasions."[1]

In science alone there was Galileo in Italy, Pascal and Descartes in
France, Francis Bacon and Newton in England, Huyghens in Hol-
land. To those names could be added many others who today would
enhance the prestige of our greatest universities. Germany's contribution to that memorable list was Johannes Kepler (1571-1630). A brilliant mathematician and astronomer, he contributed to the scientific

revolution with his work on the planetary orbits, laws of motion and scientific method. Kepler's accomplishments formed the foundation of modern theoretical astronomy. He was also a devout Christian whose unwavering faith in God sustained his life and motivated his research.

Kepler's work was all the more amazing in light of the great odds against which he fought all his life. Born into a poor family, he was constantly short of money. From infancy his health was delicate; throughout his life he suffered from fever attacks, stomach disorders, skin eruptions and poor eyesight. A Protestant amid the growing Catholic Counter-Reformation, Kepler was persecuted for his faith, banished from two cities and forced to give up his property. Frequent moves took their toll on his home life. His first wife died early of disease; fewer than half of his children lived beyond ten years.

Employment was always uncertain for Kepler. The noblemen whom he served often paid his salary late; the emperor defaulted on commitments to him. Amid those personal misfortunes came the Thirty Years' War, one of the cruelest in European history. During his last twelve years, Kepler had to conduct his research in the middle of that conflict, at times with his house occupied by soldiers and in sight of the carnage. Yet under those incredibly difficult circumstances, Kepler continued his arduous work and became one of the greatest astronomers. Through all his suffering he remained a warm-hearted human being with deep Christian commitment.

Before looking more closely at this remarkable man, we should consider the aftermath of Copernicus's achievement and the astronomical situation into which Kepler came.

After Copernicus

Although *On the Revolutions* eventually led to a radically different view of the universe and a new way of doing science, at first it made little impact. The delayed response to Copernicus's theory was due to several philosophical and scientific factors.

First, although the mathematicians who understood *On the Revolutions* were grateful for the new tables, which made their calculations easier, most of them did not accept as a physical reality Copernicus's theory that the earth moves. They had a precedent in Ptolemy, whose circles could serve as useful devices for computing planetary positions without being considered physically real.[2] So the new system was accepted simply as a more convenient mathematical model, and even in that regard it provided only slightly greater accuracy than its Ptolemaic predecessor.

Second, Copernicus's central premise that the earth moves around the sun had the status of an assumed but unproven proposition. Whatever probability it possessed came only from the mathematical discipline of geometry. Here the new system contradicted a fundamental principle of what was considered a higher discipline: physics. According to physics, a simple body could have only one proper motion; therefore the earth could not both rotate on its axis and orbit the sun.

A third and more practical reason for such slow acceptance was a reluctance to go against common sense. It was obvious to everyone that the earth is a massive, stable object around which the heavenly bodies are plainly seen to move. If the earth actually rotated on its axis, wouldn't parts fly off into space? Wouldn't the air be left behind? Wouldn't a projectile shot straight up fall west of its starting point? None of those phenomena occurred.

At first relatively few people read *On the Revolutions;* it was not a popularly written best seller of the kind Galileo produced sixty years later. Yet during the latter half of the sixteenth century it became a standard reference for astronomical research. Scholars could dispense with neither the book nor the tables based on it, even though by 1600 only ten active "Copernicans" could be counted.[3] Nevertheless, *On the Revolutions* was increasingly read and sometimes studied in both Catholic and Protestant schools. Slowly but inexorably Copernicus's system gained ground, moving toward its final victory more by infiltration than frontal assault.

The new astronomy also created problems for theologians. It seemed to contradict biblical passages that assumed the stability and centrality of the earth and mobility of the sun. The identity of humanity as God's crowning work of creation appeared to be undermined by removing the earth from its unique position among the planets. The great distance of the stars of the eighth sphere generated a feeling of anxiety in so large a universe. The reactions of church leaders to such problems during the last half of the sixteenth century, however, have frequently been misrepresented. They will be sketched in chapter 7.

Finally, Aristotle's system embraced all the phenomena of heaven and earth, so that a radically different astronomy would undermine the entire structure of knowledge about the world. Before Copernicus's view could be generally accepted, Aristotle's physics had to be overthrown on other grounds. For completion of the scientific revolution, the problem of motion in terrestrial dynamics was solved by Galileo, then correlated with the motion of heavenly bodies in the synthesis achieved by Newton.

Copernicus both closed an old era and opened a new one. He served as a bridge between the late medieval version of Aristotle's natural philosophy and the new science of the seventeenth century. The importance of his work was not only the system he produced but also the influence he exerted on others. Among those was Johannes Kepler, who assisted Tycho Brahe—the most accurate astronomical observer before the invention of the telescope—and then became custodian of Tycho's invaluable data.

Kepler's Early Years

The name Kepler had been carried by medieval knights, titled noblemen and prominent businessmen. But in the early 1500s financial reverses forced the proud family to become craftsmen. Yet Johannes's grandfather Sebald managed to succeed in business and become mayor of the Swabian town of Weil. He was a staunch Protestant in a predominantly Catholic community that had no Lutheran pastor at the time his grandson was born.

Sebald Kepler had one son who brought little credit to the family name. Heinrich was an ill-tempered, spiteful man who spent much of his life as a drifter, mostly as a mercenary soldier who kept volunteering for service far from home before he finally disappeared. He married Katherine Guldenmann, daughter of an innkeeper who was mayor of a nearby town. She was as restless and quarrelsome as her husband. They made life miserable not only for each other but also for their seven children, whom she forsook for a time to join Heinrich on one of his campaigns.

Into that atmosphere of discord and insecurity Johannes was born prematurely in 1571. From the outset he was frail and had many childhood diseases—including smallpox, which he barely survived.

In 1577 his mother showed him a spectacular comet. Three years later his father took him out to see an eclipse of the moon. So, early in childhood Johannes Kepler turned his thoughts toward the heavens, which became for him a lifelong concern.

The Keplers belonged to a small Lutheran community painfully struggling for freedom of worship. As a young boy Johannes developed a devout faith; after Latin school he decided to enter the Protestant ministry. At the age of thirteen he passed the highly competitive examinations to enter a preparatory seminary. During the next five years he continued his struggles with repeated illness, stiff academic requirements and rivalry among the students.

In autumn 1589 Kepler entered the University of Tübingen, a famous center of Protestant theological studies pervaded by a bold and speculative spirit. During the first two years he had a broad educational program in the Faculty of Arts leading to a master's degree. He then started a three-year program of theological subjects. During those years he was seldom free from headaches, skin rashes and enervating fevers. Yet he kept his scholarships and won academic distinction.

The influence of a teacher sometimes changes a student's career. For Kepler that teacher was Michael Maestlin, a professor of mathematics and astronomy who was highly regarded throughout Europe. Since the Copernican theory was too technical for classroom instruction, Maestlin explained it to an inner circle of able students. He showed how the new system accounted for the retrograde motion of the planets in a natural way, and how the planets were arranged in an elegant harmony with respect to both their distances from the sun and their periods of revolution. Young Kepler was fascinated and quick to see the advantages of the new and simplified model over the Ptolemaic system. He began to prepare notebooks of evidence that Copernicus's theory was correct. Several years later he wrote to a friend, "I became so delighted with Copernicus, whom Maestlin often mentioned in his lectures, I even wrote a painstaking disputation about the first motion, maintaining that it happens because of the rotation of the Earth."[4] Throughout his life Kepler remained devoted to Maestlin and consulted with him occasionally about technical problems in astronomy.

Despite his growing interest in science, Kepler continued his theological program to prepare for the ministry. In the course of his studies he began to question certain Lutheran doctrines, including the precise nature of the Holy Communion. But Kepler's studies were interrupted by a decision that changed his career. Early in 1594 the Protestant seminary in Graz, Austria, asked the Tübingen authorities to recommend a successor to their mathematics teacher who had just died. Kepler was selected for the position. Since he would complete his degree by the end of the year, he debated at length whether he should go. Finally, with a promise that he could return whenever he chose, Kepler took the position as teacher.

With borrowed money he set out for Austria, arriving in Graz on April 11, 1594. There he found the atmosphere brittle with religious tension. In that part of Europe the prince determined whether his domain would be Lutheran or Catholic. So a new ruler could change a country's official faith overnight. In Graz, although the nobles were Reformed, Archduke Charles was not; he summoned the Jesuits to begin a Catholic reconquest of Styria (southeastern Austria). Nevertheless, several islands of Lutheranism held out, including the *Stiftschule* (ecclesiastical school) at which Kepler taught.

In spite of his efforts Kepler never became a good teacher. Like many other creative geniuses, he was not gifted in presenting his ideas to beginners. His high standards were not appreciated by students who had little interest in mathematics and astronomy to begin with. But he received commendation from the school inspectors.

Kepler's appointment included another position, that of district mathematician (a sort of borough surveyor) and maker of calendars (almanacs). Astrological calendars provided not only dates for phases of the moon and eclipses, but also prospects for weather and harvest, the fates of kingdoms and the fortunes of war. Noblemen with little concern for astronomy had great interest in astrology, so "calendar men" were much in demand. Kepler proved to be one of the best. His predictions for the year 1595—peasant rebellion, Turkish attacks and an unusually cold winter—were on target. For the next five years his success as a horoscope-caster widened his social contacts among the nobility.

Kepler believed that the heavenly bodies influenced earthly events. Although he continued his commitment to generalized astronomical predictions, he warned against depending on such calendars alone. Actually Kepler prepared his calendars mostly on a common-sense evaluation of political and economic conditions. He also made them general enough not to get caught too far out on a limb when events sawed it off. Kepler once declared that astrology is "the foolish daughter of the respectable and reasonable mother Astronomy." Yet he played the game because he had to; it was part of his job and a means of augmenting his meager salary.

Meanwhile Kepler's main interest focused on matters far more important than predicting harvests and battles. His mind continued to dwell on the Copernican model—with its intrinsic beauty and potential insight into the order and meaning of nature.

Astronomical Discovery

Kepler's imagination was captured by two main ideas: the importance of the sun and the mathematical harmony of nature. Those convictions guided Kepler, the mystic and mathematician, in his lifework as an astronomer. Of the Copernican theory he wrote, "I have attested it as true in my deepest soul, and as I contemplate its beauty with incredible and ravishing delight."[5]

Copernicus had made a bold beginning, but he also had raised important problems. The most basic concerned the nature of the universe. As a Christian, Kepler was convinced that God had a master plan when he created this orderly, beautiful and mathematically perfect world. Kepler's own thinking reflected and reinforced the ancient Pythagorean idea that "numbers govern the world." So the underlying mathematical harmony—the music of the spheres—is the real cause of the planetary motions. God's plan is discovered in the mathematical laws he has provided.

Kepler wanted to discover all the laws in that master plan, to complete the entire jigsaw puzzle. His relentless search for scientific truth reflected the devotion of a committed Christian. On one occasion he reported, "I believe Divine Providence intervened so that by chance I found what I could never obtain by my own efforts. I believe this all the more because I have constantly prayed to God that I might succeed if what Copernicus had said was true."[6]

Kepler wove those themes into his first major book, the *Mysterium cosmographicum* ("Cosmographic Secret"). It was published in 1596 through the influence of Maestlin, who generously gave his time to editing for style and seeing the manuscript through the printing.

Kepler attempted to correlate the increasing distances of the planets from the sun with a combination of the five regular or "perfect" solids of the Greek geometrists. Using the available observations, Kepler gave a purely mathematical solution. Today we recognize that the correlation is accidental. Although the solids do not really fit the data, however, the model shows Kepler's ingenuity.

Kepler realized that although Copernicus had made the sun stationary, he did not use the sun, but rather the center of the earth's orbit, as his reference point. Thus the sun played no physical role. But Kepler believed that the sun's centrality was essential to celestial physics; the sun itself must provide the force to keep the planets moving. Kepler tried to describe mathematically how that force diminished with distance. The important physical-mathematical step had been taken. Although his physical explanation was erroneous, his idea established Kepler as the first astronomer to demand physical explanations for celestial phenomena.

On April 27, 1597, Kepler married Barbara Mueller, the daughter of a prosperous mill owner. Then in her early twenties, she had already been twice widowed and was the mother of a little girl, Regina. Although there was enough affection to keep it going, the marriage was not a happy one. Kepler was an erratic genius whose science was a consuming passion that his wife didn't appreciate. In turn, she was accustomed to a standard of living her husband couldn't maintain. Grief visited them in the early death of their first two children. Henry lived barely two months, Susanna six weeks; both died of spinal meningitis.

For a while Kepler's work went well. The *Stiftschule* was pleased with their famous mathematician and encouraged him in his research. His mind bubbled with a dozen different scientific ideas. He made friends with the nobleman von Hohenburg, who lent him many books. Kepler also kept up a lively correspondence with some who criticized his book.

Meanwhile Archduke Ferdinand had been tightening the screws of his campaign against the Protestants in his realm. In September 1598 he ordered all Lutheran theologians and teachers to leave the country within two weeks. Only Kepler was allowed to return. Then the archduke suddenly banished anyone who was not a Catholic, or who did not pledge to become one immediately, and levied a heavy property tax. When Kepler refused to convert, he was dismissed from his two positions and ordered to leave the city. On September 30, 1598, jobless, with a growing family and little cash reserve, he fled from Graz with Barbara and Regina in two small wagons carrying the only household goods they were allowed to take. He did not realize that his flight would lead him to Tycho Brahe, whose observations would provide the data he needed to pursue his astronomical research.

Tycho Brahe (1546-1601)

Three years after Copernicus's death Tycho Brahe was born into a noble Danish family. At the age of thirteen he entered the University of Copenhagen to study philosophy and rhetoric. The next year an eclipse of the sun changed his life. Tycho was fascinated by the fact that the time of the eclipse had been accurately predicted. He immediately invested some of his allowance in astronomical tables and a copy of Ptolemy's *Almagest*. During the rest of his years at the university he concentrated on mathematics and astronomy.

In 1562 Tycho continued his studies at Leipzig. He also studied at several other northern European universities under one gifted astronomy professor after another. He took up the practice of astrology, became interested in astronomical instruments and designed a new portable sextant. Tycho realized that even the most precise instrument cannot be perfectly accurate. So he calculated in advance the error inherent in his equipment—a procedure that has been followed ever since with scientific instruments. As a result, his measurements with the naked eye were five times more accurate than those of Hipparchus, the greatest observer of antiquity.

After returning to Denmark, Tycho discovered the spectacular nova of November 1572 shining in the constellation of Cassiopeia. As he collected observations from other astronomers, he discovered that the new star was much farther away than the moon. Contrary to Aristotle, changes do occur in the heavens! Tycho published his measurements and conclusions in his first book, entitled *De nova stella* ("On the New Star").

In 1576 the king of Denmark became Tycho's patron and granted generous funds for astronomical research. On the tiny island of Hven, set aside exclusively for his use, Tycho built the most elaborate observatory of the time. Uraniborg (meaning "Castle of the Heavens") was a complete city with its own residences, laboratories, printing press, paper mill and four observatories equipped with excellent instruments designed by the astronomer himself.

During twenty years of work at Uraniborg, Tycho became the leading scientific figure in Europe. He was visited by philosophers, statesmen and even an occasional king. Although kind to the sick and poor, he could be a harsh taskmaster to his workers. He insulted shallow nobles and did not hesitate to contradict a ruler. After the Danish king died, Tycho feared the loss of royal support at home. He eventually accepted the invitation of German Emperor Rudolph II to become the imperial mathematician with a generous salary. Tycho arrived in Prague in 1599.

Although Tycho had the highest admiration for Copernicus, he rejected his theory—partly for scientific reasons, but also because the Holy Scriptures repeatedly affirmed the stability of the earth. Since he couldn't accept Ptolemy's model, Tycho worked out a compromise: The earth remains stationary at the center of the universe; around it revolve the moon, sun and outer sphere of the stars, but the five planets revolve around the sun (figure 5).[7]

The hybrid version failed to gain wide acceptance. Nevertheless Tycho made an invaluable contribution to astronomy and the new science. His long series of accurate planetary observations provided an entirely new star catalog to replace that of Copernicus with its many inaccuracies.

Tycho and Kepler

Although Johannes Kepler's *Cosmological Secret* had a mixed reception, a significant response came from Tycho Brahe, to whom Kepler had sent a copy with a request for his opinion. The Dane considered the main thesis clever and interesting, but, as he observed in a letter to Maestlin, pure reasoning should be supported by observations of the heavenly bodies. He was impressed enough to invite the younger man to become his assistant. In later years Kepler observed that the direction of his whole life, study and writing took its departure from that one small book.

On February 4, 1600, Johannes Kepler and Tycho Brahe met face to face in the castle the emperor had assigned to his court mathematician. The contrast between the two astronomers could hardly

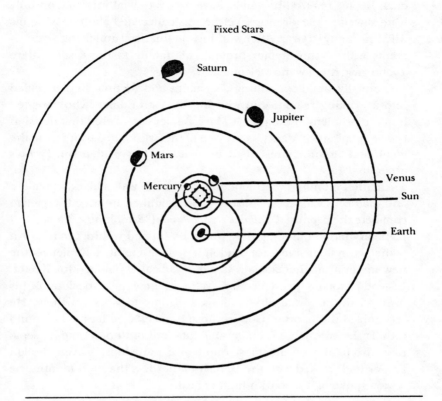

Figure 5. Tycho Brahe's Geocentric Universe
All the planets revolve around the sun, while the sun revolves around the earth.

have been greater—in age, social background and standing, temperament, and even their views of the solar system. There was a wide gulf between them, yet they desperately needed each other. Although only fifty-three, Tycho felt his strength declining and wanted a vigorous young assistant to prepare from his vast amount of observations a set of planetary tables based on his system. Kepler, in turn, needed accurate data to confirm his hypothesis of regular solids and planetary distances, and to carry out his strategy for discovering the master plan of the universe.

The following months were a period of uncertainty, friction and misunderstanding between the two men. Tycho jealously guarded his data; Kepler realized he would have access to vital information only if he stayed a year or more. Yet he was concerned about leaving his wife's property in Graz. After working out financial and living arrangements with Tycho, Kepler brought his family to the castle, where Tycho gave them warm welcome.

Gradually, amid continuing difficulties and friction, Kepler settled into a working relationship with the old astronomer, who assigned him the problem of the planet Mars. Kepler considered that decision providential, since Mars was the one planet whose departure from the ideal circular orbit prescribed by Aristotle was evident in Tycho's accurate data.

After ten months Tycho suddenly became ill with a bladder ailment and died on October 24, 1601. On his deathbed he urged Kepler to complete the proposed *Tabulae Rudolphinae* ("Rudolphine Tables") of planetary motion, hoping they would be framed within Tycho's own planetary system. Emperor Rudolph soon appointed Kepler as the new imperial mathematician. It was a radical about-face for Kepler. Instead of total dependence on Tycho, he now had a position of his own, all the accurate observations and time to work on them. He recognized the hand of God in those events: "God let me be bound with Tycho through an unalterable fate and did not let me be separated from him by the most oppressive hardships."[8] Even though Kepler had worked with the Danish master less than ten months, he always spoke of Tycho with high regard.

Conquest of Mars

What looked like a blitzkrieg turned out to be a long war of attrition. Instead of solving the problem of Mars's orbit in a matter of weeks, Kepler had to struggle for almost five years. His official responsibilities left him only about half of his time to pursue the project.

Kepler's problem was complicated by the fact that since Mars was observed from a moving earth, two orbits had to be taken into account. The astronomer tried to fit the observations with a circular orbit and equant in various positions. Through a long, tedious calculation using seventy trials he found a solution that worked for the earth. He formulated what we call his second law of motion: *the radius vector sweeps out equal areas in equal times* (figure 6b). In other words, an imaginary line connecting a planet and the sun sweeps over equal

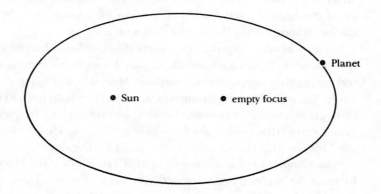

a. *First Law:* The planetary orbits are ellipses with the sun at one focus.

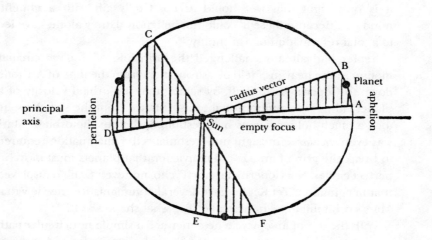

b. *Second Law:* The radius vector sweeps out equal areas in equal times. The three shaded portions are equal in area, so the planet must move through orbital arcs AB, CD and EF in equal times, therefore faster when it is nearer the sun.

Figure 6. Kepler's First and Second Laws

areas of the plane of its orbit in equal time intervals. (Kepler understood the fundamental nature of this law only later when he based the calculation of the *Rudolphine Tables* on it.)

Kepler was encouraged by his progress but realized that the struggle was not over. With characteristic humor he wrote to friends that he was succeeding in his personal war with Mars (the Roman god of war). Yet he knew that more fighting was in store. He would have to burrow through mountains of figures, checking and rechecking frequently for minor errors that could ruin the whole procedure. He would not rest until his calculations accurately accounted for the data.

When Kepler used a circular orbit with Tycho's data for Mars, it was in error by eight minutes of arc—about a quarter of the angular breadth of the full moon. The accuracy of Tycho's measurements and the rigor of Kepler's mathematical standards kept him from overlooking that relatively small difference between theory and data, which other astronomers would have ignored. Later Kepler wrote, "Divine Providence granted us such a diligent observer in Tycho Brahe that his observations convicted the Ptolemaic calculation of an error of 8′; it is only right that we should accept God's gift with a grateful mind. . . . Because these 8′ could not be ignored, they alone have led to a total reformation of astronomy."[9]

Kepler had already challenged the principle of *uniform* circular motion in the heavens, held by astronomers from the time of Aristotle down to Copernicus himself, by stating that the orbital velocity of a planet is inversely proportional to its distance from the sun. Now he took a much bolder step as he questioned whether the orbit of Mars was even *circular*. Hindsight underestimates the imagination required to break the grip of an age-old conviction that planets must move in perfect circles. Not Copernicus, nor Tycho, nor even Galileo displayed that imagination. Yet Kepler gave several arguments for the view that Mars's orbit might be noncircular. But what shape was it?[10]

With the use of an epicycle he generated a simple noncircular path similar to an ellipse but slightly egg shaped, with the fat end containing the sun. Because working with that ovoid curve presented a complex computational problem, he adopted an ellipse as an approximation, although one rather different from his final curve (figure 7). After nearly four years of labor, Kepler seemed on the brink of failure. Ill and depressed, he reported his research to date and made arrange-

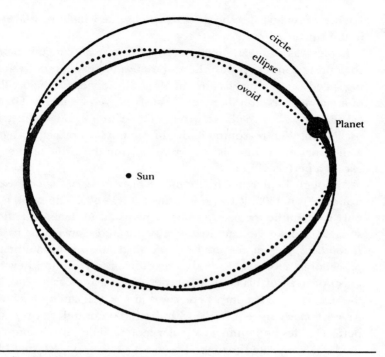

Figure 7. The Circle, Ovoid and Ellipse

ments for its publication in case he died before it was finished. Yet he continued to struggle through the winter of 1605.

Around Easter the astronomer superimposed a circular orbit on the oval-shaped orbits of the observations and studied the "new moons" between the two curves. Suddenly he saw that the figures pointed to an ellipse, previously overlooked, with one focus at the sun. He later said it was as if he had awakened from a sleep. Kepler had arrived at what we call his first law of motion: *The planets move in ellipses with the sun at one focus* (figure 6a). His victory cleared away all the complicated epicycles, deferents and equants which had cluttered astronomy since Ptolemy. For the first time a single geometric curve and a single speed law became sufficient for predictions of planetary positions, and for the first time the predictions were as accurate as the observations. The new model of the solar system was mathematically simple and aesthetically beautiful. Most important, it presented an accurate picture of physical reality. For Kepler astronomy was "a science of reality, and should reveal to us that which truly takes place in the Universe."[11]

Kepler was also searching for a *physical* cause of planetary motion— something connected with the sun that would explain both the varying speed and varying distance of Mars. He hoped that the oscillations of a magnetic axis of Mars would satisfy his requirements. Finally his calculations succeeded. He wrote, "The ellipse exists because of the oscillation. With reasoning derived from physical principles agreeing with experience there is no figure left for the orbit of the planet except a perfect ellipse."[12]

Although Kepler finished most of his *Astronomia nova* ("New Astronomy") in 1605, it was not printed until 1609. The book was not only a scientific treatise but also a personal testament of the long struggle. Unlike Ptolemy in the *Almagest* and Copernicus in *On the Revolutions*, Kepler reported significant details of the mathematical procedures he used. His book was difficult to read and beyond the grasp of most of his contemporaries. Yet it stands as a landmark in the history of astronomy. Kepler was justified in calling his book the *New Astronomy* since it broke with the two-thousand-year tradition of perfect circles and uniform angular motion. The subtitle emphasized the book's repeated theme: "Based on Causes, or Celestial Physics, Brought Out by a Commentary on the Motion of the Planet Mars." Although Kepler's theory of magnetic forces fell by the wayside, his insistence that celestial physics be based on causes has profoundly influenced contemporary science, which assumes that physical laws operate everywhere in the universe. In a long introduction defending his physical principles, Kepler described how the Copernican system could be reconciled with the Bible.

Kepler also found time to study the properties of light. His research led to a clearly defined concept of the light ray, the foundation of modern geometrical optics. In 1604 Kepler published *Astronomiae pars optica* ("The Optical Part of Astronomy"), which discussed parallax, refraction and his eclipse instruments. This work ultimately changed the course of optics, especially when Kepler applied these principles to the telescope in 1611. When Galileo sent a copy of the *Starry Messenger* with a request for an opinion about his startling telescopic discoveries, Kepler replied quickly with a long letter of approval, which he promptly published. A few months later Galileo wrote, "I thank you because you were the first one, and practically only one, to have complete faith in my dissertations."[13]

Added to Kepler's other personal problems during this period were his wife Barbara's depression and opposition from Tycho's son-in-law. Yet throughout his demanding research and trying circumstances Kepler maintained his sense of humor and faith in God.

Theology and Science

During the year 1611, Johannes Kepler's personal world fell apart. In February smallpox invaded his home, struck the three children and claimed six-year-old Frederick, who was his favorite. The child died to the sound of foreign troops pillaging Prague, now aflame with rioting and disease. Stricken with grief, Barbara soon caught typhus brought by the soldiers and died in July.

Since Emperor Rudolph had lost his political grip and been deposed, Kepler's position at court became precarious. For that reason he had been trying to get the chair of mathematics at Tübingen and succeed his old professor Maestlin, who had retired. But he received word that the Lutheran theologians had vetoed his appointment. Kepler had questioned the Formula of Concord which he was expected to affirm. It stated a view of Christ's bodily presence in the sacrament of Communion that Kepler found unsupported by his intensive study of the Bible and the early church fathers. He was accused of Calvinist leanings which disqualified him from being considered a "brother in Christ." As a result the door was shut to the one position which would have provided the professional status and financial security he desperately needed.

Early in 1612, while still supported by Rudolph, Kepler moved to Linz as district mathematician. That area was a stronghold of ultra-conservative Lutheranism. Kepler immediately applied to his new pastor, Daniel Hitzler, for admission to Communion. He honestly explained his doctrinal position, whereupon Hitzler regarded him as an "unhealthy sheep," denied him the sacrament and excluded him from the congregation. Six years later Kepler made a final appeal to the theologians at Tübingen. They officially instructed him to accept the Formula of Concord or else "steer clear of the congregation of our church and our creed." His exclusion from the Lutheran fold grieved the astronomer for the rest of his days as he was caught in a no-man's land between two opposing authoritarian religious establishments.

With his knowledge of astronomy Kepler gave attention to solving certain chronological problems in the Gospel of Luke. For example, how could Quirinius have been governor of Syria when Augustus was Caesar? By searching the Roman and Greek records along with the Hebrew and Babylonian calendars, Kepler discovered a mistake in the Latin calendar. He calculated that Jesus was actually born in the year 4 B.C. and wrote a treatise defending the reliability of Luke's record.

One bright light in Kepler's fourteen years in Linz was his marriage to Susanna Reuttinger, a twenty-four-year-old orphan, on October 30, 1613. She made a happy home for Kepler and his two children. Susanna bore him seven more children, of whom five died in infancy or childhood. Kepler was a devoted father, concerned for the religious instruction as well as the education of his children. He composed a catechism on the sacraments for them to memorize.

During his first difficult years in Linz, Kepler published no astronomical works, although he did write a significant mathematical treatise which was a forerunner of the calculus. With it he devised a new procedure for calculating the volume of wine casks.

Meanwhile Kepler's mother was arrested and accused of witchcraft. In the fall of 1617 he traveled to Württemberg to arrange for her defense. She was eventually acquitted. In September the first daughter of his second marriage died; several weeks after his return to Linz in February 1618 his second infant daughter died.

In 1618 Kepler completed a cosmological study on the harmony of the universe, which he called "a sacred sermon, a veritable hymn to God the Creator."[14] A major work of 255 pages, entitled *Harmonice mundi* ("Harmonies of the World"), it developed his theory of harmony in four areas: geometry, music, astrology and astronomy.

> With the accuracy of the researcher, who arranges and calculates observations, is united the power of shaping of an artist, who knows about the image, and the ardor of the seeker for God, who struggles with the angel. So his *Harmonice* appears as a great cosmic vision, woven out of science, poetry, philosophy, theology, mysticism.[15]

In the course of his investigation Kepler discovered what we now call his third law of motion: For any two planets, *the squares of their periods of revolution are proportional to the cubes of their mean distances from the sun.* Kepler was especially pleased with that law because it neatly linked the planetary distances with their periods or velocities. Ironically, *Harmonies* was published at a very disharmonious time: the outset of the Thirty Years' War between the Protestant Union of princes in northern Europe and the Catholic League of the south.

During his latter years in Linz, Kepler published a monumental work, *Epitome astronomiae Copernicanae* ("Epitome of Copernican Astronomy"). It was a book intended for use in schools to compete with textbooks then in use based on Ptolemy's system. Published in three parts during 1618 to 1621, it provided the strongest defense up to that time of the Copernican theory, but its difficult contents made it more a handbook for professors than a text for students. *Epitome* ranks with Ptolemy's *Almagest* and Copernicus's *On the Revolutions,* however, since from 1630 to 1650 it was the most widely read treatise on theoretical astronomy in Europe.

Despite its name, *Epitome* is far more than an introduction to Copernican theory. It is a complete astronomy including Kepler's three laws and the concept of modern celestial mechanics which he introduced. Especially significant for the problem of motion are his comments on the force we now call gravity. This volume is the theoretical handbook for Kepler's new celestial tables based on his reforms of the Copernican system. Kepler's planetary positions are about thirty times better than those of his predecessors.

Yet the astronomer's concern extends beyond the *efficient* cause, the mathematical explanation of nature's mechanisms. He pursues his search for *final* causes, the reason why things are as they are: the relative sizes and distances of the planets, the apparent size of the sun and the length of the day. In the *Epitome* as well as the *Harmonies,* we see Kepler the scientist, theologian and philosopher.

Scientific Method

Kepler made a significant contribution to the development of the new scientific method. He was the first professional astronomer to accept Copernicus's theory and work it out in mathematical detail. Kepler was convinced that mathematical laws provide the basis for explaining natural phenomena. He observed that although Aristotle traced things ultimately to *qualitative* distinctions, and gave mathematics only an intermediate place, he (Kepler) searched for *quantitative* relationships: "Nothing [about nature] can be known completely except quantities or by quantities. And so it happens that the conclusions of mathematics are most certain and indubitable."[16] That new scientific approach collided with the qualitative, symbolical, alchemical tradition.

Kepler interpreted causality in terms of mathematical simplicity and harmony discoverable in observed facts. He struggled to devise a theory that accounted for most of the data, tried to fit *all* of the data to the theory, then attempted to improve the theory to make it fit better. Earlier Kepler had come to recognize that he could go no further with theory alone; he required access to Tycho's accurate observations. "Without proper experiments I conclude nothing."[17] Valid mathematical hypotheses must be exactly verifiable through observation; they must be tested against facts rather than age-old tradition.

Further, Kepler refused to treat Copernicus's discoveries and his own merely as mathematical hypotheses. He held that they gave a true picture of the real world since the underlying structure of physical reality is mathematical. Unlike previous astronomers, Kepler sought a unified, physically acceptable model. "In Kepler's view the physical universe was not only a world of discoverable mathematical harmonies but also a world of phenomena explainable by mechanical principles."[18] He recognized, for example, that in Copernicus's system the central reference point is the center of the earth's orbit and not the stationary sun; therefore the latter plays no physical role. Kepler argued that the sun itself must provide the driving force to keep the planets moving.

In his research Kepler went one step further to discover how God the architect had planned the earth and set it in motion. Kepler's sense of order and harmony was intimately linked with his theological understanding of God the Creator. Repeatedly he affirmed that geometry and quantity are coeternal with God and that humankind shares them because human beings are created in the image of God. Kepler boldly sought to know why the universe is as it is. It must be "archetypal" laws in the mind of the divine architect and engineer that keep his construction going. Edward Rosen observes,

> Kepler's clarion call, trumpeted to receptive ears, echoed and re-
> echoes down the corridors of the seventeenth century and thereaf-

ter. It demonstrated how unswerving allegiance to the scientific quest for truth could be combined in one and the same person with unwavering loyalty to religious tradition: accept the authority of the Bible in questions of morality, but do not regard it as the final work in science.[19]

Kepler played a decisive role in the advancement of modern science. Without his strenuous work the progress of astronomy would have been delayed for a century. When Newton later deduced his law of universal gravitation, he started with Kepler's laws of motion, especially the third one. In fact, Newton's great *Principia mathematica* was introduced to the Royal Society as a "mathematical demonstration of the Copernican hypothesis as proposed by Kepler."[20]

Final Years

After the *Epitome* the astronomer devoted himself to fulfilling his long-delayed responsibility for preparing the tables of Tycho's data. The work was to be called the *Rudolphine Tables* in honor of Tycho's patron. In this tedious task Kepler encountered the old problems: the jealousy of Tycho's son-in-law, salary arrears, the need to obtain a special grant for publication, vigorous persecution of the Protestants in Linz and a city caught in the clutches of war. The scratched record of Graz and Prague was being replayed.

The gigantic project occupied most of Kepler's creative energy from 1621 to 1623, when the *Tables* were completed. Getting them printed was another matter. Although Emperor Ferdinand promised to pay for their publication, Kepler had to spend two frustrating years going from city to city to negotiate for each one's share of the cost. In the process he collected only a third of the amount needed and had to advance the rest out of his own meager savings.

In 1625 the emperor issued a sweeping new edict banishing most of the Protestants and confiscating writings not conforming to Catholic dogma. Kepler was spared because of his court title and work on the *Tables* then being printed. In 1626 the peasants rebelled against the Bavarian troops occupying Linz and laid siege to the city, whose inhabitants soon suffered hunger and disease. In June of that year, disaster struck as the printer's house in the outskirts was burned; the press and printed pages were destroyed, although the bulky manuscript was unharmed.

By November 1626, Kepler had left Linz with his family and belongings and headed for Ulm, where he found a new printer. The complicated 586-page manuscript of the *Rudolphine Tables* was finally published in September 1627. It included an enlarged star catalog and a section on the use of logarithms, invented by John Napier in 1614, too late for Kepler's use in his earlier calculations.

Kepler moved one more time. In July 1628 he and his family traveled north to the town of Sagan in Silesia. In the employ of the famous general Wallenstein, the astronomer once more turned to writing. He published his *Ephemerides,* astronomical annuals with lists of tables showing the position celestial bodies would occupy on certain dates. They gave data concerning eclipses and other facts useful to astronomers and navigators. He also wrote one of the earliest works of science fiction, called *Somnium seu astronomia lunari* ("Dream of the Moon").

Kepler felt isolated in the remote town of Sagan, far from the city life he had always known. He also continued to miss the church and its sacraments. Once again in 1629 the long arm of the Counter-Reformation reached out, directing Protestants to become Catholic or leave. Again Kepler saw many of his friends ruined or exiled as fear gripped the city. His despondency was momentarily lightened by two events in the spring of 1630: the birth of a baby daughter and the marriage of his grown daughter Suzanna.

Soon the old record played one last time: Graz, Prague, Linz and now Sagan. That summer Wallenstein was relieved of his command. The Swedes invaded Germany and headed toward Silesia. The religious situation in Sagan worsened. The imperial treasury still owed Kepler the immense sum of 12,000 gulden, and his future looked more precarious than ever. In October 1630, nearly sixty years old, he wearily set out in a hopeless mood to collect long overdue interest on bonds in Linz, to persuade the emperor to pay his debt, and to seek a new patron. He had no plans for either returning to his family or preparing a new home for them.

On November 2, Kepler rode his horse across the cold Danube River into Regensburg where he stayed with a friend. Soon he came down with a fever that grew steadily worse with occasional delirium. Although several clergymen visited him, they did not offer the Communion he had been denied so many years. Yet Kepler was not bitter.

When someone asked him in a lucid moment where he thought his salvation lay, he answered confidently, "Only and alone on the services of Jesus Christ." In Christ the astronomer found his refuge and solace.

About noon on November 15, 1630, Johannes Kepler died. He was buried in the cemetery of St. Peter's Church outside the walls of Regensburg, far from his family in Sagan. On a simple tombstone was chiseled an epitaph that Kepler had written a few months earlier:

I used to measure the heavens,
  now I shall measure the shadows of earth.
Although my soul was from heaven,
  the shadow of my body lies here.[21]

Three years later the tides of war reached the city and obliterated the churchyard. But they could no longer harm Kepler or his legacy to our understanding of the universe.

1564	Galileo's birth
1574	Family move to Florence
1581	Student at Pisa University
1585	Return to Florence
1589	Professor of mathematics at Pisa
1592	Professor of mathematics at Padua
1609	Construction and use of telescopes
1610	Return to Florence as the Grand Duke's chief mathematician and philosopher
1611	Visit to Rome with the telescope
1614	Caccini's sermon against Galileo
1615	*Letter to Christina;* third visit to Rome
1616	Admonishment by Cardinal Bellarmine
1623	Cardinal Barberini becomes Pope Urban VIII; Galileo's fourth visit to Rome
1623	Start of work on the *Dialogue on the Two Principal World Systems*
1632	*Dialogue* publication and ban; summons from the Inquisition
1633	Trial and recantation in Rome; house arrest in Arcetri
1637	Total blindness
1638	Publication of the *Discourses* at Leiden
1641	Torricelli's work with Galileo
1642	Galileo's death

Figure 8. Galileo: A Chronology

4
GALILEO: PHYSICS AND ASTRONOMY

Philosophy is written in this grand
book of the universe,
which stands continually open to our gaze. . . .
It is written in the language of mathematics.
  GALILEO GALILEI

RENAISSANCE ITALY WAS A COLLECTION OF STATES WITH A WIDE variety of governmental structures. In one the people might hold power; another would have a hereditary ruler. Such diversity fostered the idea that there could be more than one way to govern. Differences of opinion on economic and social issues flourished. In that relatively open society, ready in many areas to consider new ideas, Galileo Galilei began his education.

In two arenas, however, the strong hand of authority maintained a firm grip. The Roman Catholic Church had a monopoly on religious life, and Aristotelian philosophy dominated science in the universities. Yet in Galileo's time both institutions found themselves on the defensive against swirling currents of Reformation and Renaissance.

Those currents converged in the life and work of this controversial figure sometimes called the father of modern science. Few episodes in the history of science have generated more intense debate than the ecclesiastical condemnation of Copernicus's astronomy in 1616 and the trial of Galileo in 1633. In one form or another that controversy continues unabated almost four centuries later.

Galileo was of average height, a heavyset man quick both to anger and to return to good humor. He was a passionate, powerful character who could dominate any room or discussion. His talent and wit won a variety of illustrious friends in university, court and church circles, and among artists, musicians and craftsmen. At the same time his biting sarcasm against those whose arguments were vulnerable to his scientific discoveries made him some formidable enemies. Galileo thrived on debate, the clash of minds and words. He knew that although theories have to be proved, people have to be persuaded. His professional life was spent not only in observing and calculating but also in arguing and convincing. His goal was to promote as well as develop a new scientific world view.

Galileo's career divides easily into three main periods. The first (1564-1610) includes his life as a student and professor at Pisa and then Padua. The middle years (1610-1632) extend from his return to Florence to the publication of his *Dialogue*. The final period (1633-1643), beginning with his trial, covers the decade of his house arrest. This chapter will concentrate on the first period and Galileo's scientific achievements leading up to the condemnation of Copernicus in 1616. Chapter five will focus on the development of Galileo's theology of science during the middle period, on the trial and finally on his last decade of research and writing.

Early Years

Galileo came from an old noble Florentine family that had seen better times. His father, Vincenzio, was a musician who performed well on the lute and was also interested in music theory. He studied the new music, especially problems of instrumental music with a single voice. Conducting experiments with a specially constructed single-stringed instrument, he discovered a mathematical law contradicting the fundamental assumption of traditional music theory.

Vincenzio engaged in sharp controversy with Gioseffo Zarlino, an acknowledged musical authority with whom he had studied for two years in Venice.[1] Following an acrimonious correspondence, Vincenzio wrote a *Dialogue on Ancient and Modern Music*. When Zarlino prevented its publication in Venice, the volume was published in Florence. For Vincenzio, even an ingenious and authoritative theory could not replace a trained musician's ear. His experimental approach and polemic writing must have made an impression on his son, who dealt with issues and opponents in the same way some years later.

In 1562 Vincenzio married Giulia Ammannati, a woman of intelligence and education, in Pisa, where he settled. The first of seven children, Galileo was born on February 15, 1564, the year of Shakespeare's birth. He grew up in an artistic home, sharing many interests with his father, from whom he derived a love of music and a keen interest in mathematics. Young Galileo became a fine lute player and competent organist; his musical background may have been useful in his scientific work. He was fond of poetry and loved to draw and paint. He picked up his father's confidence in experiments and enjoyed making mechanical devices, just as Newton did a century later. Galileo's mechanical bent persisted. As a scientist he constructed instruments both to test his theories and to make practical use of his discoveries.

In 1574 the family moved to Florence. Galileo attended school at a famous Benedictine monastery, Santa Maria at Vallombrosa, where he received the usual Renaissance education and religious training. When Galileo considered entering monastic life, his father wasted no time in diverting him from that course. Nevertheless, the boy continued his studies with the monks until 1581.

At the age of seventeen Galileo entered the school of medicine at the University of Pisa. At that time Italy was rich in centers of learning, with thirteen universities (in contrast to the three in England and Scotland). Yet for all the discoveries and innovations of the Renaissance, academic instruction was largely authoritarian. Like most established powers, it discouraged creative thinking and viewed new outlooks with disfavor. With Aristotelianism reigning supreme in philosophy and science, the golden age of Greece might be recaptured but never surpassed. All teaching took place in Latin, which students were expected to speak outside class as well. The academic establishment looked back to tradition, as yet unaware of the new world on its doorstep.

As long as the only books were manuscripts, universities could maintain a monopoly on science.[2] After about 1500 that situation changed rapidly. Printers in many cities made their investments in equipment pay off by keeping their new presses running. They issued inexpensive books appealing to wider audiences, soliciting works of public interest from new authors. With new opportunities to communicate practical information, the domain of useful science spread far from the centers of learning, often independently of them.

The outpouring of cheap books benefited the universities least. Having flourished for centuries without multiple copies of texts, they continued to base their instruction on lectures and debates. Handbooks and compendiums comprised the main texts. The task of the natural philosophers (that is, the scientists) was to transmit that tradition to students, not to experiment or innovate. Except for medicine, the important scientific advances in sixteenth-century Italy occurred outside the universities. The new astronomies of Copernicus and Tycho Brahe and developments in mechanics and physics rarely made their way into the curriculum. In some respects university science was less advanced than it had been two centuries earlier because it failed to keep up with these changes.

In such an academic climate, young Galileo encountered both the tradition of the first-century Roman physician Galen and the more ancient authority of Aristotle. Even as a student he developed an independence of thought and an argumentative style that earned him the nickname "The Wrangler." His running controversy with Aristotelian professors lasted almost half a century.

Meanwhile Galileo's interest in medicine waned. When his funds ran out in 1584 he left Pisa without a degree. Wanting to concentrate on mathematics and physics, Galileo pursued the study of Euclid and Archimedes under the tutelage of his father's friend Ostilio Ricci. Within a year Galileo constructed an improved hydrostatic balance which brought him to the attention of the nobles of Florence. His new theorems concerning the center of gravity of certain solids earned Galileo his first recognition abroad. Both the problem and his method of solving it showed the influence of Archimedes, to whom Galileo frequently turned for inspiration and guidance.[3] Although not unknown during the Middle Ages, Archimedes' works had received little attention before the sixteenth century. During his stay at home Galileo also developed a love for the classics and an interest in popular literature.

Professor at Pisa and Padua

After several years of scientific successes, Galileo returned to Pisa in 1589 with a three-year appointment as professor of mathematics. As he studied natural phenomena, he recognized the crucial importance of mechanics, the science of motion which was the simplest kind of change so important in Aristotle's natural philosophy. But for Galileo an exact understanding of movement would play a much larger role: the first and indispensable kind of knowledge of the physical universe. The mathematicians, guided by Euclid and Archimedes, viewed the world in terms of geometrical shapes and mathematical laws to account for observations. But their status was inferior to that of the natural philosophers, whose province was explanation of the physical world. These Aristotelians were not prepared to have a mere mathematician invade their field of physics and argue for new concepts of motion.

Galileo soon began writing an untitled treatise, now referred to as *De motu* ("On Motion"), which was not published but circulated privately.[4] He attacked Aristotle's concept of two classes of motion: *natural,* as in the fall of an object to earth, and *violent,* as in the flight of a projectile. Galileo introduced imaginary rotations of massive spheres and defined "neutral" motions, an idea that eventually led to his concept of inertia in terrestrial physics. His genius enabled him to devise "thought experiments" by imagining idealized situations— for example, a motion without friction.

On Motion sought to negate Aristotle's two rules on the speed of a falling body: (1) that it is proportional to the body's weight, and (2) that it is inversely proportional to the density of the medium. Although he demonstrated conditions of equilibrium on inclined planes, Galileo failed at that time to recognize the importance of gravitational acceleration. As a result he was unable to reconcile his conclusions about motion with the observed facts. (The story of Galileo's experiment of dropping large and small cannonballs from the top of the tower of Pisa, told by a later biographer, is probably unfounded. Yet subsequent writers filled in the details to embellish that account, which until recently was called "the most famous of all experiments.")

Unfortunately, Galileo had a knack for antagonizing people. His outspoken criticism of the academic establishment made him many enemies. He even wrote a satire in verse on a university ordinance requiring professors to wear their academic gowns *at all times* (including the bedroom?). That bit of poetic ridicule appeared not in Latin but in everyday Italian—a medium that proved effective for Galileo in later controversies. By his last year at Pisa, his faculty colleagues had suffered so much at Galileo's hands that in revenge they attended his lectures and hissed at comments with which they disagreed.

When his appointment ended in 1592, Galileo knew it would be useless to apply for renewal. So he enlisted the support of several influential friends to secure an appointment as professor of mathematics at the University of Padua near Venice. The chair was given to him rather than an Aristotelian, Giovanni Magini, whose term at Bologna was about to end. From then on, Magini bore Galileo a grudge. Padua's freedom of thought attracted the ablest students from all over Europe, many of whom came to study with Galileo during his eighteen years at that university.

Galileo continued his work as a mathematician, experimental physicist and practical inventor.[5] In 1595 he devised a mechanical explanation for the tides that required the two circular motions of the earth assumed by Copernicus. Even though his theory turned out to be wrong, evidently it marked the beginning of Galileo's interest in astronomy. Two years later a German visitor gave him Kepler's first book, the *Cosmographic Secret*. In thanking him, Galileo affirmed that he had long accepted the new astronomy.

Investigating a way to measure temperature by constructing an air thermometer, Galileo set up a workshop and designed some of the equipment himself. To augment his salary, he offered private instruction to young foreign noblemen in military architecture, surveying, fortification and mechanics. Galileo invented a "geometric and military compass" that could be used for calculations in surveying, navigation, gunnery and sundial construction. In 1599 he hired a craftsman to make those instruments for sale.

When his father Vincenzio had died a decade earlier, Galileo had shouldered the financial responsibility for his mother, brothers and sisters. The outside income from consulting and manufacture of instruments supplemented his meager professorial salary and enabled Galileo to provide a generous dowry when his sister married in 1601. During his Paduan years Galileo had a Venetian mistress named Marina Gamba, who bore him two daughters and a son. The elder daughter, Virginia, entered a convent with her sister Livia, took the name Maria Celeste and later became her father's chief solace. The son, Vincenzio, assisted his father during the last years of his life. When Galileo went to Florence in 1610, Marina Gamba returned to Venice, and eventually married.

The Paduan years were particularly fruitful for Galileo's study of mechanics. In 1602 he investigated pendulums and the descent of bodies along arcs and chords of circles, with special interest in acceleration. His initial calculations were made under an (incorrect) assumption that the speed of a falling body is proportional to the distance traversed. His later studies of pendulums and inclined planes were integrated under his (correct) law of acceleration: the speed is proportional to the square of the elapsed time. In that research Galileo's application of mathematics to dynamics went beyond his mentor Archimedes, who had worked only with statics.

In 1604, as Galileo was writing about his law of falling bodies, a supernova appeared in the evening sky.[6] Comparing observations in other cities with his own and finding no evidence of parallax, Galileo concluded that the supernova was at a great distance among the fixed stars. Yet according to Aristotle no change could take place in the heavens. To capitalize on the general excitement over the unusual event, Galileo gave three public lectures explaining how observations and careful measurements proved that the object was indeed a new star, not just a motionless comet near the moon. It was clear that Aristotle must be wrong.

That event led to the *first* of *five crucial controversies* with university philosophers in which Galileo continued to attack the scientific establishment. Cesare Cremonini, the ranking professor of philosophy at Padua, rose to Aristotle's defense. He could hardly let a mere mathematician prove actual change in the heavens, even though the mathematician was a long-time personal friend. To engage in a public feud the two professors went into print under assumed names.

Galileo adopted a literary technique that in his hands became a sharp polemic weapon. He countered Cremonini's arguments in a dialog between two peasants written in rustic Paduan dialect. One of the peasants reasoned more effectively than the prestigious professor. To the professor's argument that measurements on earth do not apply to vast distances in the heavens, the peasant asked sarcastically, "What do philosophers know about measuring anything?"

Although the Aristotelian tradition valued observations, its concern was primarily *qualitative.* Galileo's interest, on the other hand, was *quantitative;* wherever possible, he made accurate measurements. As a pioneer of the new science, he also showed how much ingenuity and how many precautions are required to obtain useful results.[7]

Cremonini opposed that idea and stood against Galileo on the scientific issues discussed during their time together at Padua. Five years later, when Galileo reported his telescopic observations, Cremonini refused even to look at the sky through the newfangled instrument. No wonder he eventually became the model Aristotelian philosopher in Galileo's famous *Dialogue.*

Telescopic Discoveries

Although Galileo had become convinced that the earth moves around the sun, he remained a closet Copernican—much to the discomfiture of Kepler, who urged him to come out publicly with his belief.[8] Galileo continued to wait until he could make a convincing case for the public, whose ridicule he feared. Then a dramatic discovery altered his scientific interest for many years.

In mid-1609 Galileo heard that a Dutch instrument maker had put lenses together in order to make distant objects look closer.[9] Realizing the importance of such an instrument to Venice as a maritime power, Galileo quickly obtained two lenses and assembled his own telescope. After much experimentation, he built an effective instrument that magnified nine times, a little more than most ordinary modern binoculars. By late August he demonstrated to the Venetian senate a telescope that could identify approaching ships two hours before they could be spotted by trained naked-eye observers. In gratitude the doge (ruler) of Venice granted Galileo the chair at Padua for life at double the salary, a level unprecedented for mathematicians.

Galileo immediately converted his workshop facilities to telescope production, refining his techniques to meet a sudden spate of orders. No one could match the quality he achieved through painstaking efforts. He experimented with dozens of instruments and made hundreds of observations over the years. Responding to criticism of his discoveries, Galileo asserted that people had no reason to believe he had deceived them with his reported observations.

With a twenty-power telescope he scanned the heavens and discovered countless new worlds. The Milky Way became a gigantic collection of stars. The vast expanse of the universe taught by Copernicus suddenly appeared plausible. More startling were several discoveries closer to earth that flatly contradicted Aristotle's teaching. Galileo could see that the moon is not a perfect sphere shining with its own light. Rather it has imperfections, mountains and valleys, much like the earth. Galileo was able to calculate the depth of those valleys from the length of their shadows and the position of the moon. He also discovered that the planet Venus has phases like those of the moon. To make matters worse, the sun has dark spots that appear and disappear; even the sun is not the perfect, unchangeable sphere of Aristotle's astronomy. Galileo concluded that either the sun turns on its own axis or the earth must move around the sun.

Equally disturbing, and of greater importance for the Copernican theory, was the discovery of four smaller bodies moving near Jupiter. As Galileo viewed them at different times and calculated their movements, it became clear that the four bodies are moons revolving around Jupiter. Yet according to Aristotle and the scientists of the day, only the earth as the center of the universe could have a moon. Now Jupiter and its four moons could be seen as a model for Copernicus's conception of the solar system: the planets (including the earth) moving around the sun.

Although Copernicus's theory had seemed to contradict common sense, the new evidence for the Copernican system was plainly visible to anyone who could peer through a telescope. Gazing at the heavens became a favorite after-dinner activity for guests of princes and prelates. After 1609 people without mathematical training could see for themselves that Aristotle could be wrong: "The telescope did not prove the validity of Copernicus's conceptual scheme. But it did provide an immensely effective weapon for the battle. It was not proof, but it was propaganda. . . . That is the greatest importance of Galileo's astronomical work; it popularized astronomy, and the astronomy it popularized was Copernican."[10]

Galileo soon recognized the importance of his discoveries. By March 1610 he published a slim volume entitled *Sidereus nuncius* ("The Starry Messenger") with a promise of "unfolding great and marvellous sights."[11] The results were presented in a clear and compelling style. That simple metal tube with two lenses constituted a bludgeon for beating the Aristotelians and demolishing their universe. Yet the best-selling *Starry Messenger* gave no unambiguous evidence that Galileo accepted the Copernican system.

A second edition was published in Frankfurt within months. At the age of forty-five, Galileo suddenly became famous throughout Europe. In Prague the Tuscan ambassador gave Kepler a copy with a request from Galileo for comments. Kepler's pamphlet, *A Discussion with the Starry Messenger,* extolled Galileo's work. The two publications spurred a frenzy of telescope building and star watching.

Galileo soon made another remarkable discovery while observing Venus. That planet had been too close to the sun to observe when he made his first telescopic discoveries. During the last half of 1610, though, Galileo observed the entire range of phases (from a dark disk through crescent and gibbous forms to a bright disk) expected of the planet in the Copernican model. At one blow the phases of Venus falsified the Ptolemaic system.

In Galileo's *second* public controversy, his opponent was the same Giovanni Magini who had lost the chair of mathematics at Padua to Galileo eighteen years earlier. Magini, who had become professor of astronomy at Bologna, said after publication of the *Starry Messenger* that he would see Galileo's Jovian satellites "extirpated from the sky." A Magini protégé, Martin Horky, published a book denouncing Galileo's claims. Indeed, for the most part, astronomers ridiculed Galileo or accused him of fraud.

Magini became the first academic to draw the clergy into such scientific controversies. He prompted a young religious zealot, Francesco Sizi, to publish an incredible book advancing semireligious arguments that there should be only seven planets, and claiming the supposed moons orbiting Jupiter to be an illusion. Although only a popgun, Sizi's book showed the lengths to which Galileo's opponents would go. Galileo did not consider that kind of attack worthy of reply, but one of his students did answer it on his behalf.

The Gathering Storm

In June 1610 Galileo took a fateful step whose consequences were unforeseen. He resigned the life appointment and generous salary at Padua granted by the doge of Venice to whom he had presented his first telescope. Leaving the political safety of the Republic of Venice, Galileo returned to Florence to become "Philosopher and Mathematician to the Grand Duke." Galileo's new post gave him official recognition as a philosopher and a strong base for challenging the universities. Free from the demands of academic life, he could continue his experiments and proceed with his two books, "an immense design, full of philosophy, astronomy, and geometry."[12] After two decades of thought, he intended those works to establish the Copernican system on the basis of new discoveries in astronomy and physics.

Galileo moved to Florence in September, but hardly to the "perfect state of quiet of mind" he needed. For a while he thought his continuing discoveries, especially the phases of Venus he observed in October, would convince the most stubborn Aristotelian professors. But some refused to peer through his slight "optical reed"; others looked but professed to see nothing; a few argued that his "discoveries" were really due to flaws in the lenses, or were optical illusions.

Galileo perceived danger in the hardening attitude of the scientific establishment as he saw the lengths to which they would go to preserve their tradition and writings. Envious of Galileo's large salary and the favors bestowed on him by the grand duke, his opponents were out to safeguard their own professional status and properties. Galileo could feel a solid front building against him, from his alma mater of Pisa, from Padua and from Bologna.

At that point Galileo decided he needed independent confirmation of his observations. So in April 1611 he traveled to Rome, where he contacted Father Clavius and other Jesuit astronomers at the Roman College. He took along one of his telescopes, demonstrated it and then left it with them so they could check his discoveries night by night. Seeing the phenomena for themselves, those astronomers became convinced and enthusiastically honored Galileo. Old Father Clavius was shaken in his strict Ptolemaic faith. It was difficult for the undisputed leader of Jesuit astronomy to yield to new appearances in the skies, but he gave in gracefully. In a later report to a church commission chaired by Cardinal Robert Bellarmine, however, Clavius pointed out (correctly) that the observations themselves did not unequivocally support the Copernican theory.

While in Rome Galileo was elected to the Lincean Academy, a "scientific society" founded by Prince Federico Cesi.[13] At a banquet given for the visiting scientist, the word *telescope* was coined. Galileo's subsequent correspondence with other members kept him well informed of scientific developments in Rome.

On the same visit Galileo obtained an audience with Pope Paul V, whom he favorably impressed. The scientist also visited Cardinal Maffeo Barberini, a mathematician and member of a rich Florentine family who later became Pope Urban VIII. Barberini seemed to appreciate the new discoveries, and in the years to come Galileo kept hoping he might openly accept the new theory.

Overjoyed at the reception of his discoveries, Galileo returned home confident that his trip had been an unqualified success. Had not his observations been confirmed by the highest astronomical authority in the land? Further, he now had the friendship of Cardinal Bellarmine and Prince Cesi. With church and society both on his side, what was there to fear? The answer was not long in coming.

Disgruntled professors at Pisa now allied themselves with a set of courtiers at Florence in a secret and loosely organized resistance movement known as the *Liga*.[14] The leading figure was the Florentine philosopher Ludovico delle Colombe. Later in 1611 he published in Italian a treatise that began with traditional arguments against the earth's motion but ended with quotations to show that such motion was incompatible with Holy Scripture. If Galileo could not be beaten by purely scientific arguments, the *Liga* resolved to take the battle into theological terrain. Nicknamed the "pigeons" *(colombi)* after their leader, that academic group comprised the "conspiracy" of which Galileo often spoke.

With his astronomy becoming so popular, the *Liga* decided to tackle Galileo in the arena of physics, and in Florence, where he had the fewest allies. He would be engaged in open discussion where he could be defeated. They chose the villa of Galileo's friend Filippo Salviati, a frequent meeting place for courtiers and professors on leave from Pisa. The dinner-party controversies over floating bodies and their shapes soon became notorious. Colombe offered to show experimentally that his opponent was wrong. He already bore a grudge because of Galileo's attack on Colombe's book about the new star of 1604. The two exchanged letters and public experiments to support their arguments. The grand duke invited Galileo to debate the issue with a professor of philosophy at Pisa during a court dinner for two visiting cardinals. Galileo's position, which was supported by Cardinal Maffeo Barberini, was completely vindicated.

This *third* public dispute led to a book, *Discorso intorno alle cose che stanno su l'acqua* ("Discourse on Floating Bodies"), which became another best seller and went through two editions in 1612. Public interest was stimulated by the variety and appeal of experiments that required no special equipment and were amusing to perform. Galileo had again tweaked the scientific establishment. He remarked that the *authority* of Archimedes (his favorite Greek natural philosopher) was worth no more than that of Aristotle; Archimedes was right only because his propositions agreed with experiments. In the debates Galileo accused Colombe of "word spinning" in problems he didn't understand. The professor's rancor increased until he eventually sought revenge in a more serious way than scientific dispute.

Meanwhile Galileo became enmeshed in a *fourth* public controversy, one with dire consequences. Below the surface of what appeared to be simply an astronomical disagreement lurked much larger implications. Father Christopher Scheiner, a Jesuit astronomer at the University of Ingolstadt in Bavaria, constructed telescopes based on Kepler's design and in April 1611 began using them to observe the sun. Seven months later he discovered spots on the solar surface. Scheiner reasoned that the spots either lay on the sun's surface as blemishes or were caused by small orbiting planets. He favored the second possibility since dark spots on such a bright surface seemed unlikely. More important to Scheiner was their contradiction of Aristotle's teaching that celestial bodies are perfect, not subject to change or decay.

When Galileo read the printed reports in 1612 he strongly disagreed. To Galileo it was important for the spots to be on the sun; he was glad to have evidence that, like the earth, the sun was an ordinary, imperfect body. He was able to demonstrate from Scheiner's drawings as well as his own observations that the spots changed shape. They were immense clouds on the solar surface.

In 1613 Galileo's *Historia e dimonstrazioni intorno alle macchie solari* ("Letters on Sunspots") was published by the Lincean Academy. For the first time Galileo openly advocated the new astronomy. An appendix presented convincing evidence for the Copernican view: the eclipses of Jupiter's moons and a simple method to predict them.

Aristotle had taught that celestial phenomena were essentially different from the terrestrial; their explanations had entirely different bases. Against that view, Galileo interpreted heavenly phenomena by means of earthly analogies. The *Letters* made it clear that Galileo was not only anti-Aristotelian but also a thoroughgoing Copernican. Only the new theory could make sense of the telescopic discoveries. Galileo's preface, claiming priority of discovery of sunspots, angered Scheiner. Many other Jesuits were offended and supported Scheiner in a long, bitter feud.

That same year Galileo's former pupil Benedetto Castelli was appointed to the chair of mathematics at Pisa. The professors at Pisa were hostile to Castelli from the start. When warned by the university's overseer not to teach Copernicanism, Castelli replied that he had already been given that advice by Galileo.

A Flank Attack

Disappointed by their failure to break through Galileo's lines on the fronts of physics and astronomy, the *Liga* adopted a new strategy. Carrying the attack into court circles, they would make his scientific discoveries a religious issue. Late in 1613, at a formal dinner given by Grand Duke Cosimo II (Galileo's employer), the new astronomy became a subject of discussion. Since Galileo was not present, Benedetto Castelli defended his former mentor's views. During the informal debate Cosimo Bostaglia declared that any motion of the earth was impossible since it would contradict Holy Scripture. After dinner Grand Duchess Christina persistently questioned Castelli on that issue.[15] During their discussion Professor Bostaglia made no comments.

Castelli wrote Galileo a full account of the discussion. It had been customary to debate issues of natural philosophy on their own merits. Concerned that his enemies were now dragging scientific questions into the perilous waters of theology, Galileo decided the time had come to meet such a challenge head-on. In a *Letter to Castelli* just before Christmas 1613, Galileo carefully spelled out his position as a scientist and a Catholic. He reaffirmed his commitment to the truth and authority of the Bible, then raised the question of its proper interpretation. Obviously it speaks at times in figurative terms and language understandable to the average person. Galileo expressed concern about "the carrying of Holy Scripture into disputes about physical [that is, scientific] conclusions." God has given us two books, one of nature, the other of Scripture. "Both the Holy Scriptures and Nature proceed from the Divine Word, the former as the saying of the Holy Spirit and the latter as the most observant executrix of God's orders."[16] He affirmed that the "two truths can never contradict each other," even though they are expressed in different languages for different disciplines: religion and ethics in Scripture; physics in nature. Why, then, should the Bible be used to support the opinion of fallible philosophers against others, to the jeopardy of its authority?

As copies of that letter circulated freely, battle lines were drawn, with both theologians and courtiers taking sides. Although Galileo had intended to silence illogical objections to Copernicus, his enemies turned his arguments into an occasion for innuendo, misrepresentation and rumor. Throughout 1614 the scientist was accused of undermining Scripture and meddling in theology.

Galileo's *fifth* major conflict suddenly became very public. On December 20, 1614, Father Tommaso Caccini, a Dominican friar with connections to the Aristotelian professors, preached a sermon from the pulpit of a principal church in Florence. In his sermon on Joshua's miracle of making the sun stand still, Caccini strongly condemned the idea of a moving earth as being very close to heresy. He branded all "mathematicians" as agents of the devil who ought to be banned from Christendom. That was a serious charge; in the public mind "mathematicians" were identical with astrologers, who at that time were viewed with growing suspicion.

To friends in Rome Galileo wrote that he was concerned to have been the subject of a Sunday sermon. The fact that the leader of the Dominicans wrote a formal apology did little to placate him. Even though it was known that the authorities were keeping an open mind about the new discoveries, Caccini's sermon strengthened the opposition against Galileo.

Shortly after Caccini's attack, a priest named Niccolo Lorini read a copy of the *Letter to Castelli*. It was one thing for a scientist to speculate about nature; it was quite another for a layman to write a thesis interpreting Scripture to fit those speculations. Lorini may have been haunted by the specter of Protestant exegesis and private interpretation of the Bible. So on February 7, 1615, he sent a copy of the *Letter* to one of the Inquisitors-General in Rome with his concern that the followers of Galileo "were taking upon themselves to expound the Holy Scriptures according to their private lights, . . . that they were trampling underfoot all of Aristotle's philosophy. . . . I believe that the Galileans are orderly men and all good Christians, but a little wise and cocky in their opinions."[17]

When Galileo heard that his *Letter* had been submitted to the Holy Office, he immediately sent an authentic copy to his friend Archbishop Piero Dini in Rome, asking him to show it to Cardinal Bellarmine. Galileo pointed out that he had written that letter in haste and was now expanding his exposition. In June 1615 he en-titled a new treatise, *Letter to the Grand Duchess Christina*. That work was copied and widely circulated (though not published until 1636 in Strasbourg).

The ensuing discussion and events leading to the fateful condemnation of the Copernican system in 1616 will be considered in the next chapter. Before that, however, we should summarize the main elements of Galileo's scientific activity.

Galileo's Science

The most vexing problem in assessing Galileo's contribution to Western thought is the extent to which he introduced a new "scientific method." Our answer must distinguish between Galileo the scientist and Galileo the symbol. He became a legend almost in his own lifetime. For many he has become the symbol of a revolt of reason against prejudice and authority, of the clear certainties of science against murky opinions of medieval theology.

The first historians of science, the French Encyclopedists of the late eighteenth century, saw his work as a watershed between old and new ways of doing science, a sharp creative break with the past. For them the scientist was a symbol. They presented Galileo as protomartyr and patron of the cause of intellectual freedom from benighted religious authoritarianism. Not until the early twentieth century was the natural philosophy of the late medieval and Renaissance periods fully appreciated. Scholars then became aware of non-Aristotelian mathematical mechanics dating back to the fourteenth century. The pendulum swung to the opposite extreme: some saw Galileo as simply rescuing that discovery from neglect and carrying through its first general formulation.

Granting that the truth probably lies somewhere between those extremes, certain questions remain. How original was Galileo's science? What was his method? How did the results of his work contribute to the "new science" he attempted to construct?

We have already sketched the climate of Aristotelian natural philosophy within which Galileo began his work in mathematics and mechanics. We have seen some of the subjects on which he challenged the scientific establishment of his time as his steps began to diverge from the traditional path. Since Galileo's work did not take place in a vacuum, we may inquire about the sources of his inspiration. Four main influences have been suggested: (1) reading, (2) experiment, (3) conceptual formulation and (4) Copernicanism.[18]

As to the first, Galileo's early efforts at Pisa to explain motion show that he had certainly read earlier writings, especially those of the "impetus" school. As a teacher at Padua he would have been familiar with the major variations of Aristotle's dynamics worked out by earlier theorists, as well as the complicated mathematics derived from the Merton school. As to experiment, Galileo was clearly able to perform experiments, though he did not do them often. He stressed their importance. "Where mathematical demonstrations are applied to natural phenomena, . . . the principles once established by well-chosen experiments become the foundation of the entire superstructure."[19]

With respect to the third influence, Galileo frequently devised "thought experiments" to explore the implications of a hypothesis and demonstrate its logical consistency. His conceptual ability is evident in the way he reinterpreted facts already available. In the *Dialogue,* for example, he persuaded readers by helping them see familiar facts in a new light, not new facts never before discovered. As to the fourth element, Galileo's early commitment to the Copernican system as the "true" view of the universe (not just the most convenient mathematical way to describe planetary motions) provided a framework and motivation for his lifelong work in mechanics. In fact, Galileo's mechanics and astronomy were remarkably interdependent as he tackled the age-old problem of motion.

Although some scholars attribute the major role in the drama of Galileo's creative achievement to one or another of those factors, each of them played its part in the complex thought and activity of the great scientist. The tendency to oversimplify must also be resisted in explaining Galileo's scientific method. Unlike Kepler, he did not provide a systematic treatment of his views on this subject. He wrote almost nothing for publication during the crucial Paduan period (1597-1610) when a new and different mechanics gradually took shape in his mind. Galileo's ideas on procedure and epistemology at times were confused and inconsistent in the tentative fitting and trying that went on throughout his life. Like most practicing scientists, he phrased his insights according to the exigencies of the moment rather than a defined philosophy. Since Galileo could see green grass on both sides of the fence, he has been claimed by a variety of philosophical schools. Here we avoid such debate in the interest of briefly noting the main elements in Galileo's practice of science.

For Galileo mathematics was the key to unlocking the secrets of the universe.

This grand book . . . cannot be understood unless one first learns to comprehend the language and to read the alphabet in which it is composed. It is written in the language of mathematics, and its characters are triangles, circles, and other geometric figures, without which it is humanly impossible to understand a single word of it; without these, one wanders about in a dark labyrinth.[20]

As a mathematician turned physicist, Galileo equated understanding the physical world with knowing its geometrical structure. He believed that nature could be interrogated in the language of mathematics, but he was also convinced that it should be allowed to answer for itself. In other words, mathematical analysis and theory must have empirical confirmation. For Galileo scientific facts had to do with observations and measurements of "primary" characteristics such as quantity, shape, size and motion, and not "secondary" qualities such as color, sound and smell so important in Aristotelian natural philosophy. Nature replies to mathematical questions because nature is the domain of measure and order.

The role of experiment in Galileo's work has long been debated. Many of the experiments attributed to him, and some which he himself describes, were not actually carried out. He was a great interpreter, not a gatherer of facts. Some of these were "thought experiments" in which he imagined a specific situation and thought through the consequences of a given idea or hypothesis. Galileo was a true "experimenter" in this basic respect: he constantly aimed to confirm features of his theories by specially designed experiments. His clear lesson was that assumptions made in setting up a hypothesis must be verified; good scientific theories must return naturally to reality.[21] Galileo's approach is not purely mathematical; it is *physico-mathematical*. Reality is the incarnation of mathematics.

How, then, should experiments be conducted? Experimentation must be more than the simple accumulation of data. For Galileo the laboratory is not the breeding ground but the testing ground of theories. Whether real or mental, experiments are productive only if they are arranged in accordance with a hypothesis that determines the data to be obtained for mathematical analysis. Facts do not speak unless interrogated, and the kind of question one asks determines the range of meaningful answers. Experiments by themselves do not provide theoretical statements; they illustrate, confirm or falsify an existing hypothesis. Yet a well-designed critical experiment may call for a change in current theory. It may even suggest the direction such a change should take to fit the new experimental results.

One of Galileo's most important contributions to scientific methodology was his knack of *idealizing* a problem. He was able to reduce each problem to its basic, essential form; to eliminate factors not immediately relevant; to reach "laws" that did not describe the motion of any actual body, but rather stated what its behavior would be if the influence of environment were eliminated or standardized. For example, idealization treats the earth's surface as a plane, and perpendiculars to it as parallel. It ignores friction and resistance in the study of falling bodies. It conceives the idea of the mass-point. Galileo was able to distinguish between the primary and secondary qualities of Aristotle and concentrate on measuring the former. He by-passed the complex problem of *causes* in order to discover a mathematical *description*. This knack of idealizing enabled Galileo to go right to the heart of a problem and develop a simple mathematical theory.[22]

The three major elements in Galileo's scientific method are intuition, demonstration and experiment. First, he idealized a problem to identify its essential form, isolate the basic elements to be analyzed and formulate a hypothesis or model. Second, he deductively worked out a mathematical demonstration of several conclusions and devised well-chosen experiments to test them. Third, he carried out his experiments—real or mental—and evaluated the results. Galileo observed that, although such a method begins with the data of sense perception, it sometimes leads to conclusions that seem to contradict the senses. For example, in the Copernican astronomy mathematical reason (the earth moves around the sun) overrides our senses (we see the sun moving).

A New Science?

In a reaction against the sterility of sixteenth-century Aristotelian science, pioneers like Bacon and Descartes claimed to have an entirely new method. But is that what Galileo meant when in the *Discourses* he proposed a "brand-new science concerning a very old subject"? In what sense did he consider it "brand-new"? What he presented there was not a new method or conception of science but aspects of motion that "had not hitherto been remarked, let alone demonstrated."[23]

Galileo inherited and confirmed Aristotle's general conception of science as knowledge that can be "shown" or "demonstrated," that is, proved, explained and taught.[24] To qualify as fully "scientific," knowledge must fulfill all three goals, but especially be proved (established) and explained. Aristotle distinguished between two kinds of scientific knowledge, the "what" and the "why," effects and causes. One establishes the facts (that is, the behavior of a ball rolling down an inclined plane); the other "gives the why of" the facts (a mathematical explanation). Although Galileo set out to dismantle Aristotle's physics, in the *Dialogue* he was careful not to criticize the latter's conception of science. Galileo disagreed with the Greek philosopher on the consequences of "new events and observations," but he stated that if Aristotle were alive, "I have no doubt he would change his opinion."

Galileo also shared Aristotle's "scientific realism," the view that there is a uniquely true physical theory, discoverable by human reason and observation, and that alternative theories are consequently false. Galileo believed that the distinguishing features of the natural sciences are conclusions that are "true and necessary." True knowledge of causes is obtained by "certain demonstration." The *Discourses* is dotted with terms like *rigorous proof* and *demonstration.*

He disagreed with Aristotle, however, on the nature of physical reality, claiming that it is mathematical in form and that mathematical theory should determine the structure of experimental research. Only in mathematics do we find certainty. The full demonstrative ideal of science can be achieved only to the extent that a physical science can simulate mathematics. Here Galileo was guided by his mentor, Archimedes.

Unfortunately, the telescope opened up a new and puzzling realm where this "true and necessary" demonstration was not possible. The heavenly bodies demanded a different kind of science, a new and less direct mode of proof, since they were remote and unfamiliar. Causal reasoning was difficult to test since direct experiments were not possible. Galileo realized that demonstrative science could not handle questions like the nature of comets. (Nor could it operate in the realm of the "very small," with the problem of atoms.) As a result, Galileo's conclusions about features of the moon were based on analogy, inference and retroduction, which goes from effect to proximate cause and back to effect, relying on confirmation through testing predictions (see chapter 9).

In Copernican astronomy Galileo's problems with demonstrative science came to a head. He used Kepler's recommended method of getting "true knowledge" by excluding all hypotheses except one. To that end he argued against the physics of Aristotle and the astronomy of Ptolemy. He gave seven arguments to show how much simpler it is to postulate the earth's rotation rather than that of the stars. But Galileo admitted that he was not "drawing a necessary proof from them, merely a greater probability." In order to *demonstrate* the movement of the earth he would have to use a causal argument. For this proof he turned his attention to the tides, an argument with far-reaching consequences considered in the next chapter.

So two different conceptions of science animated Galileo's work. The demonstrative ideal, which he inherited from the Greek tradition, was the one he formally held and never abandoned, despite the difficulties it created in the realm of cosmology. The other conception was the principle of retroduction exemplified in his discussions of phenomena whose causes are remote (comets, sunspots), enigmatic (motions of the earth) or invisible (atoms). Although he used retro-ductive inference with great skill, Galileo refused to consider anything less than rigorous demonstration as genuine "science."[25]

While others talked about the need for new methods of science, Galileo endeavored to discover a demonstrative science of motion. He was not a philosopher but a scientist; he did not propose a new theory of science but a new science as he laid the foundations for modern mathematical physics. Yet in doing so he pioneered a path that ulti-mately led to a new conception of the scientific enterprise.

5
GALILEO:
SCIENCE AND
THEOLOGY

The doctrine attributed to Copernicus,
that the earth moves around the sun . . .
is contrary to the Holy Scriptures
and therefore cannot be defended or held.
CARDINAL BELLARMINE

GALILEO'S CONDEMNATION IN 1633 STANDS AS THE MOST DRA-matic and notorious incident in the long history of inter-action between science and theology. Concentration on the scientific issues has often obscured the political and religious context of the conflict.

Political upheavals early in the sixteenth century precipitated a crisis of confidence in the Italian mind. The sack of Rome in 1527, collapse of the Florentine Republic in 1530 and Spanish domination over most of the peninsula lowered a curtain of disillusionment. Loss of faith in political reforms led to a greater emphasis on the authority of princes.

During this period Thomas Aquinas (1224-1274), a thoroughgoing

Aristotelian, was the most popular guide to the meaning of faith. Cardinal Robert Bellarmine (1542-1621), Galileo's chief protagonist in the 1616 crisis, was appointed papal theologian and counselor to the Holy Office. As the church bureaucracy grew, Bellarmine did not hesitate to tell Catholic princes that they had a moral obligation to enforce true beliefs among their subjects.

Italian influence was decisive at the Council of Trent (1545-1563), called to formulate a response to the growing Protestant challenge. In 1559 Paul IV issued the first official Roman *Index* of prohibited books. Toward the end of the sixteenth century, church authority appeared to triumph. The Counter-Reformation soon became a continuous action of vigilance that included censorship, for example, of all translations of the Bible into popular language. The early seventeenth century produced a wave of ideological condemnation. "Individuals and governments were considered subject to a single eternal system of justice based ultimately on eternal and divine law, of which the Catholic church was the sole guardian and interpreter."[1]

In such a climate, innovations in science or any other field could easily be considered a threat to that system unless shown to agree with the church's teachings. For that reason, Galileo made a concerted effort to show that his discoveries were neither contrary to the Bible nor a challenge to the authority of the church. This chapter reviews the theology of science he developed in events that led to a crucial decision against Copernicanism in 1616, the seven years of relative calm after that, and then a stormy decade of scientific and theological efforts culminating in his trial in 1633. A brief description of Galileo's discoveries and writings during the final years of house arrest will close our account.

Science and the Bible

Ludovico delle Colombe's pamphlets of 1611 were the first indication that Galileo would be attacked on theological as well as scientific grounds. He reacted first by consulting Cardinal Conti on the problem of Aristotle and the Bible. Conti noted that several of the great philosopher's teachings—for example, on the immutability of the heavens and the eternity of the world—contradicted Scripture. On the other hand, the Copernican doctrine could be held only on the assumption that the Bible speaks (about the earth as immovable) in the ordinary language of the people—an assumption that should not be made without compelling necessity. In his 1613 *Letter to Castelli,* Galileo explained his ideas on how the Bible might be so interpreted. With that decisive step he accepted the challenge of waging the battle on theological grounds and resolving conflicts between scientific and biblical accounts of natural events.

In 1615 Galileo wrote his more careful and detailed version known as the *Letter to the Grand Duchess Christina.* There he set forth his view of the relationship between science and theology. He tried to argue three essential points: (1) The issue had been brought to the Roman court for reasons based on wrong premises. (2) Astronomical theories could not be matters of faith. (3) The new cosmology was in harmony with biblical teaching if the Bible were interpreted according to ordinary exegetical principles of long standing in church tradition, but at variance with the literal emphasis of the Council of Trent.[2]

The introduction to *Letter to Christina* describes how the controversy started: Galileo stated that his opponents in the *Liga* "have resolved to fabricate a shield for their fallacies of the mantle of pretended religion and the authority of the Bible. These they apply, with little judgment, to the refutation of arguments that they do not understand and have not even listened to."[3] Galileo notes that the Copernican system was devised by a "pious Catholic who was even consulted by the Church in the matter of the form of the calendar. He did not ignore the Bible, but knew very well that if his doctrines were proved, then they **would** not contradict the Scriptures when rightly understood."

Galileo then explains his view of the Bible's authority. "The Holy Bible can never speak untruth—whenever its true meaning is understood." But that true meaning is not always obvious from the literal sense, as anyone can see in the Bible's use of anthropomorphic terms for God's hands and feet and eyes. Such terms are inspired by the Holy Spirit "in order to accommodate them to the capacities of the common people, rude and unlearned as they are." Galileo notes that this principle of interpretation has been widespread among all theologians.

Yet the problem is whether that principle can be applied to passages where the Bible speaks of physical matters. Galileo uses the famous metaphor of the "book of nature," which plays a central role in all his thinking about theology and science: "The Holy Bible and the phenomena of nature proceed alike from the Divine Word. . . . God is known . . . by Nature in His works, and by doctrine in His revealed word." Galileo emphasizes that the Bible is written for "the primary purpose of the salvation of souls and the service of God" and not to teach science.

Therefore, "in discussions of physical problems we ought to begin not from the authority of scriptural passages, but from sense-experience and necessary demonstrations." Further, we should not be surprised that the biblical authors speak so little of physical or astronomical matters, since their purpose was religious and immediately related to revealed truths which can never be reached by reason or sense. Galileo then takes pleasure in quoting Cardinal Baronius to the effect that in the Bible the Holy Ghost intends to teach "how one goes to Heaven, not how the heavens go."

Even though the book of Scripture and the book of nature must be approached in different ways, they cannot contradict each other because they proceed from the same Author. On that score Galileo appeals to St. Augustine, who warned against setting the authority of Scripture against clear and evident reason. Why then do we find apparent contradictions between the two? Galileo states that it is the "task of wise expositors to seek out the true sense of scriptural texts. These will undoubtedly accord with the physical conclusions which manifest sense and necessary demonstrations have previously made certain to us."

Although he believes that the church has a teaching office with divine guidance, Galileo wants the theologians to stay within their proper limits. He is unhappy with a number of theologians who are "men of profound learning and devout behavior, but who nevertheless pretend to the power of constraining others by scriptural authority to follow in a physical dispute that opinion which they think best agrees with the Bible, and then believe themselves not bound to answer the opposing reasons and experiences."

In his *Letter to Christina,* however, Galileo hesitates between two quite different views of the relationship between the Bible and natural science.[4] One series of arguments leads cogently to the conclusion that the Bible uses the common language of the time. The writers express themselves according to the physical views of their time in order to be understood. A phrase such as "the sun standing still" is not intended as a scientific teaching. Incidental references to physical phenomena in the Bible are irrelevant to questions of natural science.

At the same time, Galileo uses other arguments leading to the totally different hermeneutics of Augustine: The scientist must provide a "conclusive demonstration" of his hypothesis before the theologian needs to ask whether an apparently conflicting passage of Scripture ought to be given a nonliteral interpretation. Galileo writes, "Yet even in those propositions which are not matters of faith, this authority [of the Bible] ought to be preferred over that of all human writings which are supported only by bare assertions or probable arguments, and not set forth in a demonstrative way."[5] In other words, only if a *demonstrated* scientific truth conflicts with the literal meaning of a passage can we question whether it should be interpreted literally.

Which of the two conflicting hermeneutical views did Galileo choose? Even though he probably leaned toward the first (given his sensitivity to matters of meaning and language), he realized that it was contrary to a nearly unanimous tradition on biblical interpretation. Besides, he was confident that he could provide the necessary demonstration of the earth's motion, a goal consistent with his conviction that a hypothesis did not become "science" until it was rigorously proved. So Galileo conceded to biblical authority over scientific hypotheses that are merely probable, thus setting the stage for his later encounter with Cardinal Bellarmine.

Finally, Galileo summons courage to comment on the exegetical decree of the Council of Trent, whose authority he nowhere contradicts. In a long, carefully reasoned argument, he tries to establish that the decree, as well as the consensus of the church fathers, concerns "those passages, and those alone, which pertain to faith and morals and thus concern the edification of Christian doctrine, and this is what the Council of Trent said in its fourth session."[6] He notes that the church fathers are not all agreed on astronomical questions in their interpretation of the miracle of the sun in Joshua. The last part of Galileo's letter in effect declares, Do not condemn the Copernican system without examining it.

Since this remarkable letter was written by an amateur in theology, the essential principles it sets forth can be discussed apart from any technical weaknesses in their presentation. The book of nature and the book of Scripture, since they come from the same Author, complement one another rather than contradict one another. Science is a legitimate path to truth apart from revelation, though in a different sphere. Scripture cannot be used against scientific statements proved by scientific methods. The literal sense of the Bible does not always convey its meaning. When difficulties arise, one should not consult the church fathers on questions they did not discuss. Theologians who want to reject a scientific statement must prove it false for scientific reasons. Galileo clearly enunciated all of those principles and supported them with cogent arguments in agreement with exegetical tradition. Thus his *Letter to Christina* deserves a prominent place in both the history of science and the history of theology in the Roman Catholic Church.

The 1616 Condemnation of Copernicus

Father Niccolo Lorini's note of February 1615 to Cardinal Millino in Rome had reported that certain "Galileans" taught that the earth moved, and that the Holy Scripture was concerned only with matters of faith, not with philosophical or astronomical questions. The moderate tone of the note did not deceive the cardinal, a prominent member of the Holy Office. He informed the ecclesiastical court, which began an investigation, called witnesses from far and near, and finally laid two questions before its panel of theological experts: Is the sun the center of the world and immovable? Does the earth move around the sun and turn daily? The concerns of those consultors (as they were called) were both theological and pastoral: Did these hypotheses contradict the church's interpretation of Holy Scripture? Might they lead the faithful away from the path of righteousness?

On February 24, 1616, after only a few days of deliberation, the panel reached a verdict. It held that the immobility of the sun was foolish and formally heretical because it contradicted the literal meaning of the Scriptures. The mobility of the earth it held, however, to be merely erroneous. Since *On the Revolutions* was considered an important reform of astronomy on which the calendar was based, it was not to be prohibited but only corrected. In other words, Copernicus's statements on the motion of the earth would be made hypothetical and therefore acceptable. On March 5, 1616, the Holy Office promulgated its decree to branches of the *Index* around the world: *On the*

Revolutions was "suspended for correction."

Several observations can be made about that verdict. The first concerns the speed with which the expert consultors worked to decide one of the most important questions in the science of their day. Clearly they must have regarded their task as a routine one not requiring deep scientific investigation. Second, their report shows that they considered themselves competent to judge the Copernican system from a scientific as well as a theological viewpoint: They declared the motion of the earth to be "stupid and absurd in philosophy."[7]

Galileo had decided in late 1615 that he should go to Rome where the important decisions would be made, but he stayed clear of the court's deliberations. Everyone seemed friendly, but nobody wanted to get into a discussion of controversial issues. Pope Paul V, a conservative administrator, was hostile to intellectuals. The Tuscan ambassador warned Galileo that this was no time for him to initiate arguments about the moon. Galileo's best friends urged him not to rock the boat. They recommended that he should go home, continue his research and let the Copernican issue cool down until they could give it a softer sell. But Galileo stayed and continued his behind-the-scenes lobbying.

The grounds of the panel's argument surprised Galileo, whose letters show him confident that the church would take neither side. Afterward he believed that the Holy Office had turned its back on Augustine and Aquinas, who would have declared that the true sense of the Bible supported whatever had been verified in nature. Galileo's crusade was not simply on behalf of Copernicanism itself (as often argued); he sought to keep the church, for its own good, from the mistake of making an article of faith out of *any* disputed scientific question. He wanted science to be free from the control of theology as well as philosophy. Despite his efforts, however, the theologians lent biblical authority to the traditional cosmology and prohibited teaching of the new system.

Galileo's role in the 1616 controversy had to do largely with a personal encounter with Cardinal Bellarmine. A year earlier that influential Jesuit theologian had written a long letter to another Copernican, Father Paolo Antonio Foscarini. Bellarmine's letter is an important document, showing how one of the better-informed members of the Curia approached the problem:

Further, I say that if there were a true demonstration that the sun is in the center of the universe and that the sun does not go around the earth but the earth goes around the sun, then it would be necessary to be careful in explaining the Scriptures that seemed contrary. We should rather have to say that we do not understand them than to say that something is false. But I do not think there is any such demonstration, since none has been shown me. To demonstrate that the appearances are saved by assuming the sun at the center and the earth in the heavens is not the same thing as to demonstrate that in fact the sun is in the center and the earth in the heavens.[8]

It is clear that Bellarmine was prepared to distinguish between two essential questions: (1) Was the Copernican system true in the sense of being supported by convincing evidence? (2) Was it compatible with Holy Scripture? When Galileo obtained a copy of Bellarmine's letter, he realized that the ball had bounced into his court. He must demonstrate that the new cosmology was a true physical description of the universe and not just a convenient mathematical device to "save the appearances" (fit the observed data). It was one thing to argue that the sun-centered model was compatible with the book of Scripture; it was quite another to prove that the book of nature supported that model.

As Galileo assessed his own astronomical discoveries, he must have realized that they did not *prove* the earth's motion. He had dismantled Ptolemaic astronomy and refuted the counterarguments against the Copernican system, which predicted the phases of Venus and explained many other things. But his reasoning, as we have seen, involved inference and retroduction (the beginnings of what is now called the hypothetico-deductive method: the testing of a hypothetical model which becomes more likely as it passes each test successfully). To Cardinal Bellarmine and the other theologians, Galileo's procedures were essentially inductive and potentially fallacious. Such contingent arguments were not sufficient to force a reinterpretation of Scripture. Galileo had to fight his battle on their ground of Aristotelian demonstration and Augustinian hermeneutics.

The proof that Galileo finally devised toward the end of 1615 was the action of the tides. He believed that it was due to the combined daily rotation of the earth on its axis and its annual revolution around the sun. He presented this explanation to various audiences in Rome as a conclusive physical demonstration on which he wrote a paper in January 1616.[9] Unfortunately, this path led down a dead-end street; it did not move Bellarmine to reconsider his position, and its prominence in the *Dialogue* sixteen years later gave opponents a chance to reject the book entirely. It was not until 1637 that Galileo abandoned his theory of the tides. (A physical demonstration of the earth's revolution and rotation awaited discovery until the mid-1800s—four centuries after Copernicus—with stellar parallax and the Foucault pendulum.)

In March 1616 Galileo was summoned before Cardinal Bellarmine, who admonished him against advocating "realist" Copernicanism as a cosmology. If he refused, the scientist would be enjoined before witnesses to "abstain altogether from teaching or defending this opinion and doctrine and even from discussing it."[10] Three steps would be taken if necessary—admonition, injunction and prison. If Galileo submitted to the first, that would end the matter; he would not have to make any formal declaration.

Galileo accepted Bellarmine's warning. By then he realized that he must restrain his argumentation, obey the instruction of his church and hope that some day he could persuade the authorities to change. Within a few days the scientist was granted a friendly audience by the Pope, who assured him that both his upright conduct and the plotting of his enemies was known, so he had nothing to fear. Nevertheless, Galileo was disturbed by rumors circulating in Rome that he had been officially enjoined against teaching the Copernican doctrine. To set the record straight, he requested from Bellarmine a formal note describing what had actually happened. On May 26 the cardinal gave him a personally written letter to the effect that Galileo had not publicly renounced his convictions nor been forced to do penance; he had only been informed that Copernicus's doctrine was "contrary to Holy Scripture and therefore cannot be defended or held." Galileo left Rome with the impression that he could still use the new cosmology as a hypothesis.

Back in Florence, Galileo felt that the storm had subsided, leaving his scientific integrity unquestioned. His *Letter to Christina* had not been censored. His theological statements had not even been mentioned in the decree. But since the Copernican movement had suffered a severe setback, Galileo now had to change his strategy for gaining its acceptance. In the long run, of course, the church suffered a far greater setback; having won that battle, it eventually lost the war. Rejection of a purely scientific theory of the universe was a disastrous blunder for the church. It led not only to Galileo's condemnation in 1633, but also to an antiscience reputation that has lasted for more than three centuries.

Scientific Activity

After a few weeks of dejection over the victory of "those three most powerful operators, ignorance, malice and impiety," Galileo revived his scientific activities. Not wanting to give his enemies an excuse for further action, over the next eight years he no longer discussed Copernicanism. Instead he devoted himself to a variety of scientific projects. He prepared new tables for Jupiter's satellites, hoping to devise a method for mariners to determine longitude. He continued work on his theory of the tides. Prohibited from discussing Copernican astronomy, he felt free to continue his criticism of Aristotle's physics. But work on the long-neglected treatise he had planned was interrupted by an unexpected celestial event.

In autumn 1618 three comets appeared, creating excitement and spurring debate about their nature. As books about comets came from the press, Galileo's opinion was sought. One book, published anonymously by Father Orazio Grassi, presented the views of mathematicians at the Roman College, a center of Jesuit learning. Galileo couldn't resist an opportunity to retaliate against some long-time opponents by demonstrating their errors. In an inaugural address as head of the Florentine Academy, Galileo's pupil and friend Mario Guiducci produced the arguments. Published in June 1619, they showed the hand of Galileo and received favorable comment in Rome, even from Cardinal Barberini. The Jesuits were incensed; Grassi, under the pseudonym Lothario Sarsi, responded in a slashing attack which accused Galileo of defending Copernicanism.

At that point both Galileo and the Linceans at Rome realized that they had to reply in person, to protect Guiducci and vindicate the honor of the new science. Galileo felt free to do so because comets, which were not considered by the Aristotelians to be celestial objects, had received no comment from Copernicus. He decided not to mention the Jesuits at all. Instead he attacked the straw figure of Lothario Sarsi. In January 1621 Galileo started work on *Il saggiatore* ("The Assayer") on which he spent the next two years.

These were difficult times for Galileo. Tethered by the admonition of 1616, watched by enemies for any misstep, beset by sickness, torn by hopes and fears in Florence, Galileo walked a tightrope. Yet he enjoyed the consolations of country life in his villa, the company of literary friends and the frequent correspondence of his beloved daughter, now Sister Maria Celeste.

In August 1623 Maffeo Barberini became Pope Urban VIII. Giovanni Ciampoli, a staunch supporter of Galileo, was appointed to the coveted Vatican post of Secretary of the Briefs. It seemed possible that the clouds of intellectual lethargy would disperse. When Prince Cesi made a visit to congratulate him, Barberini asked how Galileo was faring. Since the new Pope was also a Florentine and a friend of Galileo, the Lincean Academy decided to dedicate to him *The Assayer*, Galileo's book dealing with the new comets.

In *The Assayer* Galileo avoided discussing the Copernican view, yet he included such interesting remarks on the nature of science that the book has been called his scientific manifesto. Though not a great scientific treatise, it is a masterpiece of Italian polemic prose.[11] Without meeting Grassi's main argument, Galileo ridiculed his opponent with a variety of literary devices, including destructive irony and sparkling wit. His mastery of language matched his facility with mathematics. His literary skill and scientific perception ranged over a wide variety of problems as he hammered away at the false logic of scientific authorities.

After seven years Galileo had returned to the polemical arena. *The Assayer* was an immediate success; even the Pope had it read to him at mealtimes. Yet this sarcastic lampoon on Grassi alienated the Jesuit astronomers, once his strongest support. After the trial of 1633 it was said that if Galileo had known how to keep the favor of the Roman College, he would have still been living in freedom and "able to write on any subject he wished, even the rotation of the earth." Although exaggerated, this statement highlights the fact that the scientist's vanity, quarrels over priority of discovery, contemptuous attitude and effective sarcasm cost him dearly in the long run.[12]

Pulverized in the public eye, Grassi was ordered to keep a low profile even though he had voiced the accepted views of Jesuit astronomers. In 1626, however, he published a reply to Galileo, apparently peaceful but beneath the surface full of venom. Six years later Grassi did more than write; with his academic colleague Scheiner he helped bring about Galileo's trial.

In April 1624 Galileo again went to Rome, where he was warmly received by Barberini (Urban VIII). The Pope complimented him on his new book and granted him five more audiences. The scientist tactfully broached the subject of a moving earth while giving his explanation of the tides. He also alluded to the malice of his enemies and the difficulties under which he labored. Galileo, hoping that the decree of 1616 might be rescinded, soon realized that he was no longer talking with Maffeo Barberini but with Pope Urban VIII. The Pope was not about to take such a step. He did encourage Galileo to publish his tide theory, though, if he could make it clear that the earth's motions were considered only hypothetically, not as a reality that could be proved.

Although Galileo did not achieve his main objective, he was grateful that at last he could openly discuss the Copernican doctrines once more. Eight years of prudence had taught him how to express his convictions by ingenious implication. He had come through *The Assayer* flap unscathed; now he could proceed with his book on the tides.[13] He had confidence in the power of truth, once it was committed to writing. Galileo returned to Florence with favors, holy medals and pensions for his family.

Dialogue on the Two Principal World Systems

From 1624 to 1630 Galileo worked intermittently on a remarkable classic of scientific and philosophical literature, *Dialogo dei due massimi sistemi del mondo—Tolemaico e Copernicano* ("Dialogue on the Two Principal World Systems—Ptolemaic and Copernican"). Covering a wide range of subjects, it reveals much about the mind of Galileo. "It is the mind of a man who knew very well where he was going. In the work there is all of him; the physicist, the astronomer, the man of the world, the literateur, the polemicist, even at times the sophist; there is, above all, the totally expressive and expressed Renaissance man."[14]

Though compelled to present Copernicanism hypothetically, Galileo tried to make it as persuasive as possible. He chose the dialogue format, at that time a popular but sometimes dull educational approach. It was a way for an author to express objectionable views in a detached manner through the words of someone else. Galileo gave it a twist by introducing two experts, an Aristotelian and a Copernican, vying for the support of a third neutral participant. Galileo could thus present his strongest case for the Copernican system without explicitly committing himself to its truth. He obeyed the letter, if not the spirit, of Cardinal Bellarmine's admonition of 1616.

The conversations of the *Dialogue* take place over four "days" of arguing the merits of the old and new astronomies. On the first day, for example, Aristotle's distinction between celestial and elemental substances is criticized. The second day focuses on the earth's daily rotation, the third on the earth's annual revolution around the sun, the fourth on the tides. The close connection between the Copernican view and the new mechanics is presented for the cultured layman, intelligent but often without much formal education. Galileo wrote in colloquial Italian with a conversational tone, repetitions, irony, cutting criticism and wit. Many years earlier Galileo had described the audience he wanted to reach:

> Though well provided with horse sense, as Ruzzante would say, such men, being unable to read things written in Latin, become convinced that these wretched pamphlets containing the latest discoveries of logic and philosophy must remain forever over their head. Now, I want them to see that just as Nature has given them, as well as the philosophers, eyes to see her works, so she has also given them brains capable of grasping and understanding them.[15]

Resolved this time to be covered by the standard ecclesiastical publishing procedure, Galileo went to Rome in May 1630 to get his book licensed by the proper authorities. Urban VIII endorsed the idea of an astronomical dialogue provided it was strictly hypothetical. He objected to the proposed title, *Dialogue on the Tides*, because that would emphasize a physical argument for the earth's motion. The sudden death of Galileo's patron, Prince Cesi, and poor communications during the bubonic plague both caused delays. Eventually the Florentine Inquisitor read and approved the book. By that time the Jesuits had swung into action, managing to cause bureaucratic delays for a full year. It took until July 1631 for the book to be cleared with a proper preface and imprimatur. In February 1632 Galileo finally presented the first printed copy to the grand duke.

Like Galileo's earlier books, the *Dialogue* quickly engendered a chorus of praise and literally sold out as it came off the press. In spite of the general interest it aroused among cultured readers, though, it hardly persuaded the Vatican authorities to change their position of 1616. In fact, within a few months rumors of disapproval by the church began to circulate. In August an order came from the Roman Inquisitor to stop all sales. A commission of experts examined the *Dialogue* to assess, as the author's enemies charged, its Copernican character. On October 1, Galileo was officially summoned to Rome to report to the Holy Office.

The Trial and Its Verdict

As the prolog of this book suggested, Galileo's trial of 1633 was not the simple conflict between science and religion so commonly pictured. It was a complex power struggle of personal and professional pride, envy and ambition, affected by pressures of bureaucratic politics. The deliberations seemed to take on a life of their own, moving toward an inevitable conclusion with elements of a Greek tragedy.

At the outset both judges and defendant were confused by the contradictory documents of 1616. Galileo's presentation of the admonition from Cardinal Bellarmine, milder than the official injunction found in the files, challenged the very basis for his trial.[16] When the questioning shifted to the recently published *Dialogue,* it was obvious where the author himself stood. The arguments for the Copernican system were cogent, the refutation weak; so when Galileo declared that he had not defended Copernicus, the judges became indignant. Whom did he think he was fooling? It took only five days for them to declare that Galileo had maintained and defended the Copernican view; they had a "vehement suspicion" that he still held it.

But then weeks passed as the judges continued to deliberate. They had a clear case but were divided over what to do about it. Cardinal Francesco Barberini, the Pope's nephew and closest collaborator, was one of the ten judges. He put discreet pressure on Commissary Maculano to find a way out. Maculano asked the Holy Congregation's permission to deal extrajudicially with Galileo; if a confession could be obtained, the court could be more lenient with him. After a long discussion the defendant agreed to make a confession.

On April 30, 1633, Galileo was again summoned by the judges. He stated that a rereading of his book had made him realize his errors, which he then confessed. The Commissary released the prisoner in the custody of ambassador Niccolini.

At the next interrogation, on May 10, Galileo was allowed to present his case if he wished. He submitted a long statement which in guarded language was a strong defense, even though he confessed his error and promised to correct it in the future. Galileo concluded with a plea for mercy in view of his poor health, advanced age and anxiety over the attacks of his enemies.

Galileo's defense was accepted and everything seemed set for a mild sentence. But when the case was sent up to higher authorities for a final decision it hit a snag. A crisis arose from conflicting forces in a complex political struggle. The decision making took a sudden turn against Galileo, and the Commissary's recommendation was over-ruled. On June 16 the following verdict was recorded:

> Galileo . . . is to abjure on vehement suspicion of heresy in a ple-
> nary assembly of the Congregation of the Holy Office, then is to
> be condemned to imprisonment at the pleasure of the Holy Con-
> gregation, and ordered not to treat further, in whatever manner,
> either in words or in writing, of the mobility of the Earth and the
> stability of the Sun; otherwise he will incur the penalties of relapse.
> The book entitled the *Dialogue* . . . is to be prohibited.[17]

The verdict was implemented on June 21 when Galileo was summoned for a final interrogation. He was told that his book showed him to hold the Copernican view. He must now tell the truth about his views or face the consequences. After further questioning, Galileo finally renounced the Copernican view. Maculano, still in charge, passed over certain passages in the *Dialogue* that could have been used to prove the author guilty of heresy. The session lasted only an hour; it concluded with Galileo's signing the deposition.

The next day Galileo heard his sentence, which declared at length the errors in his book, banned the *Dialogue* and condemned him to the "formal prison of this Holy Office." Galileo begged the cardinals to leave out two points. First, he should not be made to state that he was not a good Catholic, for he was and intended to remain one despite all the accusations of his enemies. Second, he would not confess that he had ever deceived anyone, especially in publishing the

Dialogue, which he had submitted for ecclesiastical approval and printed only after obtaining a license. After winning those two points, Galileo knelt again and read aloud the corrected version of the confession.

> I, Galileo, son of the late Vincenzio Galilei, Florentine, aged seventy years . . . have been pronounced by the Holy Office to be vehemently suspected of heresy, that is to say, of having held and believed that the Sun is the center of the world and immovable and that the Earth is not the center and moves. . . . With sincere heart and unfeigned faith I abjure, curse and detest the aforesaid errors and heresies.[18]

Galileo had become resigned to the banning of his book, but he had not expected such a harsh verdict. In line with an out-of-court settlement in April, he had pleaded guilty to error in his writing and cast himself on the mercy of the court. Now he felt as if he had been hit with a brick.

The Protagonists

The principal roles in that unfolding tragedy were played by Galileo, the Aristotelian scientists, the Jesuits, the Dominicans and Pope Urban VIII. It is hard to sort out the precise nature and interrelationship of their roles, but each was significant to the drama.

1. *Galileo.* The central character was a mathematician, physicist, experimenter, inventor, entrepreneur, musician, writer, polemicist and debater. Galileo was a crusader, but he was not a zealot who rushed into a fray without a strategy or knowledge of his foes. His letters and books reflect a personality that was prudent though feisty. In his polemical writing as well as his scientific research, Galileo weighed the evidence and framed careful conclusions. He was aware of social customs and political realities in both state and church. Over his long life he formed lasting friendships with a wide variety of intelligent and powerful men who remained loyal to him through thick and thin. As a polemicist Galileo was a potential danger to the university, state and church. Yet two grand dukes and many high church officials, including three judges who declined to sign his sentence, continued to trust him, knowing that he fought for just causes.

Galileo's long crusade was not waged primarily for Copernicanism, at least not as a new philosophy. Giordano Bruno (1548-1600) had refuted Aristotle's natural philosophy and broadened Copernican theory into a new metaphysics, without introducing another scientific methodology. For Galileo, however, the Copernican conception offered the focal point for a new unified science drawing together mathematics, mechanics and astronomy. He advocated the pursuit of science to explain natural events, free from the control of *any* philosophy, whether old or new.

During his campaign Galileo was concerned not only for science but also for his church. When his academic enemies made their controversy a theological issue, he fought to keep the church from tying biblical teaching to Aristotelian science. Galileo was pressing less for ecclesiastical approval of Copernicanism than for the right of science to develop in its own domain free from the authority of theology. Yet he saw no need for a breach between science and theology since God is the Author of both books—of nature and of Scripture. If the church were to forbid anything, it should be the imposition of scriptural authority in scientific debates, which should be settled by experience and reason.

2. *University scientists.* For almost thirty years before the conflict took a theological turn, Galileo waged a running battle against the Aristotelianism of the scientific establishment. He effectively used the media of private discussion, public lecture and polemic writing. Although his attacks were not personal, Galileo's opponents were understandably hurt and angered as he undermined their scientific system and professional reputations.

Imagine a similar situation today in the physics department of a prestigious university. A new assistant professor with a three-year, non-tenure-track appointment turns his students against the fundamental presuppositions of their textbooks, openly criticizing the theories of the department head, a Nobel Prize winner. For good measure, the upstart broadens his attack in public lectures and the popular language of a best seller. How long would he be allowed to continue such a campaign? Attempts by his department to break or buy out his contract after the first semester might make the Pisa professors of the seventeenth century look broad-minded by comparison.

It is curious that, despite the evidence, historians of science have seldom blamed the university professors for their part in the decision against Copernicus and Galileo, their opposition to freedom of scientific inquiry. Yet it was they, the leading scientists, who urged the theologians to intervene, confident that the church would be on their side. In a letter to a friend in 1635, Galileo wrote about the events leading to the church's fateful decision against the Copernican system in 1616. Galileo did not blame the young priest, Caccini, who had denounced him from the pulpit in his own city of Florence; he indicted the men whose "slanders, frauds, stratagems, and trickeries were used eighteen years ago in Rome to deceive the authorities." As for the present, "You have certainly understood from my writings which was the true and real motive that caused, under the lying mask of religion, this war against me, that continually restrains and undercuts me in all directions."[19]

3. *Dominicans.* Thomas Aquinas, the thirteenth-century "Angelic Doctor" from whom Thomism gets its name, had embraced Aristotle's natural philosophy. Aquinas was a Dominican, and his order remained faithful to his teaching. Suspicious of any innovation, even if only astronomical, they vigorously opposed Galileo. Some, like Lorini and Caccini, preached against him. Other Dominicans, however, authorized the publication of Galileo's *Dialogue* in 1632.

4. *Jesuits.* At the beginning of the seventeenth century the Jesuit order exerted great cultural influence within the church. Their ranks at the Roman College had eminent scholars of mathematics, physics and astronomy. They sought to keep new research within the pale of orthodoxy so that it would enhance the church's authority. During the period in question the Jesuits vacillated on the issue of Copernican astronomy. Officially they stayed on the sidelines of the 1616 controversy, although several influential Jesuits gave Galileo indirect support.

Ironically the two orders changed positions in 1632. The Jesuits inspired accusations against Galileo and criticized the Dominicans for authorizing publication of the *Dialogue.* Two Jesuit astronomers on the faculty of the Roman College, Scheiner and Grassi, were definitely Galileo's enemies. Angry over his attacks on their scientific views, they considered Galileo's writings in Italian a threat to their educational program; they may have been influential in bringing him to trial.

It was the Jesuits who informed the Pope that under a rhetorical mask the *Dialogue* made a convincing case for Copernicanism. They also told Urban that he was being ridiculed by having his argument against the tidal theory put into the mouth of Simplicio. Since Urban had presented that argument directly to Galileo, he felt his friendship betrayed.

There is no evidence that Galileo meant to ridicule the Pope, but the damage had been done. The Pope, who considered himself an intellectual, felt that he was not being taken seriously. Out of favor with the Jesuits for allowing the *Dialogue* to be published, he feared they might turn on him, especially after they assured him the issue was potentially more dangerous than Luther or Calvin. Thus the one group that should have been warning the Pope not to take the fateful step of drawing the church into scientific controversy instead led him into the quicksand.

5. *Pope Urban VIII.* In the end, the Pope proved to be the pivotal figure, though his turning against Galileo was largely the result of forces beyond his control. The astronomers Scheiner and Grassi were motivated by long-term malice; Urban's anger sprang from a frustration suddenly produced by converging pressures.

Urban's international politics had backfired. His undercover alliance with the Protestant Gustavus Adolphus of Sweden became known when that king suddenly died. The Pope had alienated Austria with nothing to show for it, and had been ill-used by Cardinal Richelieu of France. On the home front he faced criticism for sacrificing the church's interests to personal ambition, the greed of his relatives and interests of the house of Barberini. Moreover, he had been forced to move swiftly to crush a political plot within his own Curia. He began to see enemies everywhere and lived in fear of poison.

Galileo's apparent perfidy was the last straw. The Vatican had given permission for publication of the *Dialogue* after assurance that all would go well. Now Urban felt deceived by his old friend and began to worry about repercussions from such a popular book. After trying to aid the new science, he felt double-crossed by Galileo's mobilizing of lay opinion against the intellectual authority of the church. It was time to act decisively, he thought, to recoup some prestige and to reaffirm his position as head of the church. So he appointed a commission of theologians to review the *Dialogue,* the action that led directly to Galileo's summons and trial.

Two other events hardened Urban's opposition to Galileo. First, the injunction of 1616 was recovered from the files, possibly by Scheiner, and shown to the Pope. As an unsigned memorandum, it was of no legal value, but it declared that Galileo should not discuss Copernicanism "in any way whatever." It appeared that Galileo had disobeyed a legal order of the Holy Office and, despite their many conversations, had failed to tell Urban of the injunction. Second, the report of the trial delivered to the Pope in June 1633, supposed to be objective, gave an inaccurate and biased picture of Galileo's case. Sent up without the actual trial documents, it served to confirm the Pope's grievance against Galileo and stiffen his resolve for strong action.

The Verdict on the Verdict

The decision was made on June 16 after Urban returned to Rome and met with the Congregation, the highest tribunal. He overturned the arrangement with Galileo approved by the judges (most of whom were Dominican), issuing a decree that the defendant should be interrogated, required to recant and then imprisoned. The Jesuits had won the day against both a scientific enemy and a rival religious order.

In the light of those facts, one should be wary of accepting the traditional interpretation of the trial, exemplified by Colin Ronan's conclusion: "Galileo does stand as a classic example of the evils of a totalitarian regime. . . . [He] cut right across the religious authority of the Church. . . . It was essentially Galileo's danger to an authoritarian outlook that caused his downfall."[20] Ronan cites as a parallel the Lysenko case in Russia, when scientists were tried for daring to hold Mendelian concepts.

Ronan's conclusion is a curious mixture of truth and error. He is close to the truth when he calls Galileo the victim of an authoritarian outlook. The problem is that he points the guilty finger in the wrong direction. To call the Catholic Church in the Italy of that time (a collection of independent states) a totalitarian regime is an anachronism. The Pope hardly had the power of a modern dictator. For example, if Galileo had stayed in the Republic of Venice, which had recently expelled the Jesuits for political intrigue, he would have been safe.

The real authoritarianism that engineered Galileo's downfall was that of the Aristotelian scientific outlook in the universities. Only after Galileo had attacked that establishment for decades did his enemies turn their controversy into a theological issue. Even then it was the natural philosophers who worked behind the scenes with pliable church authorities to foment Galileo's trial, and finally to rob him of the reasonable solution worked out by the Inquisition. Those activities are dismissed by Ronan simply as "human nature." A more accurate assessment is given by Santillana:

> In reality it was a confused free-for-all in which prejudice, inveterate rancor, and all sorts of special and corporate interests were prime movers. . . . It has been known for a long time that a major part of the church intellectuals were on the side of Galileo, while the clearest opposition to him came from secular ideas. . . . The tragedy was the result of a plot of which the hierarchies themselves turned out to be the victims no less than Galileo—an intrigue engineered by a group of obscure and disparate characters in strange collusion.[21]

Galileo's Last Years

On June 30, 1633, Galileo was released to the custody of a friend and former pupil, Archbishop Ascanio Piccolomini in Siena. Despite strict instructions that Galileo should see no one, his host invited many visitors to the palace. Soon the two friends were busy at work on new scientific projects.

In December 1633 the Pope allowed Galileo to return to Florence, instead of going to prison, and stay at Galileo's small farm near Arcetri. Urban kept his promise that the old man should "suffer as little as possible" and continued the pension he had granted in happier days. Although under house arrest for the remainder of his life, Galileo was glad to be home and near his daughter Virginia (Sister Maria Celeste). Her regular letters had helped sustain him in Rome, and now she could personally attend her father's needs. Her death in April 1634 was a grievous loss to the old scientist.

Despite his new sense of loneliness, he resumed his scientific activity. Prohibited from discussing Copernicus, Galileo returned to the questions of motion and applied mechanics. Those subjects allowed him to chip away at established views and demonstrate the power of mathematical reasoning. They would also prepare the ground for discussing planetary motion again, if the edict should be rescinded or forgotten. Most of all Galileo wanted to complete a long-planned book, which became his greatest contribution to the new science. All this was a remarkable agenda for a man of sixty-nine who had just emerged from years of controversy and trial by the Inquisition.

Galileo's *Discorsi e dimostrazioni matematiche intorno a due nuove scienze* ("Discourses and Mathematical Demonstrations Concerning Two New Sciences") was a masterpiece of scientific prose. Like the *Dialogue* it took the form of a discussion and with the same three participants—Salviati, Sagredo and Simplicio—considering various topics over a number of days. On the first two days, they discuss the new science of strength of materials. Then they spend a few days on the problem of motion. During the last two days they consider the theory of proportion and percussion. Throughout, Aristotle's teachings sustain a thorough going-over. Galileo comes remarkably close to the first law of motion that Newton defined fifty years later. *Discourses* was substantially completed in 1634, although Galileo continued to perfect it over the next three years. The manuscript was smuggled out of Italy and published in Leiden in 1637. Although he chafed under house arrest and the prohibition against replying to his Aristotelian opponents, in the end Galileo had the last word.

During 1637, though, a progressive disease deprived the scientist of the sight in his right eye; it finally made him blind as he was planning to conclude his career with two more books. His son Vincenzio and a pupil named Viviani became stenographers for his prodigious correspondence with scholars all over Europe. During his last years Galileo enjoyed a constant stream of stimulating visitors. He also continued research on sound, on problems of dissonance and mathematics and on a mechanism for a pendulum clock.

Galileo had been deeply hurt by the trial verdict's "vehement suspicion of heresy." Yet he did not withdraw from the church; he went on praying and asking his friends to pray for him. He even planned a pilgrimage to the shrine of Loreto. Galileo's own conscience as a Catholic and as a scientist was clear. Even though the church had turned its back on him, he blamed only some "wrong-headed individuals."

I have two sources of perpetual comfort—first, that in my writings there cannot be found the faintest shadow of irreverence toward the Holy Church; and second, the testimony of my own conscience, which only I and God in Heaven thoroughly know. And he knows that in this cause for which I suffer, though many might have spoken with more learning, none, not even the ancient Fathers, have spoken with more piety or with greater zeal for the Church than I.[22]

The real cause for which he suffered was freedom of scientific inquiry from both the university and ecclesiastical establishments.

In November 1641 Galileo was confined to bed by kidney pains, heart palpitations and a slow fever. His two pupils Viviani and Torricelli stayed with him constantly. Although weak, he enjoyed listening to their scientific discussions.

On January 8, 1642, a month before Galileo's seventy-eighth birthday, Viviani wrote,

With philosophic and Christian firmness he rendered up his soul to its Creator, sending it, as he liked to believe, to enjoy and to watch from a closer vantage point those eternal and immutable marvels which he, by means of a fragile device, had brought closer to our mortal eyes with such eagerness and impatience.[23]

6
NEWTON: UNIVERSAL GRAVITATION

*No sciences are
better attested than
the religion
of the Bible.*
ISAAC NEWTON

FROM 1558 TO 1603 THE DYNAMIC REIGN OF QUEEN ELIZABETH strengthened England and gave it a golden age. Elizabeth defeated the Spanish Armada, placed English finances on a sound basis and re-established the Anglican church free of Roman Catholic control. At home Shakespeare and Spenser wrote, while on the high seas Francis Drake and Walter Raleigh searched for new lands and wealth. But the strong queen left a legacy of struggle between king and parliament that dominated the 1600s.

In June 1642 parliament delivered an ultimatum to Charles I, which he promptly rejected. The following month parliament voted to raise an army, whereupon the king rallied his loyal followers to begin England's first civil war. Eventually Oliver Cromwell's "roundheads" defeated the royal cavaliers, and Charles I was beheaded. The year 1642 also witnessed both the death of Galileo in Italy and the birth of Isaac Newton in England.

Newton's parents were country folk who lived on a small farm in Woolsthorpe north of London.[1] Hannah Newton's husband died soon after their marriage, stricken with a fatal illness at the age of thirty-six. On Christmas day, 1642, friends came to assist the young widow with the birth of her son Isaac. About two years later, Hannah married the Reverend Barnabas Smith. Instead of moving with his mother, the child stayed on at the isolated farm, with his grandmother caring for him. Isaac grew up without the companionship (or rivalry) of brothers and sisters.

Instead of taking part in the rougher games at school, young Isaac became an avid reader, devising his own games that could be played without partners or opponents. Early in life he developed self-sufficiency and resourcefulness, which served him well during later years of research. Newton developed unusual skill in constructing mechanical toys. He had the same propensity for invention that was characteristic of Galileo, although in other respects the two men were radically different. Galileo showed a zest for social life and for crusading against opponents of his ideas; Newton became a recluse who preferred to keep his discoveries private rather than have to defend them.

In September 1654, at the age of twelve, Newton entered the Old King's School in nearby Grantham. Established in 1528 during the reign of Henry VII, it had a good reputation for preparing students to enter Cambridge and Oxford. Newton reached the top of his class, became interested in chemistry and continued building intricate mechanisms, including a windmill and water clock. After four years he returned to Woolsthorpe to help his mother with the farm, since his stepfather had died. Despite his good intentions, the boy spent more time keeping a notebook of observations on nature and reading mathematics than looking after the animals. After two years of frustration his mother decided he should complete his course at Old King's and prepare for university.

Cambridge University

In June 1661 Newton entered Trinity College, Cambridge. The kind of instruction that had frustrated Galileo eighty years earlier still prevailed in the English as well as continental universities. The new theories of Copernicus and Kepler were ignored, Galileo's work was unrecognized, and most people still believed that the sun revolved around the earth. A number of scientific societies sprang up outside the academic establishment. They were started largely by amateur scientists who wished to exchange new ideas and foster research. The Royal Society of London for Improving Natural Knowledge was chartered by Charles II in 1662. Its counterpart in France was the Paris Academy of Sciences founded by Louis XIV in 1666. The Royal Society, which became Newton's platform for launching his discoveries, stimulated most of England's scientific exploration. The society's motto, *Nullius in verba* (freely translated, "We don't take anybody's word for it"), expressed its approach to science.

For three years Newton followed the prescribed course at Trinity, which included mathematics (algebra, geometry and trigonometry), Latin and Greek. He also studied physics and optics under a remarkable man, Dr. Isaac Barrow, who held the prestigious Lucasian chair of mathematics and was also a Greek scholar. He was the first to recognize Newton's genius, introducing his student to telescopes and the current theories of light. The slumbering giant of Newton's intellect suddenly awoke. He mastered Kepler's *Optics* and read nearly everything written about light. Since the subject called for experimenting, grinding lenses and building ingenious apparatus, it was made to order for his mathematical mind and deft fingers. During his student years Newton observed the stars and began making notes that later led to a new theory of light and color.

In 1655 classes at Cambridge were suddenly suspended by an onslaught of bubonic plague. Flea-bearing rats carried the dread disease into congested London, where a fifth of the population died that summer. As the plague spread, students and teachers were sent home. Newton, with his new bachelor's degree, packed his notebooks for a return to Woolsthorpe. For the next two years he continued doing experiments that became the basis for many future scientific achievements. As with Copernicus, Kepler and Galileo, some of Newton's most brilliant insights came during university years.

In his study of light Newton did many experiments with prisms and kept accurate records of the data. He discovered that white sunlight contains the whole spectrum of colors. He showed that a prism will separate white light into its component colors, which a second prism can recombine to make white light again. (That result was puzzling because white sunlight was considered pure and perfect, like Aristotle's celestial spheres.) Newton also demonstrated the phenomenon of chromatic aberration: portions of light passing through a lens are refracted in different degrees. Eventually he invented and built a reflecting telescope, using a curved mirror instead of a lens to bring light from distant stars into sharp focus.

Another project captured Newton's attention during his unexpected "vacation" at home. At Cambridge he had discovered the binomial theorem, an accomplishment that alone would have established his prestige in the history of mathematics. Now he pursued a new way of calculating the areas of curved shapes. It was a difficult problem to determine how many square inches, for example, are in an arc of a circle or an ellipse. The greatest Greek mathematicians had tried and failed. Yet a student in his early twenties succeeded by using the available knowledge and following a hunch about an entirely new approach. With remarkable energy he calculated the area of a hyperbola to "two-and-fifty figures by the same method." Newton thus laid the foundations for his method of "fluxions." That method later developed into differential and integral calculus, the cornerstone of modern mathematics and an indispensable tool for scientific research.

A third discovery during his "plague vacation" eventually led to the solution of the age-old problem of motion in the heavens and on earth. Newton was puzzled by the moon's motion, wondering what kept it moving so evenly around the earth in an orbit of twenty-seven and one-eighth days. Fifty years earlier Kepler had discovered that the inverse-square principle applied, and that there must be some kind of attraction between the sun and the planets. (Gravity was not considered a problem in the Ptolemaic system; it had become one with the Copernican model of a moving earth and with Kepler's search for a motive force.) Newton analyzed the moon's motion in terms of centrifugal force, an endeavor to recede from the earth balanced by gravity. He discovered that for circular motion, the centrifugal force is measured by v^2/r where v is the velocity of the orbiting body and r is the radius of rotation. (Huyghens also discovered this relation and published it in a supplement to a book on the pendulum clock in 1673).

According to popular reports, during this time at home Newton was sitting one day under a favorite apple tree not far from the house, pondering a variety of questions. When an apple landed at his feet, he started thinking about the motion of the moon. The attractive force that caused the apple to fall extended to the top of the tree; did it also extend as far as the moon? If so, what would the attraction amount to at such a great distance?

Newton knew that, once set in motion, an object travels in a straight line unless some force causes it to deviate from its course. Both the moon and a projectile tend to move in a straight line. Then why don't they fly off into space like mud thrown from a rapidly rotating wheel? Because both are constantly falling toward the center of the earth. Newton undertook a series of calculations which showed that the moon moves as if it were attracted to the earth with a force 1/3600 of the strength with which the earth pulls on objects at its surface. Since the moon is 60 times farther from the center of the earth than objects on the earth's surface, the factor of 1/3600 is consistent with the deduction that the earth's gravity extends to the moon and decreases with the square of the distance.

Controversy has swirled around this apple-and-moon story. Is it fact or fiction? Although the account is found in supposedly reliable reports of Newton's discoveries, documents of the 1660s indicate that he was not then even comparing the "falling" of the moon in its orbit with the falling of objects on the earth. Rather, he was comparing the "centrifugal endeavor" (a moving *away from* the earth) of the orbiting moon and of an object on the earth's surface rotating along with the daily motion of the earth. It has been suggested that in 1717, to ensure his own priority in discovering the inverse-square law of gravitation, Newton invented this mid-1660s scenario and circulated the familiar story of the falling apple.[2]

Although the timing and sequence of the steps in Newton's calculations are not exactly known, several facts are clear. He did discover the inverse-square law for circular orbits in the 1660s and laid the foundation for his later work in mathematics, optics and astronomy (celestial mechanics). Yet the often-repeated account of an *annus mirabilis* ("miraculous year") in which Newton was supposed to have worked out his whole theory of universal gravitation, then kept it in cold storage for about twenty years, is a myth. Although his achievements during this brief period were phenomenal, Newton had ahead of him many years of meticulous research before he could publish his theory of universal gravitation.

Lucasian Professor

By the spring of 1667 the plague had subsided, having taken 31,000 lives in London. Cambridge reopened and six months later Newton was elected a Trinity Fellow with an annual stipend of one hundred pounds. He went home for Christmas with the good news.

During 1668 Newton immersed himself in the construction of his new reflecting telescope. He also continued his work on optics and made plans to set up a chemistry laboratory. In July he received the Master of Arts degree, opening the way to academic advancement. Life at Cambridge perfectly suited his temperament and ambition. He wanted nothing more than the opportunity to apply himself whole-heartedly to the pursuit of new ideas, surrounded by books and laboratory equipment.

At the request of Professor Barrow, Newton reported his mathematical research in a paper entitled *On Analysis of Equations with an Infinite Number of Terms*. So impressed was Barrow with its originality and value that he asked Newton's permission to send it to John Collins in London for circulation among the world's leading mathematicians. The young scientist was obviously pleased, but asked that his name not be attached to the paper. When Collins later requested the author's name for distribution of the paper, Newton reluctantly consented, at the urging of Barrow. In 1669 all the outstanding mathematicians throughout Europe learned about his unusual contribution.

On October 29 Newton was appointed Lucasian professor of mathematics largely on the basis of Barrow's enthusiastic recommendation. The retiring professor was anxious to devote the rest of his life to theological studies. So Isaac Newton, at the age of twenty-seven, occupied one of the world's most famous chairs of mathematics. He held that position for another twenty-seven years until his appointment by the king as warden of the Mint in 1696.

Newton's professorship called for one lecture a week during one term of the academic year, plus conferences with students twice a week, leaving him ample time for studying and experimenting. As both teachers and students became interested in Newton's telescope, his colleagues urged him to send the instrument to the Royal Society. He was surprised by the intense excitement the telescope created. The members requested that he construct another one for showing to the public in 1671. The most important personages in the land, including King Charles II, looked through Newton's instrument, which performed as well as those several times longer. In January 1672 Newton, now thirty, received his first public honor—election as a Fellow of the Royal Society.

The next month Newton's *New Theory about Light and Colors* was read before the society. It was a masterful example of scientific method with carefully planned and executed experiments from which the conclusions logically followed. There were many theories to explain color, but none had been confirmed by experiments of that kind. For once Newton was enthusiastic over one of his achievements. His paper was warmly received and referred to three prominent men for their evaluation. One was Robert Hooke, an excellent microscopist and mechanical genius, who commented negatively. Newton was about to learn that for every action in human affairs (as well as in nature), one should expect an opposite (though not always equal) reaction. He discovered that, in their pride and ambition, scientists are no less human than others. Like Galileo, he suffered the most sustained opposition from within the scientific establishment.

Hooke referred to Newton's theory as a "hypothesis" (that is, a conjecture) for which he could see no undeniable argument. Seven years older than Newton, Hooke had a brilliant, inquiring mind that investigated a wide variety of scientific disciplines. But he was temperamental and jealous about his own work. He had done experiments with light and published a report in 1665. Now he regarded the younger man's paper as a refutation of that work.

Hooke's negative reaction did not keep Newton's paper from being published, however. It was soon attacked by leading scientists on the continent, including Christian Huyghens. British scientists also sent letters of protest to the Royal Society, not only about Newton's conclusions but also about his mathematical-experimental approach. He was shocked and mystified by such opposition since he had simply presented the facts, thinking they would be rationally accepted. Although his lifestyle of intense concentration on a problem for months at a time had taught Newton much concerning physical phenomena, it left him naive about human nature. He went to his mentor Barrow for an explanation. The older man, who had suffered much persecution himself, explained that even great scientists will defend an old and cherished concept as they would their dearest possession. He told Newton that a pioneer must expect rebuffs from people in high places.

Gradually most of the critics came around to Newton's view. But in 1675, when he presented his *Hypothesis Explaining the Properties of Light* to the Royal Society, Hooke attacked not only the Trinity professor's theories but also his integrity, claiming that the main part of the work "was contained in his [Hooke's] *Micrographia*, which Mr. Newton had only carried farther in some particulars."[3] Furious over the charge of plagiarism, Newton wrote a masterful reply demolishing Hooke's arguments one by one. Although the two officially reconciled, the wounds on both sides remained unhealed. This prolonged and heated polemic was largely responsible for the nearly pathological aversion to all publications Newton developed in his later years. Once again he withdrew from the world to the satisfying solitude of analysis, experiment and meditation.

During the next few years Newton devoted his time to other subjects, including chemistry, practical inventions and theology. His work on optics led him into a study of alchemy and the nature of matter. He experimented with formulas used by alchemists in their pursuit of a method to transmute base metals into gold. The extent of Newton's keen interest in alchemy, long an embarrassment to his admirers, became generally known only in 1936 when these writings (of about 650,000 words) were put on sale.[4] Widely scattered and until recently considered unimportant, these manuscripts have been collected and are being studied with new interest. Scholars disagree on the extent to which Newton's study of alchemy influenced his science; but it seems evident that even though he separated them from his "purely scientific" research, his alchemical views influenced his willingness to accept the notion of "action at a distance" (the centripetal pull of gravity) which he resisted for so long.

Newton and Hooke

While Newton continued his solitary work, events in the outside world took a turn that led to his publishing his greatest work. By late 1677 his two good friends Isaac Barrow and Henry Oldenburg had died. Hooke, who had continued his study of planetary orbits, was elected secretary of the Royal Society. After two years of promoting correspondence with scientists at home and abroad, he wrote a cordial letter to Newton inviting him to resume his former relationship with the Royal Society and participate in the exchange of scientific information with its members. Hooke suggested that they engage in private correspondence on scientific topics of mutual interest. He then asked for comment on his own work, "particularly if you will let me know your thought of that of compounding the celestiall motions of the planetts of a direct motion by the tangent and an attractive motion towards the centrall body."[5]

At this point Hooke was ahead of Newton conceptually. In 1674 Hooke had published his *Attempt to Prove the Motion of the Earth by Observation*. His intuition and boldness of thought were evident in a proposed new "system of the world" with three basic suppositions. (1) "All celestial bodies whatsoever have an attraction or a gravitating power toward their own centers." (2) "All bodies whatsoever that are put into a direct and simple motion will so continue to move forward in a straight line, till they are by some other effectual powers deflected." (3) "These attractive powers are so much the more powerful in operating by how much the nearer the body wrought upon is to their own centers. Now what these several degrees are, I have not yet experimentally verified" (p. 233). Unfortunately, Hooke did not have the mathematical ability to verify his suppositions.

Although Newton did not want to be drawn into the swirl of another debate, he felt he should not refuse Hooke's invitation. So he quickly replied with the outline of an experiment to show that the path of a body falling from a great height to the center of the earth would be a spiral. The proposed experiment was read to the society and aroused great interest. When Hooke discovered that the suggested curve was wrong, he lost no time in making the mistake known in a public lecture to the society.

When the news reached Cambridge, Newton's anger had two targets: himself for carelessness and Hooke for breaking his promise to handle any future disagreements in private. In a second letter Newton showed that the path would not be an ellipse, as Hooke had proposed, but rather a rotating "ellipti-spiral." Hooke's response on

January 6, 1680, was significant: "Your calculation of the curve described by a body attracted by an aequall power at all distances from the center . . . is right . . . but my supposition is that the attraction always is in duplicate proportion to the distance from the center reciprocall" (pp. 252-53). Apparently, in conversations with others involved in efforts to work out Kepler's laws, Hooke had been able to guess at the relationship of the inverse-square centripetal force and the orbital ellipse.

Newton did not reply to this letter. Then on January 17 Hooke sent a short supplementary letter with a further comment on the problem. He asked, "If a central attractive force causes an object to fall away from its inertial path and move in a curve, what kind of curve results if the attractive force varies inversely as the square of the distance?" (p. 260, paraphrased). He concluded by expressing confidence that Newton could calculate what the curve must be and suggest a physical reason for this proportion.

Even though Newton did not reply to Hooke, it would be hard to imagine that such a precise statement of the main concept of the *Principles,* made six years before its publication, had no impact on Newton. He wrote to Edmund Halley years later that Hooke's "correcting my spiral occasioned my finding the theorem, by which I afterwards examined the ellipsis" (p. 251, n. 3).

Although scholars disagree on the extent to which those letters contributed to Newton's thinking at that point, Hooke's method of analyzing curved motion may well have steered Newton down the right track. And at a time when he was still speaking of orbital motion in terms of centrifugal force, Hooke's emphasis on *attraction* (centripetal force) was a key concept that gained ground in Newton's thinking.[6]

Stimulated by the correspondence, Newton tackled a complicated mathematical puzzle that dominated his thinking for weeks. Kepler had shown that the ellipse fits the observations of planetary orbits. Would it now be possible to calculate the exact curve on the basis of the inverse-square law: The attraction between two bodies varies inversely as the square of the distance between them? Newton proved that an ellipse would satisfy the conditions, but he did not communicate this result to Hooke or anyone else until August 1684.

These mathematical derivations were unprecedented. From his inverse-square law and the techniques of calculation that related it to motion, Newton could compute for the first time with great precision the shape and speed of both celestial and terrestrial trajectories. "The resemblance of cannon ball, earth, moon and planet was now seen, not in a vision, but in numbers and measurement."[7]

That great discovery might have remained buried much longer if a certain coffee-house conversation had not occurred in January 1684. On an afternoon following a Royal Society meeting, three important members met for informal discussion. The noted architect (and astronomer) Christopher Wren was accompanied by Robert Hooke and a young astronomer, Edmund Halley. Their discussion turned to the great unanswered question confronting natural philosophy, the derivation of Kepler's laws of planetary motion from the principles of dynamics.[8] Although they believed that the inverse-square law was the key, no one had yet produced a mathematical demonstration. Hooke claimed that he could demonstrate all the laws of celestial motion from the inverse-square relation and would present the proof when the time was ripe. A skeptical Wren responded with the offer of a prize for anyone who could demonstrate within two months an answer to the question: Given the inverse-square force law, what will be the orbital shape? Two months passed, and no one, not even Hooke, had produced the answer.

Halley was so disappointed that in late summer he went to Cambridge and propounded the question to Newton, who replied that he had already calculated the curve to be an ellipse. The scientist promised to rework his demonstration and send it to the delighted Halley in London. In November the young astronomer received more than he expected, a nine-page treatise entitled *De motu corporum in gyrum* ("On the Motion of Bodies in an Orbit"). It sketched a demonstration of the original problem: An inverse-square force requires an elliptical orbit for velocities below a certain limit. Based on principles of dynamics, the treatise also demonstrated Kepler's second and third laws. It pointed to a general science of dynamics by further deriving the trajectory of a projectile through a resisting medium.

Halley recognized that the precise mathematical analyses of *On Motion* constituted a revolutionary advance in celestial mechanics. He lost no time in returning to Cambridge to secure Newton's permission for its presentation to the whole Royal Society and publication. Well aware of the professor's aversion to publicity, Halley took time to assure him of the importance of the discovery and the warm reception it would receive. Newton consented and in February 1685 sent a revised draft of the manuscript which took the momentous step from an interactive two-body system to an interactive many-boay system.

The Principia

Newton was now launched on a program that devoured his time and energy for a year and a half. As a student he had discovered the inverse-square relation from Kepler's third law. Hooke's stimulus led him to extend the inverse-square force to explain Kepler's first law. Halley's August 1684 visit precipitated the calculations which produced the theorems and problems of *On Motion* and broadened Newton's horizons. He wrote the astronomer Flamsteed for data to make his demonstrations more precise, remarking, "Now that I am upon this subject, I would gladly know the bottom of it before I publish my papers."[9]

In getting to the bottom of the problem, Newton virtually cut himself off from human society. Aside from a few letters and a brief visit to Woolsthorpe for family responsibilities, he immersed himself totally in propositions and theorems, mathematical problems and proofs, until the spring of 1686. Using his mastery of mathematics, Newton demonstrated through an incredibly difficult calculation that the combined gravitational effect of each cubic foot of the earth was exactly the same as though its entire mass were concentrated at the center. At last he had the proof of an assumption he had made twenty years earlier. He could now publish his law of universal gravitation: Every particle in the universe is attracted to every other particle by a force proportional to a product of their masses and inversely proportional to the square of the distance between them $(F = Gm_1 m_2/r_2)$.

Newton completed a three-part work that was officially presented to the Royal Society in April 1686.[10] A committee was immediately appointed to oversee its printing. Because the society was short of funds, Halley volunteered to assume financial responsibility, even though he had only moderate means. In July 1687 the *Philosophiae Naturalis Principia Mathematica* ("Mathematical Principles of Natural Philosophy") came from the printer. Like Copernicus's *On the Revolutions*, the *Principles* was written in Latin mainly for mathematicians;

it was at first comprehensible to only a few, even though Newton used classic geometry and not the new calculus.

The first volume sets forth three laws of motion which extend Galileo's work and break with the ideas of Aristotle and the medieval philosophers. Here is the first clear description of the way multiple forces operate together, the impact of one body on another and the law of universal gravitation.

1. Every body persists in its state of rest or of uniform motion in a straight line, unless it is acted upon by an external force.

2. Change in motion (acceleration) is directly proportional to, and in the same direction as, the external force.

3. To every action there is an equal and opposite reaction.

These laws provide the basis for the science of mechanics, a major division of physics. Dealing essentially with forces and their effects, that science is foundational for modern technology.

The second volume explores what happens when motion takes place through a resisting medium such as air or water. Newton was somewhat less successful in that part of the work, much of which had to be revised in succeeding decades.

The third volume, entitled *System of the World,* is Newton's crowning achievement and the part most accessible (in translation) to an ordinary reader. In it the principles of the first two books are applied. Newton explains the orbits of Jupiter's satellites discovered by Galileo, shows how Kepler's three planetary laws are a consequence of universal gravitation, discusses the earth's daily rotation and the movement of its axis in space, and explains how the gravitational pull of the sun and moon causes the tides. Finally he calculates the precise motion of the moon.

Newton's *Principles* is unexcelled among scientific writings. With his logic, detailed mathematical analyses, clarity of text and breadth of content, Newton runs the whole gamut of physical science in its application to the seventeenth-century universe. His demonstrations introduced a radically new celestial dynamics based on novel concepts of mass and inertia, force, momentum and an entirely new quantitative measure of dynamical force. Newton's writings dominated scientific thinking for the next two centuries. The principles articulated and the method by which they were determined—the interaction of mathematical theory with observed data—firmly established the new scientific approach to describing nature.

Publication of the *Principles* generated great interest, especially in England, where other than the scientifically minded attempted to read it. It went into three editions and within ten years was being taught at Cambridge. Yet the new synthesis was by no means welcomed everywhere; in France the followers of Descartes resisted Newtonian ideas for about twenty years. On the continent a century later, however, the great mathematicians Laplace and Lagrange devoted their lives to completing and extending Newton's work.

For Edmund Halley, without whose encouragement the *Principles* would not have been published, Newton's work brought a special reward. For years the young astronomer had been intrigued by the problem of comets, which were thought never to return. But Newton showed that they also are subject to the law of gravity and move in elliptical orbits as do the planets. Therefore a comet should be expected to return, but when? A brilliant comet of 1682 gave Halley a chance to make his own observations and be the first to apply the law of universal gravitation to a practical astronomical problem. For the next twenty years he devoted his spare time to searching old manuscripts for the record of a similar comet. He found one observed by Kepler in 1607 that seemed to match, making a period of between seventy-five and seventy-six years. Then with a sharper focus for his search Halley discovered similar reports in 1531, 1456 and 1305. He jubilantly published his discovery in 1705 with an unprecedented prediction of the comet's return in December 1758. On Christmas night, sixteen years after his death, eager astronomers all over the world greeted the expected return of "Halley's comet." Its next appearance for the twentieth century is scheduled for 1986.

Scientific Method

The *Principles* marks the climax of the scientific revolution started a hundred and fifty years earlier by *On the Revolutions*. Copernicus and Kepler began to undermine Aristotle's system on the celestial front by their discoveries in astronomy. Galileo's attack initially was more down-to-earth in the field of mechanics, although his telescopic discoveries supported the Copernican system. With his law of universal gravitation Newton finally invalidated Aristotle's concept that the laws governing motion in the perfect region of the heavens are different from those on an imperfect earth. Newton synthesized celestial and terrestrial movements in his laws of motion and universal gravitation: hence the heavenly bodies do not have a special, divine nature. Newton's synthesis was unrivaled until the twentieth century, when Albert Einstein related matter and energy in an equally universal and elegant formula: $E = mc^2$.

Like Copernicus, Kepler and Galileo, Newton was a superb mathematician. But unlike the latter two, he had no a priori conviction that the nature of the world is essentially mathematical. Newton would say, the world is what it is; let us try to explain all that we can by exact mathematical laws (the language of science). At the same time, let us be open to other approaches. Although mathematics plays the central role in scientific inquiry, theories must be confirmed by experiment. Mathematical truths must not ride roughshod over physical facts but be constantly updated as new data become available.

Newton's scientific method steadily oscillates between theory and empirical data. How does one combine mathematics and experiment? The preface to the *Principles* states, "The whole burden of philosophy [science] seems to consist in this—from the phenomena of motions to investigate the forces of nature, and then from these forces to demonstrate the other phenomena."[11]

Since Newton wrote little about his actual method, it must be discovered largely from his practice. But because philosophers of science bring to investigation their own convictions about the nature of the scientific enterprise, the problem is complicated (see chapter 7). Although the inductive method is currently out of favor, Newton used it in some of his most important scientific work. His formulation occurs in his two major published books on natural philosophy, the *Principles* and the *Opticks*.

As in Mathematics, so in Natural Philosophy, the Investigation of difficult Things by the Method of Analysis, ought ever to precede the Method of Composition. This Analysis consists in making Experiments and Observations, and in drawing general Conclusions from them by Induction, and admitting of no Objections against the Conclusions, but such as are taken from Experiments, or other certain Truths.[12]

Newton's painstaking experimentation was based on his confidence in his inductive method, which undergirds the objectivity and the cumulative character of science.

Newton also used what today is called the retroductive method: (1) *formulation* of a hypothesis, (2) *deduction* of the consequences and (3) *testing* of these consequences by observation and experiment.[13] From the outset of his career Newton had an extraordinary flair for devising "crucial experiments" whose results could be extrapolated into a general, usually mathematical, formula. With a specific subject like gravity or light, he took the known facts and formulated a mathematical hypothesis or theory to fit them; he then deduced mathematical and logical consequences, which he compared with data gained by observation and experiment to confirm the degree of fit. Newton's procedure featured a repeated give-and-take between mathematical construct (model) and physical reality. Because he did not assume that his initial construct of gravity exactly represented reality, he was free to explore the characteristics of a mathematical attractive force even though he believed that the concept of a grasping force "acting at a distance" was not good physics. Repeated modification of his mathematical construct eventually led Newton to formulate his law of universal gravitation. It worked so well in explaining and predicting observed phenomena that he concluded this attractive force must "truly exist," despite the fact that it could not be allowed in the physical system to which Newton was committed.

Newton distinguished between "natural philosophy" (science) and "hypothesis" (assumption, speculation). For him the mission of science was to discover mathematical laws of nature's behavior—laws clearly deducible from and verifiable by observations of phenomena. He objected to "hypothesis" in the sense of a fiction ("I do not feign hypotheses") or as a statement that cannot be proved ("demonstrated" or "deduced") from experience. (This use of the word *hypothesis* is different from the currently accepted meaning: a plausible proposition to be tested by experiment, the first step of the hypothetico-deductive method.) Newton made his position clear in the second edition of the *Principles*. He explained to Cotes, who was overseeing the printing, "And the word hypothesis is here used by me to signify only such a proposition as is not a phenomenon nor deduced from any phenomenon but assumed or supposed without any experimental proof."[14] Newton then added his famous pronouncement:

But hitherto I have not been able to discover the cause of those properties of gravity from phenomena, and I frame [feign] no hypotheses, for whatever is not deduced from the phenomena is to be called an hypothesis, whether metaphysical or physical, whether occult qualities or mechanical, and has no place in experimental philosophy [science]. . . . It is enough that gravity does really exist, and act according to the laws which we have explained, and abundantly serves to account for all the motions of the celestial bodies, and of our sea.[15]

For example, Newton's science described *how* the attraction between two bodies occurs but does not explain *why*. On one occasion he wrote, "You sometimes speak of gravity as essential and inherent to matter. Pray do not ascribe that notion to me; for the cause of gravity is what I do not pretend to know, and therefore would take more time to consider it."[16] Newton's law of universal gravitation provided a mathematical explanation without having to account for its nature or ultimate cause.

Biblical Studies

For Newton the world of science was by no means the whole of life. He was deeply committed to his faith in the Creator of the world who also revealed himself in history and Scripture. A member of the Anglican church, Newton attended the services and participated in special projects such as paying for the distribution of Bibles among the poor and serving on a commission to build fifty new churches in the London area. Yet the scientist's public pronouncements on his Christian faith were few and far between. Shortly after his death a pamphlet with everything he had published on religion under his name ran a paltry thirty-one pages.[17]

Yet during his life Newton spent more time on theology than on science. He wrote about 1,300,000 words on biblical subjects. This vast manuscript legacy lay hidden from public view for two centuries until the Southeby sale of the Portsmouth Collection in 1936. Since then, the bulk of Newton's nonscientific manuscripts have been reassembled in three major collections in England, Israel and the United States.

Newton's religion was no mere appendage to his science; he would have been a theist no matter what his profession. His understanding of God came primarily from the Bible, over which he pored days and weeks at a time. The subjects of miracles and prophecy were prominent in discussions of the time and in Newton's study. He made many calculations to determine the dates of various Old Testament Books and textual analyses to discover their authorship. He also discussed New Testament prophecies with particular attention to those in the book of Revelation.

In contrast to most popular interpretations of prophecy, Newton's purpose and procedure are instructive. In commenting on Daniel he notes the "folly of interpreters who foretell times and things by this prophecy"; it was far from God's intent to "gratify men's curiosities by enabling them to foreknow things." Rather, those prophecies stand as witnesses to God's providence when "after they were fulfilled, they might be interpreted by events. . . . The event of things predicted many ages before, will then be a convincing argument that the world is governed by providence."[18] Newton stresses the importance of understanding the nature of prophetic language and its principles of interpretation (see chapter 8). "It is only through want of skill therein that Interpreters so frequently turn the Prophetic types and phrases to signify whatever their fancies and hypotheses lead them to."[19]

In the next section we will consider the influence of Newton's theology on his scientific activity. Here we note the seldom-asked question of the effect of his scientific method on his biblical studies. In a manuscript on rules for interpreting prophecy, Newton notes the similarity between the goals of the scientist and those of the prophecy expositor. They are identical in their quest for simplicity and unity.

Truth is ever to be found in simplicity, and not in the multiplicity and confusion of things. As the world, which to the naked eye exhibits the greatest variety of objects, appears very simple in its internal constitution when surveyed by a philosophic [scientific] understanding . . . so it is in these [prophetic] visions. It is the perfection of God's works that they are all done with simplicity. He is the God of order and not confusion.[20]

Newton's rules for biblical interpretation are similar to those he gives at the beginning of book 3 of the *Principles*.

Newton's historical learning, including a knowledge of Jewish customs, was extensive; the work he published was considered a valuable addition to religious knowledge. Newton also set out to master the writings of the church fathers. His interest in the doctrine of the

Trinity led him to study particularly the works of Athanasius, Gregory and Augustine, who formulated trinitarianism. He became fascinated with Athanasius and his passionate, bloody conflict in the fourth century with Arius, who denied the Trinity and the status of Christ in the Godhead. Newton, convinced that a massive fraud had perverted the legacy of the church and certain Scriptures, adopted the Arian position well before 1675. He recognized Christ as a divine mediator between God and humankind, but subordinate to the Father who created him. Christ had earned the right to be worshiped (though not on a par with the Father) through his obedience and death.[21]

Although his Arianism became known with the publication of his long-dormant theological manuscripts, during his lifetime nobody cast aspersions on Newton's Anglican orthodoxy. And it certainly never occurred to Newton—any more than it did to Copernicus, Kepler and Galileo—that there might be a conflict between his commitment to the revelation of God in the Bible and his scientific investigation of nature.

Theology and Science

Although Newton spent much of his time studying the special revelation of God in Scripture, he had a high view of general revelation—the knowledge of God that can be gained through the study of creation. The scientist had a strong commitment to natural theology, to which he believed his discoveries made a significant contribution. At the end of the *Principles* he wrote:

> This most beautiful system of the sun, planets, and comets, could only proceed from the counsel and dominion of an intelligent and powerful Being. . . . This Being governs all things, not as the soul of the world, but as Lord over all; and on account of his dominion he is wont to be called Lord God.[22]

The second sentence is particularly significant. Newton's God was no deist "watchmaker," no "eternal principle"; he was to be worshiped "not so much for his essence as for his actions, the creating, preserving, and governing of all things according to his good will and pleasure."[23] God used natural causes, but they were not sufficient to explain all phenomena. Thus Newton invoked the immediate action of God to prevent the fixed stars from collapsing into the middle of space and to make occasional adjustments in certain irregular motions of the planets. God's perfection entailed the constant activity of the divine will, for which, in a kind of "evangelistic" concern, Newton believed he provided evidence. "When I wrote my treatise about our Systeme, I had an eye upon such Principles as might work with considering men for the beliefe of a Deity & nothing can rejoyce me more than to find it usefull for that purpose."[24]

Newton observed the distinction between religion and science set forth in Bacon's classic statement about the book of God's word and the book of God's works, and his warning not to confuse their learnings. Newton refused to use the Bible as an authority on scientific matters; during his years as president of the Royal Society he banned anything remotely touching religion, even apologetics. On one occasion he wrote, "We are not to introduce divine revelations into philosophy [science], nor philosophical opinions into religion."[25] Yet this distinction was not a divorce. Although the books were not to provide the content for each other's teachings, they were bound together in many ways. Newton did not consider one to be sacred and the other secular. They were of equal worth as their respective teachings about God supplemented each other.

Newton's approach to understanding nature guided his interpretation of Scripture, especially prophecy. In both books he discovered a divine simplicity. His theology also profoundly influenced his scientific method which was characterized by induction rather than pure speculation. Newton's voluntarism emphasized the will and dominion of God, who freely created the world and continues to reign over it.

These [laws of nature] therefore we must not seek from uncertain conjectures, but learn them from observations and experiments . . . not by the force alone of our own mind, and the internal light of our reason. . . . All sound and true philosophy [science] is founded on the appearances of things [observations].[26]

Newton's God was not merely a philosopher's impersonal first cause; he was the God of the Bible who creates and rules his world, who speaks and acts in history. "To Newton the public scientist we owe so much of the modern understanding of nature, but to Newton the private theologian we owe no less: the attitude that what God has freely done can be learned not by inventing it, but by discovering it."[27] The biblical doctrine of creation undergirded his empirico-mathematical science.

Public Life

The last third of Newton's life was radically different from his isolated years of scientific endeavor and from the final years of the other three scientists we have studied. Copernicus became increasingly lonely in his small Polish town and barely glimpsed his book before he died. Kepler, equally isolated in Silesia, fought his battle against ill health, poverty and professional frustration to the bitter end. Galileo's last decade was spent under house arrest, his work repudiated by his church and his sight failing. In contrast, Newton's last years brought him a prestigious position, honors bestowed by his country, social life in London and the acclaim of the world.

In the spring of 1687, James II caused turmoil at Cambridge University by ordering the admission of Father Alban Francis, a Benedictine monk, without the customary oaths required by statute. That action was part of the new king's program to return England to Roman Catholicism. The Cambridge officials protested and sent a delegation to appear before the court in London. Newton played a significant role in arguing the case. The university was able to hold out against the king, who was soon forced to flee the country. In 1689 Cambridge elected its famous scientist to parliament; consequently, Newton spent much of his time in London on this assignment. After twenty-five years of grappling with ideas the scholar now entered the arena of politicians and courtiers.

Newton became restless as he continued his professorial duties and asked friends to find a suitable position for him in London. Meanwhile he continued his study of lunar theory, worked in his laboratory and discovered laws of heat transfer. By 1692 the strain under which he had been living for many years drove him into a nervous depression that lasted two years. Finally, in 1696, Newton received word that the king had appointed him warden of the Mint, a new assignment that brought to the fore his administrative ability.

Like Copernicus one hundred and fifty years earlier, Newton was drawn into a currency crisis. Silver coins had long been debased by clipping or filing down the thicker sections. Since the edges were not milled and there was no inscription along the rims, such tampering was not easily detected. The practice continued to be widespread despite its severe penalty, hanging. Now the government decided on the drastic action of calling in all the old coinage in exchange for newly minted, tamperproof coins with a legend close to milled edges. In order to succeed, the program had to flood the country with enough new coins to keep up with business activities.

With his ability, energy and integrity, Newton was just the person to supervise the project. During the first critical months he had new furnaces built and increased coin production almost tenfold to satisfy the demand and maintain confidence in the markets. By 1699 the entire recoinage project had been successfully completed, and Newton was appointed master of the Mint. Two years later he resigned his professorship at Cambridge and moved to London where his niece Catherine Barton kept house for him.

In 1703 Newton was elected president of the Royal Society, a position to which he was re-elected annually for the rest of his life. After an interlude of absentee presidents selected for their political prominence, the scientist's administrative ability provided a strong hand at the helm to steer the society's course. Unfortunately, Newton's lifelong impatience with contradiction produced a despotic dominion during his later years.

Two great arguments marred this period. The first was a decade-long feud with the first Astronomer Royal, John Flamsteed. Newton fanned the flames with a growing arrogance in requesting of Flamsteed observations for his calculations. He and Halley published these observations in an unauthorized printing in 1712, most of which Flamsteed burned four years later. The second conflict had international repercussions as Newton became entangled with the German mathematician Leibniz in a long, bitter argument over who invented the calculus—a controversy perpetuated by their followers. Actually the two men developed the concept about the same time but used different systems of notation. The conflict was complicated by profound philosophical and theological differences.

In 1705 Newton was knighted by Queen Anne. Renowned scientist, master of the Mint and president of the Royal Society. Sir Isaac Newton had become a personage of consequence. Newtonian science, initially opposed, gradually swept the field. Toward the end of the eighteenth century the mathematician LaPlace declared the *Principles* to be the greatest production of the human mind. With deep conviction Halley wrote, "Nearer the gods no mortal may approach." No wonder Alexander Pope exclaimed:

Nature and Nature's laws lay hid in night:
God said, *Let Newton be!* and all was light.

Although for eighty years Newton's body had served him remarkably well, illness now took its toll. During his last years of enforced rest he returned to the problem of the moon's motion, worked on a revision of the *Principles* and carried on the study he loved best, his biblical research.

Isaac Newton died on March 20, 1727, in his eighty-fifth year. He was buried in Westminster Abbey with full honors. His death was regarded as a national loss. Yet Newton's own view of his achievements was modest: "I don't know what I may seem to the world, but, as to myself, I seem to have been only like a boy playing on the sea shore, and diverting myself in now and then finding a smoother pebble or a prettier shell than ordinary, whilst the great ocean of truth lay all undiscovered before me."[28]

7
MODERN SCIENCE: A NEW PERSPECTIVE

*The function of setting up
goals and passing statements
of value transcends
the domain of science.*
ALBERT EINSTEIN

SCIENCE HAS WON ITS INFLUENTIAL ROLE IN THE DEVELOPMENT OF Western thought through a new way of looking at the world. Its pioneers in the sixteenth and seventeenth centuries devised a radically different method of accounting for the workings of nature. It broke with Aristotle's approach, which had reigned for almost two thousand years. Natural philosophy—what we now call science—became a new game, with its own rules for scoring.

In this chapter the term *modern* is used in contrast to *Aristotelian* with reference to a *method,* not a specific *result.* For example, we are concerned primarily with the kind of mathematical approach Copernicus used to produce and justify his model of the universe, not just the fact that he placed the sun rather than the earth in the center. It was

Newton's view of the relationship between theory and experimental data, as much as his law of universal gravitation, that firmly established the new scientific method of describing natural forces. In fact, Newton's once-modern model of the universe is now called classical (that is, old-time) physics, inadequate to describe the "very large" expanding universe or "very small" subatomic phenomena. Explanation of those phenomena calls for entirely new concepts like relativity and quantum mechanics. Nevertheless, today's "modern physics" employs the same mathematical approach tying together theory and data, hypothesis and observation or experiment, which was advanced by Copernicus, Kepler, Galileo and Newton.

In the following pages, we briefly review salient features of Medieval and Renaissance science, then consider the nature of scientific discovery, scientific presuppositions and the role of Christianity in developing the new science.

Medieval Science
Following the fall of Rome, the writings of Aristotle and many other Greek philosophers were largely lost to the Western world, although the ideas of Plato had made their way into Christian theology. Augustine (A.D. 354-430) had been a Neoplatonist before he became a Christian. His combination of elements from that philosophy with Christianity formed the first Christian synthesis of knowledge, which prevailed until the time of Aquinas.

Rediscovery of classical Greek learning occurred first in the Arab world during the ninth century. Both Greek and Hindu scientific works (including Ptolemy's *Almagest*) were translated into Arabic. Scholars popularized the so-called Arabic numerals (borrowed from the Hindus) along with the decimal system and the concept of zero. Those innovations dealt with large numbers far more effectively than did the old cumbersome Roman numerals. (Imagine having to do multiplication with LXXVII and DCCLXXVI instead of 77 and 776.) That new system of mathematics was vital to the scientific revolution six hundred years later.

Classical learning followed in the wake of Islamic conquests that swept across North Africa, then into Spain. There schools and colleges enjoyed an intellectual freedom that encouraged the interaction of Islamic, Jewish and Christian thought. During the twelfth century the ideas of Aristotle, through the influence of the pantheistic Arab philosopher Averroës, infiltrated the universities of Christendom. Those teachings began to capture the thinking of the student generation and intelligentsia of the rising mercantile classes.

By the early thirteenth century the complete works of Aristotle were translated into Latin, opening up a new world to the medieval mind. Thomas Aquinas (1225-1274), following the direction pointed by his teacher Albertus Magnus, proceeded to synthesize Aristotelian natural philosophy with Christian theology. Since Aristotle's system led to a better account of the external world than did the traditional framework based on Plato's thought, Aquinas generally accepted it.[1] With courage and skill he set out to reconcile that system with Christian doctrine. Turning the new thinking of his day into a weapon for the defense of Christianity, he achieved a revolution in religious thought.

In his great works *Summa contra Gentiles* ("Compendium against the Gentiles") and *Summa Theologica* ("Compendium of Theology"), Aquinas taught that philosophy and theology, human wisdom and divine revelation, must be compatible. Although the existence of God can be demonstrated by natural reason, the doctrines of the Trinity and Incarnation are mysteries received by faith based on a rational revelation. Aquinas developed his system within the framework of Aristotle's science and logic, which strives to provide rigorous proof from accepted premises. The resulting method produces a commitment to knowledge derived by reason—from philosophical axioms on the one hand, from biblical authority on the other. In that comprehensive synthesis, science and philosophy are combined with theology into one system, hardly conducive to the free investigation of either nature or Scripture.

Although some of Aquinas's teaching was condemned shortly after his death, the ban was later lifted, and in the sixteenth century it became the official philosophy of the church. Aristotle and the Bible had been so completely harmonized in that medieval synthesis that any attack on its astronomy or physics seemed to the Aristotelian philosophers to be a rejection of the biblical revelation as well. The marriage of Aristotelian philosophy to Christian theology set the stage for the domestic quarrels of the scientific revolution, one might say— producing children who reacted strongly against their home environment.

Aristotle's science distinguished four causes of natural phenomena: formal (plan), final (purpose), material (passive materials) and efficient (change agent). But his method was most concerned with the first two, the plan and purpose, the ultimate meaning of the phenomena. For example, why does an acorn grow? To become an oak. The behavior of each creature follows from its essential nature and future goal. The central feature of all change is from *potentiality* into *actuality*. The universe itself moves to realize its ultimate purpose or end. According to Aristotle, therefore, science is not primarily concerned with the detailed *process* of change from moment to moment. The categories of its explanations are essence and potentiality, not mass and force related by laws in space and time.

The medieval search for purpose was based on a conviction that every object has its place in a cosmic hierarchy, since the universe is the creation of a purposeful God. Within Aristotle's comprehensive system, science became more *deductive* (starting from general principles and reasoning to conclusions) than *inductive* (starting from specific observations and generalizing from them). Natural philosophers worked out *logical connections* among events rather than experimenting to discover their *mechanism*. For them the ultimate *why* of the meaning of each part to the whole was more important than the immediate *how* of its action. The basic image of nature was that of an *organism* developing its potential—in contrast to the *machine* of the Newtonian era.

Modern Science

Whereas medieval science was primarily interested in the purpose of natural events, the new science concerned itself with process, the efficient cause or mechanism. Its method was not logical reasoning from first principles but mathematical analysis of experimental data. Its basic language consisted not of syllogisms constructed with words but of calculations with numbers. Measurement of quantities like velocity, mass and time; calculations based on observations and experiments; description in generalized mathematical formulas—such procedures lay at the heart of the new science as it shook itself free from control by philosophy and theology.

Although Copernicus worked largely with the same celestial observations as his fellow astronomers, he had the imagination and courage to see the solar system from a new perspective. Dissatisfied with the Ptolemaic system and its equant, he worked out the mathematics for a model with a central sun. The result was a mathematically simpler system which beautifully correlated the distances of the planets from the sun with the times of their revolutions. Kepler had available the more accurate observations of Tycho Brahe. To that "chaos of data" he applied his mathematical genius, not resting until he discovered a good fit of the data to a theory based on an elliptical planetary orbit. Copernicus and Kepler replaced the geocentric system with a heliocentric model on the basis of a mathematical demonstration—without any need to explain its plan and purpose in nature.

It remained for Galileo and Newton, however, to refine the working relationship between mathematics and experiment. As outlined in chapter four, Galileo wanted to understand the physical world by knowing its geometrical structure, yet he sought experimental confirmation for his mathematical analysis. He emphasized the hard work required to unlock nature's secrets. His approach combined hypothesis, mathematical demonstration and experiment. Galileo said the way to begin is to look for immediate rather than remote causes, devise a hypothesis capable of being tested and formulate a theory that is useful for prediction.

Newton's scientific method also rested squarely on both mathematics and observation. Although he was a superb mathematician, his emphasis on the empirical side was equally strong. Newton invented and used the calculus; he was an ingenious experimenter in mechanics, optics and chemistry. His approach applied mathematics to the physical world as it was revealed by experiment and critical observation. In discovering his law of universal gravitation he blended theory, observation and calculation in a repeated give-and-take (retroduction) between mathematical construct and physical reality.

Even though he had performed the feat of describing both celestial and terrestrial motion by a single law of gravity, he was criticized. Continental scientists like Huyghens and Leibniz assailed him for offering no explanation of how gravity works. To such criticism Newton replied:

> Our purpose is only to trace out the quantity and properties of this force [attraction] from the phenomena [data] and to apply what we

discover in some simple cases, as principles by which, in a mathematical way, we may estimate the effects thereof in more involved cases. . . . We said, in a *mathematical way*, to avoid all questions about the nature or quality of this force [attraction].[2]

Newton emphasized the term *mathematical* to make it clear that his science dealt with quantity and not quality in formulating laws that described the mechanisms of nature. It was enough for him that gravity "really exists and suffices to explain the phenomena of the heavens and the tides," even though he did not know its cause and therefore would "feign no hypotheses," that is, conjectures about its essence. Significantly, the following three centuries failed to produce a satisfactory explanation of gravity, although its behavior has been described and utilized.

Scientific Discovery

Our discussion of modern scientific method so far has not told us how scientific laws are formulated. What means does a scientist use to arrive at a new hypothesis? The answer is more difficult than it might seem at first glance.

In brief, the Aristotelians of Galileo's day used the method of deduction as they reasoned logically from first principles. Aristotle himself was a great observer of nature, but his purpose was to derive ultimate forms or ideas from which deductions could then be made to account for natural phenomena. His disciples two thousand years later did not value experimentation, since their explanations came through logical reasoning.

At the other end of the scale is the method of induction, which makes observations, summarizes them and produces generalizations. That procedure was advocated by Francis Bacon (1561-1626), the Lord Chancellor of England, who vigorously criticized the Aristotelian method of reaching scientific conclusions without observation or experiment. He insisted that progress would come from looking forward to new principles and practice, not back to ancient authority and method. Bacon promoted the inductive, observational approach of scientific inquiry and encouraged experimenters in various fields to get together for mutual encouragement. Although he stressed the need for directing experiments with proper organization, Bacon did not have the ability to give them mathematical direction and analysis. He believed that discovery could be a routine, automatic process carried out "as if by machinery." Although it hardly did justice to real scientific investigation, Bacon's view became popular.[3] Bacon contributed little to the heart of the new science, but his writings became something of a manifesto in the campaign against Aristotle.

The great discoveries we have examined here did not come by simple deduction or induction. Rather they emerged through the process of *retroduction* or *abduction*, the interaction between hypothesis and observation: fitting together a possible explanation and the data, modifying when necessary, testing to see if the theory is confirmed.[4] For example, Galileo struggled for thirty-four years before he was confident in his constant acceleration hypothesis.

Scientists usually start with the current theory, the "reigning paradigm," which no longer adequately accounts for at least some of the data. They frame a new hypothesis, often simply a hunch or intuition, then test it against available observations or new data provided by carefully devised experiments. An important criterion of any hypothesis is its ability to predict certain consequences. Scientists do not observe so-called brute facts; quite the contrary, all facts are "theory laden." The initial hypothesis determines what data are significant and guides the observations as well as correlates the results.

Scientific discovery sometimes involves a sudden new way of seeing the same data in a different configuration.[5] Through retroduction an imaginative new concept may be born. If not, "back to the drawing board" to discover whether the procedure was done incorrectly, not enough facts were available, or the single factor cannot be isolated for study.

Historically, new theories have appeared in various ways. While taking a bath, Archimedes pondered how to determine the purity of gold in the king's crown. He suddenly realized that a body immersed in liquid is buoyed up by a force equal to the weight of the liquid displaced. According to legend, he ran into the street naked shouting *Eureka!* ("I have found it!"). In contrast, Kepler labored over Tycho's observations for almost five years, like a man possessed, until he finally perceived the form of an ellipse in his diagram.[6] Although there is a logic for testing scientific laws, none exists for conceiving them. Nevertheless, by whatever means the discovery arrives, it is given a mathematical formulation and tested by experimental data.

A scientific revolution essentially repeats the same process on a very large scale. Thomas Kuhn has described such a revolution's characteristics and structure. He challenges the traditional concept of scientific "development-by-accumulation," a gradual process of adding piecemeal to a constellation of facts, theories and methods. He sees in the early stages of a science continual competition among distinct views of nature (ways of seeing the world and practicing science in it), combined with an apparently arbitrary element compounded of personal and historical accident.

A scientific revolution results in the replacement of one time-honored scientific theory by another. As new problems arise, they bring about a transformation of the world view within which scientific work is done. Kuhn calls the new view a *paradigm*, an achievement with two essential characteristics: "sufficiently unprecedented to attract an enduring group of adherents away from competing modes of scientific activity . . . [and] sufficiently open-ended to leave all sorts of problems for the redefined group of practitioners to solve."[7] Examples we have seen are Aristotle's *Physics*, Ptolemy's *Almagest* and Newton's *Principles* (for which Copernicus's *On the Revolutions*, Kepler's *New Astronomy* and Galileo's *Discourses* prepared the way). The paradigm—including law, theory, application and instrumentation—provides models for future scientific research.

Kuhn uses the term *normal science* to describe the activity of those within the community who base their work on shared paradigms with accepted rules and standards for practice. Most research is normal science working within a paradigm to solve the problems or puzzles it poses. Members of the community resist new ideas that challenge the accepted framework. Those who are unwilling or unable to accommodate their work to the prevailing paradigm must proceed alone or join some other group. Such departures can be the pivot for a new scientific revolution, which is much more than an accumulation of new theories. It is nothing less than a new way of seeing the world, marking a discontinuity with the past.

Nevertheless, an emphasis on discontinuity should not obscure the significance of certain elements of continuity. The newer work builds on and often incorporates what has been done before. For example, when a new scientific theory like Einstein's field physics is accepted, the older classical physics of Newton is not simply rejected. Except for the "very small" and "very fast," Newtonian theory correctly describes the physical world; in fact, classical physics still provides most of our technical knowledge in the fields of mechanics, sound, light, magnetism and electricity. Often the older scientific theory is more firmly established on *its own level as a limiting case* within a clearly defined range of application. This kind of continuity makes possible a genuine *progressivity* in scientific enterprise amidst the radical discontinuities that occur.[8]

It has now become clear that the strength of modern science lies in its quantitative approach to nature, measuring and calculating to provide mathematical descriptions of how the physical universe functions. Unlike Aristotle's science, it is not concerned with questions of ultimate purpose. Just as the scientific method and its results are no longer controlled by the overriding authority of philosophy or theology, so science has no right to make pronouncements on questions of values and the meaning of life.

> This, in turn, implies the disappearance—or the violent expulsion—from scientific thought of all considerations based on value, perfection, harmony, meaning and aim. . . . All formal and final causes as modes of explanation disappear—or are rejected by—the new science and are replaced by efficient and even material ones.[9]

Although noted by some of the most eminent scientists (such as Einstein), that fact is commonly overlooked. Many writers fail to distinguish between their scientific discoveries and their philosophical and religious preferences. Obviously the four scientists we have studied were not free from philosophical presuppositions, but they recognized a profound difference between natural-scientific and philosophical questions. Further, they considered their science to be only one perspective on the physical world; it did not purport to give a total explanation. Devotees of Newton in the eighteenth century who made a philosophy out of his mechanical universe did violence to his convictions at that point.

By the same token, the revolution we have been examining freed science from the overriding authority of theology. Galileo lost his battle to keep the church from becoming entangled in judging scientific theories, but his view eventually prevailed. Regrettably, that lesson has been lost in some of the current controversies over creation and evolution (chapter 12).

Yet even though science has freed itself from domination by philosophy and theology, it by no means proceeds without presuppositions.

Scientific Presuppositions

The myth of objectivity attributed to science in the eighteenth and nineteenth centuries has been discredited, although most people continue to think of science in this way. Not only do scientists as a group have certain philosophical presuppositions without which they cannot operate, but individual scientists have their own subjective values and goals.

Most working scientists seldom think about the presuppositions undergirding their work. Yet certain philosophical principles shared by members of the scientific community are almost "articles of faith" without which there would be no community. Some (such as 1 and 2 below) are presuppositions basic to any kind of scientific endeavor. Some (3 and 4) are really methodological principles, and still others (5 and 6) can be seen as moral and social principles necessary for science to proceed as a community enterprise.

1. *Order in nature.* Nature has an underlying order, shown in patterns and regularities that can be discovered. Such knowledge is attainable, and human intellect is capable of acquiring it, even though infinite variations exist.

2. *Uniformity of nature.* The forces of nature are uniform throughout space and time. What happens here in one laboratory also occurs in other countries around the world (in both the past and present) under the same conditions.

3. *Validity of sense perception.* Reliable data can be obtained by using the human senses or their extensions (for example, by reading a thermometer or voltmeter).

4. *Simplicity.* If two theories or explanations fit the data, the simpler is usually to be preferred. For example, although Copernicus's system did not provide a better fit than that of Ptolemy to the available data, or make more accurate predictions of celestial phenomena, it was mathematically simpler; it was preferred because it could account for the observations with a less complicated scheme.

5. *Moral responsibility.* All scientists are expected to report honestly the results of their experiments so that others can have confidence

in their data and use those results in their own research.

6. *Consensus of acceptance.* Scientists around the world engaged in research in the same discipline, using similar procedures and equipment, test research results and give them relative objectivity. Acceptance is based on the agreed competence of experts, a group of trained, skilled observers.

Several fundamental characteristics of the universe make scientific work possible.[10] The entities observed are real; that is, they exist independently of the observer. They also form a coherent whole and are subject to a consistent interaction. An equally important factor is that the form in which the universe exists is *not necessary,* but is only one of several conceivable forms. Therefore, science discovers its patterns and regularities by investigating the universe as it is, testing hypotheses and models in the arena of experimentation.

Science cannot tell us why such a real and rational universe exists; it simply makes these assumptions in order to carry on its investigations. The dependence of such beliefs, both historically and philosophically, on the biblical doctrine of creation leads directly to the role of Christianity in the scientific revolution.

Christianity and the New Science

The myth of "Galileo versus the church" as the prime example of Christianity's age-old antagonism toward science reached its zenith at the end of the nineteenth century. In 1896 Andrew White, cofounder and first president of Cornell University, published a two-volume work entitled *A History of the Warfare of Science with Theology in Christendom.* Like Galileo, the author produced for the general reader a polemic at times scathing and sarcastic. White's book became a classic and was reprinted in 1960 as "a complete and monumental history of the most important conflict man has known."

In a chapter on astronomy, White describes "the war on Galileo" as an increasingly bitter conflict; he accuses the church of using every available weapon to crush the scientist. "The heavy artillery of general denunciation may be seen on all the scientific battlefields." Galileo was finally defeated, and "hardly a generation since has not seen some ecclesiastic suppressing evidence, or torturing expressions, or inventing theories to blacken the memory of Galileo."[11] Although such vehement prose has largely passed from the scene, White's thesis continues to be promoted in both scholarly and popular journals. The basic relationship between science and Christianity is often described as one of hostility and inevitable conflict. Such a description ignores the fact that the attitude of hostility originated amid philosophical developments of the eighteenth and nineteenth centuries, not in the minds of the great pioneers of modern science.

Several lines of evidence show that Christianity was more a senior partner of the new science than its enemy. First, it is a historical reality that science developed within a civilization whose prevailing philosophy was Christian theism. The biblical revelation portrays a God who is consistent in character and orderly in creative activity. A belief that all reality is intrinsically orderly, therefore intelligible and predictable, is the basis of any rational or scientific activity.[12]

Second, the important concept of the contingency of nature has a Christian source. The whole universe in its regularity has been created and is sustained by God—a belief prominent in Newton's thought and cogently expressed in his writing. The concept of contingent intelligibility, based on the biblical doctrine of creation, became the foundation on which the empirical science rests.[13] In other words, nature is not understood through inherent, self-explanatory principles but by scientific observation and experiment. The world is what it is, not what we think it must be. The universe exists as a result of God's free, independent creativity. It is what God has made it to be: a contingent, open-structured order reaching beyond what we can grasp or define within the limitations of our propositions or equations.[14] Hence the surprising character of the universe, the unexpected twists and turns taken in the course of scientific theory.

Science is always traveling but never arriving. Scientific knowledge, of even a small portion of reality, can never be complete or exhaustive. Nevertheless, though scientists can know it only partially, they do gain insight into "real truth" in their continuing tour of the universe. The scientists we have studied were convinced that their theories were not figments of mathematical imagination conveniently correlating the data, but actual descriptions of the physical world as created by God.

Those four leaders of the scientific revolution were Christians, as were many others such as Bacon, Boyle, Pascal and Ray. It never occurred to them that their scientific research and its results could be at odds with their Christian faith. On the contrary, they viewed their investigation of nature as a sacred duty and privilege. Of the four, only Galileo came into conflict with church leaders; Galileo's struggle was largely due to the prolonged opposition of the scientific establishment, intensified by the scientist's pugnacious personality and a complex political situation. Far from being the classic example of inevitable warfare between science and theology, Galileo's conflict was an exception.

Finally, contrary to popular impression, the Protestant Reformation made an invaluable contribution to the new science.[14] On the continent the reformers had a positive view of science in a theological setting. John Calvin wrote, "If we regard the Spirit of God as the sole fountain of truth, we shall neither reject the truth itself, nor despise it wherever it shall appear, unless we wish to dishonor the Spirit of God."[15] Again, "For astronomy is not only pleasant, but also very useful to be known; it cannot be denied that this art unfolds the admirable wisdom of God."[16] Nevertheless, both Calvin and Martin Luther were concerned that concentration on science might divert attention from the Creator and give people the impression that natural processes are outside God's control.

Calvin and Luther accepted the Ptolemaic system, as did most astronomers in the decades following Copernicus. But they did not tie their theological understanding to acceptance of the current cosmology. The use of biblical proof texts to defend astronomical theories was a later development. Luther's single comment on Copernicus is usually taken out of context and misrepresented. One of his students, who took notes on dinner conversations, later wrote in *Table-Talk* for June 1539 that Luther dismissed Copernicus with the words, "The fool would upset the whole art of astronomy."[17] Although it is possible that the reformer could have said something like that, the remark does not appear in the notes of another reporter. The alleged comment was not published until 1566. An offhand remark attributed to Luther twenty years after his death hardly constitutes evidence that he was about to crusade against the new astronomy—as reported in many books on the history of science.

Seventeenth-century England presented an entirely different scene. Far from being in the conflict historians used to suppose, science and religion interacted with each other in a positive way. Mainstream

Protestants gradually embraced a version of the new science that supported traditional Christian philosophy as scientists purged the mechanical view of nature of materialistic tendencies. Puritans took the lead in establishing Newtonian science, making inroads into many of the universities. In the biblical tradition of high regard for manual work performed for the glory of God, the mechanical arts and experimentation were fostered. Even before Newton's time the Copernican system was widely accepted by Puritan thinkers in both Old and New England. Toward the end of the seventeenth century they constituted a majority of the Royal Society.[18]

Intellectual change rarely occurs in minds divorced from everyday reality. Scientists and theologians alike were also confronted by new and unsettling economic and political forces. "For nearly a century, beginning in the 1890s, Newton's science provided the intellectual foundation for a unique version of European Protestantism, one particularly suited to the maintenance of political stability and an unprecedented degree of religious toleration, all within the context of a rapidly expanding commercial society."[19]

So far we have concentrated on the development of the new science, in its pilgrimage from Aristotle to Newton, toward a radically different understanding of the physical world. In the next major section of this book we explore what the Bible intends to teach about the natural world and how its perspective can be related to the scientific approach.

II
THE BIBLICAL
PERSPECTIVE

8
INTERPRETING
THE
BIBLE

*The Spirit of God who spoke
through them did not choose to
teach about the heavens to men,
as it was of no use for salvation.*
AUGUSTINE

FOR HUNDREDS OF YEARS CHRISTIANS HAVE AFFIRMED TWO "BOOKS of God": his word in Scripture and his works in nature. The first concerns the destiny of humanity and leads to salvation. The second reveals the created order and is investigated by science. That distinction, which preserves the integrity of both theology and science, helps to avoid unnecessary confrontations between the two messages. In 1605 Francis Bacon wrote, "Let no one think or maintain that a man can search too far or be too well studied in the book of God's Word or in the book of God's Works, divinity or philosophy. . . . [We should] not unwisely mingle or confound these learnings together."[1]

In the first section of this book we have witnessed the rise of modern science, whose perspective on the natural world focuses on what can be observed, measured and explained mathematically. We now consider the Bible, whose primary concern is the arena of human history, within which God reveals himself and his purposes. Nevertheless, Scripture has significant teaching about the created order even though its perspective is different from that of science. In chapters eight to ten we will consider the biblical view of nature, outline some principles of biblical interpretation, take up the problem of miracles and scientific laws and examine the Genesis 1 account of creation.

To some people the Bible seems oddly outdated. Yet when properly understood, the biblical message has special relevance for our scientific and technological culture. It provides answers to urgent contemporary questions of meaning, values and purpose in life—issues outside the purview of modern physical science.

Biblical Revelation

In the Old Testament the key person was not a philosopher but a prophet. Unlike the modern scholar, who must have a keen intellect and rigorous training, the biblical prophet did not need such qualifications. He might be a court-educated leader (Moses), a writer of great literary ability (Isaiah) or a shepherd and tender of sycamore trees (Amos). One thing those individuals had in common was reception of a message from God, who took the initiative to communicate to his people. So we frequently read that "the word of the Lord came to" a certain person.

The role of the prophet was described by two New Testament writers:

In the past God spoke to our forefathers through the prophets at many times and in various ways. (Heb 1:1)

Above all, you must understand that no prophecy of Scripture came about by the prophet's own interpretation. For prophecy never had its origin in the will of man, but men spoke from God as they were carried along by the Holy Spirit. (2 Pet 1:20-21)

In a prophecy both the initiative and the authority belong to God. That constitutes a major difference between biblical prophets and modern scholars, whose research stems from their own initiative and is accepted on the authority their earlier work has achieved.

Although in the popular mind prophecy means predicting the future, the biblical concept has other, more important, elements. First, the prophets were the religious and social reformers of their time. They proclaimed God's protest against the idolatry of his people, their social injustice and economic oppression. The prophetic message called for repentance, forsaking unrighteousness and returning to worship the true God. At times there was also the element of prediction—usually of impending punishment if the people continued in their evil ways. But whatever the message, the prophets' authority did not ultimately depend on their own ability and analysis, but on God whose word they proclaimed.

Through the prophets God has taken the initiative to reveal himself and his purposes in the world he has created. The Bible records the prophetic message about God, human beings and nature in their mutual relationships. The key term in this revelatory action is *word,* a symbol of communication. The *spoken* word is proclaimed and then committed to writing; the *written* word, as Holy Scripture, is preserved and transmitted to future generations.

Yet God's revelation is not solely verbal. As the Lord and judge of human history, God also reveals himself in mighty acts of judgment and mercy. Both *act* and *word,* events and their interpretation, constitute the biblical revelation, which is firmly grounded in history.[2] On one hand, unexplained actions are ambiguous; their meaning can only be guessed. Conversely, words by themselves often seem unrelated to life. The combination of *divine act* and *prophetic word* effectively communicates God's character and purpose—the *who* and *why* of the created world.

God and Humanity in History

Meaningful revelation of God to his people encounters a fundamental problem. Jesus taught that "God is spirit, and his worshipers must worship in spirit and in truth" (Jn 4:24). The apostle Paul wrote about God "who alone is immortal and who lives in unapproachable light, whom no one has seen or can see" (1 Tim 6:16). The Israelites were not allowed to make any "graven image" or "likeness" of God for use in their worship. What comprehension, then, can we have of someone who is spirit and cannot be seen or approached?

In making himself known, God uses the principle of analogy—a partial resemblance, or similarity in certain respects, between things that otherwise are unlike. "God chooses those elements within our area of experience and language which can serve as relevant analogies of the truth of his own area of experience and self-expression."[3] In other words, God uses a model—a systematic set of analogies drawn from a more familiar situation.[4] (The same method is used in science. For example, in order to explain the behavior of gas molecules far too small to see, physicists use the model or analogy of billiard balls colliding with one another. Although they are not actually miniature balls, molecules move and interact in a similar manner. See chapter 9.)

In the biblical revelation, the central model for God is a person. The analogies are called anthropomorphisms since they picture God's activities as if he were human. Thus the Old Testament represents God as walking among his people, seeing their iniquities, hearing their cries, fighting for them in battle.

In order to understand what a model intends to communicate, we must distinguish the aspects that are relevant to the reality (the *behavior* of the colliding billiard balls) from those that are irrelevant (their *color*). The biblical terms are meant to communicate God's concern and activity on behalf of his people, not the idea that he has feet, eyes, ears and arms. God is also represented as having human emotions such as love, anger and jealousy. The human model, sometimes scorned as primitive and crude by modern scholars (who seem able to accept the billiard-ball model of a molecule), has a vividness and dramatic power to reveal God to ordinary people in every culture and century. Often the Bible uses as a model for God a specific role in society (such as ruler, judge, employer, parent) in order to emphasize some characteristic of God. Unlike scientific models, however, such metaphors (for example, "the Lord is my shepherd") have emotional overtones; they influence attitudes and actions. Language becomes event when the reader is personally involved as a participant.

Of course there are dangers in using models for God, especially in a literalism that identifies a metaphor with the reality it portrays. The prohibition against graven images in worship is more than a warning against idolatry; it is also a conviction that God is spiritual and cannot be captured in any visual form. He is always *beyond* our comprehension: "For my thoughts are not your thoughts, neither are your ways my ways" (Is 55:8). One reason for the multiplicity of metaphors in the Bible may be the fact that they are mutually self-correcting.[5]

The supreme model for God in the New Testament is Jesus Christ. He is the *living* Word who reveals the character and purposes of God.

> In the beginning was the Word, and . . . the Word became flesh and lived for a while among us. (Jn 1:1, 14)

> In these last days [God] has spoken to us by his Son . . . the radiance of God's glory and the exact representation of his being. (Heb 1:2-3)

Christ is God's great Act as well as Word, known through his life and ministry of healing and teaching. The focal point of the Gospels is the death, resurrection and ascension of Christ, the climax of God's redemptive activity. The apostles proclaim those events and their meaning. Their message is not good advice but good news: "Christ died for our sins according to the Scriptures, . . . he was buried, . . . he was raised on the third day according to the Scriptures" (1 Cor 15:3-4). The human predicament is not primarily our ignorance of right and wrong, which only requires education, but rather our sinful revolt against God which requires atonement and reconciliation. The Christian message proclaims God's act of love and mercy in Christ, calling us to respond in repentance, faith and a new way of living.

The Bible presents a linear, durative view of human history—with a purpose and goal. It begins with Adam and Eve, progresses to the new covenant in Christ and ends with God's universal reign. Unlike the Greek view of recurring cycles, none of which has unique significance, biblical history consists of unique, decisive events fulfilling a purpose. Approximately sixty per cent of the Old Testament is historical narrative—a record of events in the lives of individuals, families, tribes and nations. In the New Testament, the Gospels and Acts comprise about the same proportion; the other books have considerable theological interpretation of history, through letters to specific individuals or churches. God reveals his character and purpose for humanity primarily in and through the medium of history. In that arena archeology and historical research have consistently demonstrated the reliability of the biblical records.[6]

Interpreting the Bible

In order to benefit future generations, the *spoken* word from God became the *written* word. Such a record has several advantages. The message is given durability; free from errors of memory, it can be preserved over a long period. The message also has a finality and normativeness that other forms of communication cannot achieve. Finally, a written record can be universally disseminated through translation and reproduction.

Just as God revealed his character and purpose in his message through the prophets, so he guided its commitment to writing. In one of his letters the apostle Paul wrote to a younger colleague, "From infancy you have known the holy Scriptures, which are able to make you wise for salvation through faith in Christ Jesus. All Scripture is God-breathed [inspired] and is useful for teaching, rebuking, correcting and training in righteousness, so that the man of God may be thoroughly equipped for every good work" (2 Tim 3:15-17).

That succinct statement makes two essential points. First, not just the authors but the writings themselves are inspired. Such a doctrine by no means implies mechanical dictation (as often asserted), since the writers obviously employ their individual vocabularies and a variety of literary styles. Although we are not told exactly how God did it, we can be confident that he influenced the process to ensure the reliability of the intended message. The Word of God is communicated in human words; they accurately convey the intended ideas just as composers' notes express their music and scientists' formulas embody their theories. In each case our acceptance of the symbols enables us to receive the message they convey.

Equally important is the second point—the purposes for which the Bible is inspired. Paul notes two: understanding, for salvation through faith in Christ; and equipping, for a life of good works. Scripture embodies teaching (doctrine) designed to rebuke, correct and train in righteousness. Historically, the Bible has been accepted as "final authority in matters of faith and conduct." The Inter-Varsity Christian Fellowship basis of faith includes "the unique, divine authority, inspiration and entire trustworthiness of the Bible."[7] It is essential to remember that those characteristics relate to the *purpose* of Scripture.[8] Unfortunately, as in Galileo's time, biblical authority and reliability are often mistakenly extended to the realm of scientific explanation.

The view of the Bible presented above leads directly to the crucial question of interpretation. How can we understand the message we are supposed to trust? The Bible was produced by many different writers in a variety of circumstances over a period of fifteen hundred years. Its message was expressed in their individual thought patterns with a vocabulary embedded in the culture of the time. So the task of interpreting the Bible and applying it to our own cultural context appears formidable indeed. Yet it can be done—by carefully following the guidelines applicable to any kind of literature.

A two-stage process is required: First, we try to discover what the message meant to its first hearers or readers; then we try to decide what it has to say to us. God's Word initially came to people through events and language they could understand, but which we do not speak now. We need to discern what was intended by the author at that time. Only then can we see how it may apply to our own situation. Too often in our eagerness for guidance, we neglect or skip over the first step.

The whole process of interpretation and application is usually called *hermeneutics*. Some authors prefer to use the term *exegesis* (critical analysis) for discovering the historical particularity of the message, and limit "hermeneutics" to determining its universal relevance—the contemporary application of an ancient text.[9]

1. *Interpretation.* The key to good exegesis is reading the text carefully and asking the right questions. First, the *historical context* must be considered. What do we know about the period of the author and readers, their geographical, political, social and religious circumstances? What was going on in ancient Israel (or, in New Testament times, in the church) to call for such a message? The most basic question is the intention behind the passage: For what purpose was the author writing? The importance of this initial step will become evident in chapter 10 with the interpretation of Genesis 1.

Second, we must consider *literary context*. Frequently Christians are asked, "Do you take the Bible literally?" The appropriate answer is "Sometimes. That depends on the kind of literature." One should take the literal parts literally and the figurative parts figuratively, aware that the biblical writers use a variety of literary forms to convey God's truth. It is generally recognized that Scripture contains figures of speech. Yet many readers seem to ignore the wide differences among the Bible's literary forms (called genres). Major passages and entire books can belong to different genres; each must be interpreted in its own way.

"To communicate His Word to all conditions, God chose to use almost every available kind of communication: narrative history, genealogies, chronicles, laws of all kinds, poetry of all kinds, proverbs, prophetic oracles, riddles, drama, biographical sketches, parables, letters, sermons, and apocalypses."[10]

Once the historical and literary *contexts* are understood, a third step considers the *content* of the passage (although in practice the three steps may overlap). The meanings of the words and phrases, and the grammatical construction of sentences, paragraphs and larger units of thought are considered. The aim continues to be discovery of what that particular message meant to its first readers. Another important principle is that Scripture must be interpreted by Scripture. In other words, where does this passage or book fit into the Bible as a whole?

The whole process is often called the *grammatico-historical* method of exegesis. Good interpretation does not aim for uniqueness, for discovery of what no one else has ever seen. It strives to uncover the "plain meaning" of the text. Granted that a given meaning may not be "plain" to every student, that is still the goal. Good interpretation makes good sense of the text.

2. *Application.* The next task is to determine the contemporary relevance of the biblical message. How does the original meaning apply to our situation? At this point some new differences of opinion and controversies may emerge. Scholars who have traveled together along the exegetical path may now strike off in different directions. In fact, the subject of hermeneutics has become a major focus of theological debate. Some of the questions about the relationship between text and interpreter have proved very difficult.[11]

Hermeneutics must always be guided and controlled by the author's theological intent, which provides the basis for its application today. It is true that the significance of some Old Testament prophecies, for example, has been more fully understood in later centuries. Nevertheless, one must guard against any tendency to read into a text a meaning quite different from that intended by the writer. Otherwise a passage can be made to teach whatever is meaningful to any reader at any time. Ingenious ideas are sometimes smuggled in by the back door or side windows of the hermeneutical house, then brought out the front door as if they were legitimate residents.

Unbridled interpretative imagination, unchecked by the principles outlined above, became prevalent in the early church, largely through Alexandrian influence. Alexandria not only achieved a high level of culture, philosophy and science (chapter 1), but also became for a time the theological and ecclesiastical center of Christendom. Its most influential leader was Origen (A.D. 185-254), one of the greatest of the Greek church fathers, who headed a school for new converts. Later authors commented on his many writings, known to us mostly by fragments. He was among the first to present the gospel in terms understandable to people familiar with Greek culture. A creative theologian, Origen exerted a profound influence on biblical scholarship. Using his method of interpretation, massive biblical commentaries were compiled. Sermons tended to illustrate Origen's theory that any biblical text has three levels of meaning: literal (to see), moral (to do) and allegorical or spiritual (to believe).

> The Scriptures were composed through the Spirit of God, and have both a meaning which is obvious, and another which is hidden from most readers. For the contents of Scripture are the outward forms of certain mysteries, and the reflection of divine things . . . [understood] only by those who are gifted with the grace of the Holy Spirit in the word of wisdom and knowledge.[12]

That theory, reflecting Platonic philosophy, enabled Origen to discover secret teaching beneath the surface of the plain sense, or readily understandable meaning.[13] The allegorical method places a premium on imagination and leads to speculation about dramatic, even fantastic, meanings in a biblical passage. It tends to become "gnostic" or elitist—producing a select circle of "superspiritual" Christians who know about the "deep things" of God.

During the medieval period, in what was called the *quadriga* (a chariot drawn by four horses), a fourth meaning was added. To Origen's literal, moral and spiritual meaning was added the *anagogical,* a mystical meaning of future hope. For example, in any passage, "Jerusalem" could have four different meanings: the capital of Judea; the human soul; the church; and heaven.[14] The Bible became a goldmine of "spiritual" truths for sermons, waiting only to be discovered and refined by a vivid imagination. Martin Luther firmly opposed that procedure on the principle "Do not carry a meaning into the Scripture but draw it out." Although largely discredited in mainstream Christianity, allegorical interpretation persists in many quarters, sometimes producing heresies or cults.[15]

For some Old Testament prophecies, a fuller, longer-range significance became evident in New Testament times. But that reinterpretation had the built-in control of specific teaching by the inspired biblical authors. Today it is wise to adhere firmly to this hermeneutical principle: what God intended a biblical text to mean to the original hearers is the most important meaning for us today. Otherwise our biblical understanding, with neither chart nor compass, could sail directionless on a sea of subjectivity.

That principle sometimes seems difficult to employ, since the original message does not always apply directly to the church today. For example, although elements of moral law in the Pentateuch (such as the Ten Commandments) are universally valid, other commands (including the ceremonial and civil laws) were meant only for Israel as an ancient theocracy. Hermeneutics must be guided by such concepts as the progress of revelation through the old and new covenants, with both their continuity and their discontinuity. The application of Old Testament examples and teachings to the life of Christians today is particularly difficult.

For our purpose of considering the biblical view of nature, however, the issues are somewhat simpler. For one thing, the most complex hermeneutical problems lie in the areas of the Bible's own primary concern: the relationship between God and human beings, and of individuals in community, within the unfolding drama of history. Also, the languages of both Old and New Testaments with respect to natural phenomena have some of the same basic characteristics.

Biblical Language of Nature

Even though their major concern is the arena of human history, both Old and New Testaments abound with references to nature. In particular the Hebrews, who were not great artists or readers of literature, took their illustrations largely from the natural world.

The book of Scripture (like the book of nature) has its own way of looking at natural phenomena. Actually the Bible knows nothing of "nature" as either the living, divine organism of the Greeks or the machine of Newtonian science, with an existence of its own. The Bible speaks instead of the whole creation as absolutely dependent for its origin and continuing existence on the will of God.[16]

We have seen how Galileo and Newton stressed the fact that science uses the language of mathematics to measure and calculate quantities like mass, velocity and distance. Students of modern science must learn the meaning of such terms, plus other concepts like atom, proton and electron as well as hypothesis, law and theory. Only then are they equipped to explain the mechanisms of natural forces through mathematical equations. In scientific discussions about the natural world, neglecting to "learn the language" is not tolerated—even in a freshman course. Likewise students of the Bible must take time to understand its language and the kinds of statements it makes about nature. So let us consider several basic characteristics of *biblical* language concerning nature.[17]

1. *Cultural usage.* The Old Testament has come to us not only in the Hebrew language but also in the historical particularity of the way that language functioned in ancient Israel. For example, Hebrew measurement of time was imprecise by our standards. Alternating light and darkness (sundown to sundown) marked the day; the phases of the moon indicated the month; the cycle of seasons and the movements of stars determined the year. Because the extra fraction of a day in the earth's annual revolution around the sun could not be detected or measured, the calendar had to be patched up periodically. Such measurements, which would never satisfy a need for split-second timing in science and technology, were adequate for the purpose of daily living. Clearly, the ancient lifestyle did not suffer from its lack of precision.

Another example is Hebrew mathematics. In its system of counting, numbers frequently stood for our words *few, some* and *many*. Three meant "few"; ten, "several"; forty, "many"; seventy, a large but uncertain number. And, like us, the biblical writers at times rounded off their figures.

The ancients used physical organs such as the heart, liver and bowels to represent psychological functions. That kind of description is inadequate for modern psychology or physiology (though a correlation is often recognized). Yet we still make good use of such "primitive" expressions; even a modern cardiologist might admit being "brokenhearted" over the death of a child.

2. *Popular language of appearance.* Biblical language concerning the natural world is clearly popular rather than technical. It is the vernac-

ular of social gatherings with the kind of vocabulary used by ordinary people in everyday communication. The New Testament was not written in the classical Greek of 350 B.C. (nor in a special "Holy Ghost" Greek, as thought a century ago) but in *koine*, the common marketplace dialect of the first century. *Koine* had about the same relationship to classical Greek as modern American has to Elizabethan English. Since the Bible is a book for all people of all ages, its popular language about nature is intended to be understood by anyone.

Technical and popular languages serve different purposes. A philosopher or scientist, for example, uses technical language to communicate with colleagues and to publish in professional journals. But in ordinary conversation that same individual uses everyday language. It is unreasonable to interpret the popular writing of the Bible as though its terminology were technical. It is equally irresponsible to find hidden references to modern science in the Bible. The Holy Spirit never intended to communicate such things through the biblical writers.

John Calvin observed that the biblical writers describe natural events as they appear to the senses, not in scientific terms: "The Holy Spirit had no intention to teach astronomy; and in proposing instruction meant to be common to the simplest and most uneducated person, he made use by Moses and other prophets of the popular language that none might shelter himself under the pretext of obscurity."[18] For everyday communication scientists, like others, use phenomenal or common-sense terminology. Astronomers have no objection to using the phrase "the sun rises." Ptolemy, Copernicus and Einstein had radically different scientific concepts of the universe; yet to go fishing together they would have had no difficulty agreeing to meet "at sunrise."

3. *Nontheoretical terminology.* The biblical writers make no effort to describe the mechanism of natural events. Their concern is not with Aristotle's *efficient* cause, but with the *formal* and *final* causes—the plan and purpose. The Bible ignores the immediate *how;* rather, it stresses the *who* and *why* of the Creator and his goals. Given the human propensity to speculate, that restraint was noted by a Christian geologist a century ago during the conflict over evolution: "A remarkable point in Biblical references to nature is that we find no definite *explanation* anywhere of natural things. The writers of the Bible do not

go beyond the description of what they actually see around them, and the correct way in which they describe what they do see is beyond praise."[19]

The biblical language of nature is usually called "prescientific," sometimes with a tone of condescension. In spite of its chronological accuracy, the term *prescientific* obscures the main point about the difference between biblical and scientific language. Modern scientific language is not a standard against which ancient Hebrew writing, any more than Greek drama or Roman poetry, should be measured. Each literary form has its own characteristics and purpose. It is more accurate to say that biblical language is "nonscientific" or "nontechnical."

For two reasons, that characteristic is not a primitive defect but a universal virtue. First, can any modern writer using up-to-date scientific descriptions of nature hope to be universally understood, to communicate with all cultures regardless of their scientific sophistication? Second, how long can such a writer expect today's theories to remain "modern," acceptable to succeeding generations of scientists? Moses' purpose in describing the physical world was different from Aristotle's. The Greek philosopher managed to dominate Western scientific thought for two millennia; the Hebrew prophet met deeper human needs and his influence continues to be more pervasive.

To summarize, biblical language regarding nature is cultural, popular and nontheoretical. The third characteristic is especially significant for its relationship to science. To the assertion that the Bible is scientifically accurate, one should ask, Whose science? That of Aristotle or Copernicus? Newton or Einstein? Or a future genius whose theories may replace even our "modern" views? Since scientific theories are provisional and not permanent, subject to change or even replacement, the Bible's supposed "scientific accuracy" in any generation could be a ticket to obsolescence in the next and a loss of confidence in its trustworthiness.

Although the Bible offers no systematic explanation of the natural world, several basic attitudes are evident. First, belief in the creation of the universe by God pervades its pages. Prophets and apostles repeatedly affirm that reality. The pagan gods are powerless; only the Lord God of Israel is the "Maker of heaven and earth" (Ps 146:6).

Second, nature is not to be worshiped. It is to be admired as God's work but never adored. Any form of nature worship is a forbidden idolatry. Because the Hebrews were strict monotheists, their writings are free from the often grotesque animal and plant mythology characteristic of the nations surrounding them.

Third, the biblical writers assume the regularity and predictability of nature based on God's character (Jer 31:35-36). The same conviction of order in the world, the uniformity of natural forces, also undergirds the scientific enterprise. Yet the biblical writers do not speculate about the mechanism of those regulating forces.

Fourth, a conviction of God's providence in maintaining the universe pervades the Old and New Testaments. Biblical theism opposes both pantheism and deism; God is neither just a part of the world nor is he locked out of its activity. He is constantly working within nature as well as human history to achieve his purposes. The biblical writers attribute *all* events in nature—both the recurring and the miraculous, the predictable and the unexpected—to the power of God.

The possibility of miracles, and of answered prayer, is grounded in God's providential care of his world. Can scientific laws and biblical miracles be related to each other in a way that does justice to each? That is the issue to which we now turn.

9
MIRACLES AND SCIENTIFIC LAWS

*The divine art of miracle is
not an art of suspending the pattern
to which events conform but of feeding
new events into that pattern.*
C. S. LEWIS

AN A SCIENTIST, OR ANYONE BROUGHT UP IN OUR SCIENTIFIC age, accept the biblical concept of miracles? The eighteenth-century philosopher David Hume, who thought of miracles as violations of natural law, concluded that a miracle is a scientific impossibility. Yet the word *miracle* keeps cropping up in daily conversation. The morning newspaper may report the discovery of a miracle drug to cure cancer or a miraculous escape from a flaming crash.

Miracles are recorded in the Bible. But what constitutes a miracle? Is it, as Hume defined it, a supernatural action that violates or interferes with the laws of nature? Is it an extraordinary event once attributed to God but now explainable by science? Or is a miracle simply a rare occurrence or coincidence that is improbable and unpredictable?

Much controversy over miracles and scientific laws comes from misunderstanding, because terms are not clearly defined. First we shall consider what a scientific law is and how it describes the forces of nature. Then we shall look at the biblical meaning of miracle, and try to relate the two.

SCIENTIFIC LAWS

Scientific Terminology

Words and phrases have multiple meanings. For example, *bar* can mean a long rod; unit of atmospheric pressure; ridge of sand in the water; the legal profession; a line on a musical score; or a place of liquid refreshment. At first glance it may seem difficult, perhaps impossible, to determine the correct meaning, but that meaning usually becomes clear from the context. If we read of someone stopping at a bar on the way home from work, we can be reasonably sure that the action had little to do with meteorology or law.

Although the word *science* does not have such diverse usage, it does convey three related but distinct meanings. It may refer to (1) a *specific branch* of knowledge or study (such as astronomy, botany or chemistry) with its observable data; (2) an *exact way* of studying and explaining a body of data—for example, the modern scientific method whose development we have traced; or (3) a *systematized body of knowledge* resulting from a precise way of studying natural phenomena. Many authors write about "science" without making clear which meaning they intend.

There is no one "scientific method" for understanding natural phenomena, nor one standard formula for producing a scientific theory. We have considered the modern scientific *perspective* on the natural world, with its mathematical *procedure* for interaction of theory with observation and experiment. Now we shall look more closely at the *purpose* of scientific endeavor.

We have seen that Aristotle's science dealt with four causes of natural phenomena: formal, material, efficient and final. Following Galileo and Newton, science narrowed its focus to the material and efficient causes, relegating questions of plan and purpose to the do-

mains of philosophy and theology. Today's scientist studies the phenomena of a particular field—say astronomy or physics—to discover
what forces are at work and how they function. In that venture certain
words and ideas are important.

For example, what constitutes a "scientific fact"? Every day we make
hundreds of observations, few of which could be called scientific. At
some risk of oversimplifying, one can distinguish between *general description* and *mathematical explanation.*[1] The former is usually a qualitative report of a sense perception—something we see or hear or feel.
For example, when white light passes through a prism we can see that
it is composed of many colors. Although in a general sense that observation is a "scientific" fact, it does not provide a basis for devising
an optical theory. Only when we measure the colors in some way,
specifying their wavelengths or angles of diffraction, can we make the
calculations necessary for a mathematical explanation. Insofar as
science uses the language of mathematics (measurement and calculation), its method requires quantifiable data. In the arena of the
physical sciences a fact is defined as a measurable quantity. Since a
scientist looks for patterns of activity, a phenomenon must also recur
or be experimentally repeatable. The life sciences and social sciences
tend to be more qualitative, but move toward quantification.

Consider a liquid heated by an electric coil. A general description
might report, "I put some water in a flask and heated it. After a while
it felt very hot." Those observed facts do not constitute scientific data;
they cannot be precisely reproduced, analyzed or used to develop a
law of heat transfer. To be more useful scientifically, the report should
state, "I poured 500 ml of water into a one-liter borosilicate glass flask,
placed it on a 1,000-watt electric heating element, and observed that
after 5 minutes the temperature had risen from 25° C to 95° C."

The second account is no more "true" than the first *qualitative*
account, which is perfectly adequate for making a cup of coffee. But
such *quantitative* measurements are necessary to calculate the rate of
heat transfer and the thermal characteristics of the flask and liquid.
In addition, these quantitative measurements provide a basis for
generalization and prediction. In other words, the resulting equations
should also enable us to describe the heating characteristics of other
liquids and predict their temperatures at given times (as well as the
energy required to produce any desired amount of coffee).

Science begins with questions suggested by everyday observations or with some problem with a currently accepted theory. Among its essential tools are *constructs* like specific heat, energy and mass, which are *unexplained* fundamental abstractions. Such concepts help to organize and interpret observations; they also guide in designing experiments and selecting the quantities (variables) to be measured. Scientists do not look around the laboratory and measure whatever happens to meet the eye, as if their minds were mental vacuum cleaners sweeping up data indiscriminately.

In the example above, the investigator was not the least interested in the height of the lab bench, weight of the heating element or length of the thermometer. He or she started with a concept of heat transfer that called for measuring the volume and temperature of the water, wattage of the element and duration of heating. It is obvious that a scientist does not simply observe "brute facts." From the outset, all observed data are "theory-laden,"[2] since a prior concept arranges for their selection and interpretation. Nevertheless, the data are in the public domain, available to other scientists for testing their own theories. The link between a theoretical concept and an experimental observation is sometimes called a "rule of correspondence."[3]

With that brief overview of scientific facts and constructs, we now consider three other terms vital to the scientific method: hypothesis, law, theory.

1. *Hypothesis.* We begin with the embryonic form of a scientific law or theory. A hypothesis is a conjecture, an educated guess or hunch, that guides an experimental design for its testing. It often takes the form of a mathematical model telling us what the phenomenon is like. Repeated testing does not establish the "truth" of the hypothesis (as commonly believed) but determines whether it can be "falsified."[4] A lifetime could be required to verify a hypothesis under many different circumstances, but even then it would not be absolutely established. Scientists want to know how far they can go with a new hypothesis; they look for the degree of fit with experience and probe the limits of its applicability.

The procedure is somewhat like building a foundation in soft, muddy soil. The contractor drives pilings down far enough to sustain the weight of the building. The higher the structure, the deeper the pilings must go. Likewise, the greater the weight to be placed on a scientific theory, the more it must be tested to see where it may fail to hold up. But a theory never achieves the certainty and security of a bedrock foundation.

Copernicus tested the hypothesis that the sun rather than the earth is the center of the solar system. After many other possibilities, Kepler tried the hypothesis that the ellipse is the shape of Mars's orbit. Galileo first thought that acceleration was a function of the distance a body fell, but finally found it to depend on the time of fall. Newton's preliminary calculation for his hypothesis of gravitation showed an error of 15 per cent; something was wrong. He put his calculations aside until he could determine whether his hypothesis or the observations were incorrect. In each case an effort was made to falsify the hypothesis by testing its degree of fit with the data.

2. *Experimental law.* The label *law of nature* (or *scientific law,* or *natural law*), though widely accepted, is not a precisely defined technical term. Its historical meaning has undergone many changes; even today it is variously defined within the scientific community.[5] Nevertheless, it is agreed that the term applies to a considerable class of universal statements.

A scientific law provides an understanding of some systematic order underlying natural events. Its final test as an instrument of explanation and prediction is its concordance or harmony with observations. An example is the law that the boiling point of a liquid rises as the atmospheric pressure increases. Some laws used in comprehensive systems deal with matters not directly observable. Thus when boiling is explained on the basis of the molecular constitution of water, the law does not stem from observation—since neither molecules nor their motions can be directly observed.

The first kind of law may be called an experimental law, the latter a theoretical law (or simply theory) because it uses terms like "molecule" which cannot be observed or confirmed directly by experiments. That is not to say that a theory is entirely speculative or unsupported by cogent evidence. The distinction may seem vague, but it is as valid as the difference between the front and back of a person's head, even though no exact line separates the two. No precise criterion can be stated for distinguishing between a law and a theory, but certain features of each can be identified.

A law deals with experimental or observational evidence in a relatively restricted arena. Two examples are Kepler's laws of planetary motion and Galileo's law of acceleration. Scientific laws may take the form of equations or graphs or quantitative verbal expressions. They describe regularities in nature in a way that accounts for large amounts of data. An "experimental law" encompasses more than the immediate data of a series of experiments; it formulates a universal relationship. For example, although Kepler's calculation of an elliptical orbit was based on observations for Mars, it is valid for all the planets.

Since laws are based directly on experimental data, they can be tested at any time. They not only describe present natural phenomena but also precisely predict future results for a given set of conditions. Thus they provide the basis for technology, the use of science for practical purposes.

Finally, an experimental law has a large measure of staying power. Even when incorporated into the structure of a comprehensive theory, it retains a meaning of its own, independent of that theory. Since a law is based on observational evidence, it can survive the demise of a particular theory and find a place under the umbrella of that theory's successor. For example, Newton's three laws of motion are still valid for most areas of physics even though the Newtonian theory or model of the universe has given way to a radically different modern view.

3. *Theory.* A scientific theory is more than an inductive generalization based on observed data. Theories are sometimes called free creations of the mind, although they are usually *suggested* by observations. Newton's discovery of universal gravitation, for example, illustrates a fundamental characteristic of scientific breakthroughs: "the creation of something new by the transformation of existing notions."[6]

A theory can be fruitful despite the fact that the evidence for it is necessarily indirect. Sometimes a new theory is adopted by scientists without fresh experimental evidence; the basis for accepting it is that it offers a better correlation of data already available. An example is the Copernican theory of the solar system, for which physical evidence of the earth's motion was not discovered until the mid 1800s.

Although a law is formulated in a single statement, a theory is a system of several related statements that are more general and inclusive. Outstanding scientific theories incorporate a wide variety of experimental laws and deal with an extensive range of dissimilar materials. A theory provides connections between constructs and laws by constructing a *model* (often mathematical) to account for the experimental data.

How is a theory to be judged? Albert Einstein proposed two criteria: "external validation" and "inner perfection."[7] The first is "concerned with the validation of the theoretical foundations by means of the material of experience lying at hand." The theory must not contradict empirical fact; this is a principle of *disconfirmation* or *falsification* and not of *verification*. The second criterion is concerned with the "naturalness or logical simplicity" of the theory's premises (the basic concepts and the relations between them). The requirement of "unity and parsimony" selects the theory with the "simplest foundation, logically speaking." Einstein also referred to another process of importance in the growth of theories, the consensus of groups within the scientific community regarding the degree of external validation and inner perfection (chapter 13).

Two other criteria are used for the acceptance of theories: *comprehensiveness* and *predictive power*. As noted above, a theory is expected to relate a wide variety of phenomena. Further, a valid theory should be simple and direct; if two theories are equal on other grounds, the simpler is accepted. Finally, a theory must predict observable results of experiments not yet performed.

Scientific theories provide a perspective on the physical world that does more than describe the way it works. They attempt to provide mathematical explanations that lie below the surface of correlation.

Status of Scientific Theories

Newton's view of a mechanistic universe dominated scientific thought during the eighteenth and nineteenth centuries. His science even became a philosophy of Newtonianism that prevailed in the Western world. As time went on, deterministic and materialistic philosophers made the new science into a metaphysics with no room for God. In France the *philosophes* taught that Newton's system showed reality to be a great machine in which human beings themselves—body and soul—were part of a mechanical necessity. The growing conflict between science and Christianity in the nineteenth century is better understood in the light of that development. It was not science itself but the wolf of anti-Christian philosophy in scientific clothing which rejected biblical teachings. The roles familiar from Galileo's struggle were reversed as naturalistic philosophers used the scientific establishment to conduct an inquisition of theology.

The nineteenth century perceived science as an absolute whose concepts were final and unchangeable. A prominent physicist publicly lamented that there was only one universe to be explained and Newton had already completed the task. Such confidence was shattered by developments in both science and philosophy early in the twentieth century. Succeeding decades have forced a re-evaluation of the status of scientific theories.[8] Although *realism* retained its following in some scientific circles, it was challenged by *instrumentalism*. More recently a mediating view of *critical realism* has gained wide acceptance.

1. *Realism.* Following Newton's discoveries, the universe became a giant machine running smoothly and predictably according to built-in mechanical laws. Robert Boyle likened it to a "Strasbourg clock" on an immense scale. Newtonian mechanics was seen as the ultimate system, giving the true and final picture of the world. Scientists adopted a realist perspective in which theories were thought to be literal descriptions of the way the world really is. For example, a science-class model of the atom using ping-pong balls and marbles was thought to represent the way neutrons and electrons actually behave on a much smaller scale. As late as 1922 a comprehensive treatise on chemistry stated that evidence had almost demonstrated "the real existence of tangible atoms."

2. *Instrumentalism.* The realistic view was challenged in the 1890s by *instrumentalism* (or "operationalism"), although that philosophy found a following only after the turn of the century.[9] It holds that a scientific theory is *not* a genuine assertion about the nature of the world. Rather it is an instrument (like a convention or definition) that simply correlates the data and predicts phenomena: "What we have called the laws of nature are the laws of our methods of representing it."[10]

To an instrumentalist, what is an electron? Certainly not the infinitesimal marble of the realist. The electron is simply a useful term for something whose effects we measure. If we suppose "electrons" to be active in a black box impenetrable to our view, we can measure a certain energy input and the resultant output by appropriate instruments. But the law we formulate tells us nothing about what actually happens within the box, nor does it need to. According to this view the aim of science is not to discover "truth" or "reality"; therefore it is meaningless to talk about an electron itself apart from our mathematical equations describing its function.

3. *Critical Realism.* A mediating position between realism and instrumentalism regards a scientific theory as a *model,* which serves as an analogy or metaphor. Even though it is not a literal description, it tells us something about reality. A model gives a partial view of a system, highlighting certain features of interest so that they can be understood and studied more easily. The model (usually mathematical or logical) is determined by natural forces and so tells us something about them. In other words, what science calls an electron actually *exists* (contrary to instrumentalism), but science does not tell us what an electron really *is* (contrary to realism).

In many respects a scientific theory is like a *map.*[11] A geographical territory can be described by different kinds of maps, such as highway, topographical or demographic. Each map tells us something about the area without being a literal or complete description. For example, the road map uses a red line to describe the direction and curves of a highway, but not its color; the highway itself isn't red. The map may depict the towns as yellow circles; yet though they are at the indicated spots, the towns are neither circular nor yellow. The map is not the terrain itself, but is so related to it that we can learn some of its features and find our way about.

Whether model or map, such an understanding of scientific theories is satisfying and useful. It has largely replaced both the older realistic (ping-pong ball) and the more recent instrumentalist (black box) views. As a partial view of reality, a scientific theory satisfies our desire to understand more about the natural world. Critical realism recognizes that although scientific language is symbolic and often abstract, it does represent experimental observation and endeavor to describe the realities of nature.[12]

To summarize, a scientific theory offers one perspective (among many) on the physical world. It provides a *partial view* of nature's forces through a mathematical lens that discovers nature's mechanisms.

Scientific accounts are often *abstract,* not representing phenomena the way they appear to the senses. For example, we may describe a beautiful sunset as it appears to us: a red sun, moving downward, just at the horizon. The scientist tells us we are mistaken on all three counts. First, the sun is not red; its light is really white, though some of the wavelengths have been filtered out by the earth's atmosphere. Second, it is not the sun that moves, but the earth that rotates on its axis. Third, the sun is not really where it appears to be; allowing for the time its light took to reach the earth, the sun was actually "at the horizon" about eight minutes ago. Nowadays we readily accept that scientific picture—even though it clearly contradicts our senses. Apparently "seeing is *not* believing." No wonder Copernicus feared public ridicule of his new idea that the earth rotates on its axis and revolves around the sun; anyone with eyes could see it is the sun that moves!

Finally, a scientific theory is *provisional* and not permanent. In other words, it is the best explanation we have to work with until a better one is discovered. Any theory is subject to revision or replacement as the reigning paradigm. Nevertheless, scientific knowledge is *progressive* or cumulative. Even though a theory is not permanent, it may continue to be useful in a revised or more limited form. Each new theory preserves and adds to a core of knowledge embodied in its predecessors.

MIRACLES

Creation and Providence

"In the beginning God created the heavens and the earth" (Gen 1:1). The Bible opens with a simple yet profound statement attributing the existence of the universe to God. Most current discussions of Genesis 1 focus on the chronological aspect of creation—when and how the world began in the distant past. Yet the past tense of creation is not the only significant aspect of the biblical teaching. A New Testament writer declares that God has spoken by his Son "through whom he made the universe . . . sustaining all things by his powerful word" (Heb 1:2-3). According to the Bible, our universe depends for its entire existence—past, present, future—on the creative power of God.

But what is the ongoing relationship between God and the world? An answer to that question can provide a basis for relating miracles to scientific laws. First, though, we go back again to Aristotle.

Like other Greek thinkers, Aristotle regarded the universe as non-created and therefore eternally existent. He recognized two main aspects of nature: it is intelligible and it is a living organism, divine or semi-divine. Aristotle wrote, "Nature makes everything to a certain purpose."[13] His god, the Prime Mover, was not an *efficient* cause (the creator) but only a *final* cause, related to purpose. The divine nature was immanent in the world.

Biblical teaching presents a radical contrast to both the Greek deification of nature and the cruder nature-worship of Israel's pagan neighbors. Genesis 1 makes it clear that only God has any claim to divinity; even the sun and moon (supreme gods of other nations) serve humankind. "The moon marks off the seasons, and the sun knows when to go down" (Ps 104:19). Further, after creating the universe God did not withdraw and leave everything to "innate laws of nature." The biblical view of God as Creator includes his continuing sustenance and renewal of the world.[14] The Hebrew participles used for God's creative work indicate a person engaged in the continual uninterrupted exercise of an activity. (That English translations do not convey this meaning may reflect a latent deism in modern Western thought, tending to relegate all God's creative activity to a once-for-all action in the past).[15] Isaiah speaks in one breath of what we call creation and providence.

This is what God the LORD says—
he who created the heavens and stretched them out,
who spread out the earth and all that comes out of it,
who gives breath to its people,
and life to those who walk on it. (Is 42:5)

In the New Testament, the apostle Paul says of Christ, "He is both the first principle and the upholding principle of the whole scheme of creation" (Col 1:17 Phillips). The Bible speaks of "creatures" (animate and inanimate) entirely dependent for their origin and continuing existence on the will and activity of God. An independent "nature" is not a biblical concept.

In the biblical language of God's continuing activity, we must distinguish between the *who* and *what* on one hand, and the *how* on the other. The writers are clear about who is performing and what he accomplishes; they show little if any concern about how he does it—

the mechanism or "scientific" explanation. Their aim is not to satisfy curiosity but to stimulate worship:

> He makes clouds rise from the ends of the earth;
>> he sends lightning with the rain
>> and brings out the wind from his storehouses. . . .
> O house of Israel, praise the LORD;
>> O house of Aaron, praise the LORD. (Ps 135:7, 19)

The same principle is true of God's activity in the realm of plants and animals.[16]

> He makes grass grow for the cattle,
>> and plants for man to cultivate—
>> bringing forth food from the earth. . . .
> The lions roar for their prey
>> and seek their food from God. . . .
> These all look to you
>> to give them their food at the proper time. . . .
> When you take away their breath,
>> they die and return to the dust.
> When you send your Spirit,
>> they are created,
>> and you renew the face of the earth. . . .
> Praise the LORD, O my soul. (Ps 104:14-35)

Jesus spoke of the continuing activity of God in what we would call natural events: "Look at the birds of the air; they do not sow or reap or store away in barns, and yet your heavenly Father feeds them" (Mt 6:26).

The biblical language of God's care for his creation has been understood by countless generations in various cultures. Scientists are free to observe, experiment and theorize in order to explain *how* natural phenomena take place. That enterprise provides plenty of work for astronomers, meteorologists, zoologists, botanists, agronomists and so on. But the essential point is made by communication theorist Donald MacKay:

> I find nothing in what the Bible says about the dependence of our world on God to suggest that this dependence should be demonstrable by some scientific peculiarity of its past or present behaviour. . . . Any idea that God's being active in our world means that there must be "something science can't explain" . . . is a complete

non sequitur. The laws of nature we discover are not *alternatives* to divine activity, but only our *codification* of that activity in its normal manifestations.[17]

We have seen how Thomas Aquinas around A.D. 1250 coped with the wave of Greek philosophy inundating the Western universities. His *Summa Theologica* effected a magnificent synthesis of Aristotle's natural philosophy and Christian theology. With regard to the natural world, the biblical view was superimposed on Aristotelian concepts. Aquinas was a staunch believer in the Creator who continues to rule over nature and sustain it. He also believed in miracles. But he made a marked distinction between reason and faith, between "natural" and "supernatural."

Aquinas started with reason (applied to general revelation) to explain as much as possible about the physical world, after which faith took over to accept revealed doctrines such as the creation, Trinity and Incarnation. According to Aquinas the regular order of nature has been instituted by God, who from time to time overrules it in a *super*natural way—with a miracle. Study of the natural realm (where miracles normally don't happen) is needed, partly so we can recognize supernatural actions which only God can perform.

Aquinas's distinction paved the way for a "God-of-the-gaps" concept, which gained acceptance during the following centuries—and still persists. If, as science learns more and more about nature, God is less and less needed to explain its workings, his activity becomes limited to the current gaps in our knowledge. That concept has moved God from the position of founder and director of the organization to part-time employee and finally to the ranks of the unemployed. Those who distinguish the natural from the supernatural in the way Aquinas did seldom realize that they put God in the same position as a skilled craftsman who is reduced to the role of trouble-shooter on an assembly line, then finally replaced by a robot.

In Aquinas's time, nature was viewed as a graded hierarchy with the earth at the center of the universe, surrounded by celestial spheres carrying the planets and stars. Above the stars was heaven; below the earth was hell. After Newton, that medieval concept was replaced by the model of a law-abiding machine, a mechanism following immutable laws with every detail precisely predictable.

Newton himself believed that the world-machine was designed by an intelligent Creator and expressed God's purpose. He considered a special action by God necessary to adjust certain unexplained irregularities in planetary motion, and at several points to keep the universe from collapsing. Within a century, however, both problems were scientifically accounted for. Once built and set ticking, the universe no longer seemed to need the attention of its Maker. The stage was thus set for deterministic and materialistic philosophies to turn a scientific *method* into *metaphysics*. One perspective on nature was turned into a total account of the universe.

Eventually the machine concept was attacked from two sides. Nineteenth-century biology and geology gave nature a developmental past and future. Twentieth-century science then found Newtonian physics inadequate to explain the "very large" and the "very small." Einstein's relativity and Heisenberg's indeterminacy took their toll; no one model has been able to replace the concepts of Aristotle, Aquinas and Newton. The law-abiding machine still has a popular following, however. Discussions of miracle usually bog down over the claim that a miracle must violate or break the laws of nature, as God intervenes in their operation. But is that a reasonable description of what must occur?

Biblical Miracles

The word *miracle* appears about forty times in the English Bible. An understanding of the concept depends on the meaning of the Hebrew and Greek words and the context in which they are used.

In the Old Testament three words are translated "miracle." *Mopheth* comes from a root meaning conspicuous; it is a "miracle" or "wonder" and occurs twice in connection with Moses: "When Pharaoh says to you, 'Perform a miracle,' then say to Aaron, 'Take your staff and throw it down before Pharaoh,' and it will become a snake" (Ex 7:9). In his valedictory to Israel at the borders of Canaan, Moses declared, "With your own eyes you saw those great trials, those miraculous signs and great wonders" (Deut 29:3).

A second word, *oth*, signifies a "sign" or beacon that points beyond itself. Its two occurrences also refer to events of the exodus: "The miraculous signs I performed in Egypt and in the desert . . . The signs he performed and the things he did in the heart of Egypt" (Num 14:22; Deut 11:3). The third word is *pala*, which occurs in Judges 6:13

and conveys the idea of a difficult accomplishment: Gideon asked the angel, "Where are all his wonders that our fathers told us about?" (Judg 6:13).

In the New Testament two words are generally translated "miracle." *Dynamis* means a power, might, strength or force, and appears about 120 times; it is usually translated "power" but appears as "miracle" about 8 times. Like *pala* it conveys the idea of a mighty act. The other word is *sēmeion,* which means a sign or token. Usually translated "sign," it appears as "miracle" 22 times; the concept is that of the Hebrew *oth.* These two Greek words appear mostly in the Gospels in connection with Jesus' ministry, although in Acts and several of the letters they also figure in the ministry of the apostles. A third synonym, although not translated "miracle," is *teras,* which means "wonder," "prodigy," "portent"; it appears 16 times. Significantly, all three Greek words occur in Peter's sermon at Pentecost: "Men of Israel, listen to this: Jesus of Nazareth was a man accredited by God to you by miracles, wonders and signs, which God did among you through him, as you yourselves know" (Acts 2:22).

When the six words are taken together, their etymology, context and usage show two main characteristics of a biblical miracle. It is an extraordinary, powerful event that produces wonder; it is a sign or token pointing beyond itself.

Another characteristic of miracles is their precise timing. Moses' rod becoming a snake, the Red Sea parting, Jesus raising Lazarus and multiplying the loaves and fish—all occurred just as the need required and the word was spoken. In each case the event was a command performance. That element is especially significant in those biblical miracles that one can regard as unusual but "natural"; take, for example, Peter's catching of a fish with a coin in its mouth in order to pay the temple tax. Jesus had commanded, "Take the first fish you catch; open its mouth and you will find a four-drachma coin" (Mt 17:27). The extraordinary element was the timing, as well as the coin's value.

Several additional observations about miracles can be made. First, they are not so common in the Bible as popularly believed. In the Old Testament most of them occur in three great clusters: (1) in Egypt and the exodus; (2) in Canaan during the time of Elijah and Elisha; (3) in Babylon at the time of Daniel. In each circumstance the question was whether a pagan god (Re, Baal, Marduk) would prove more powerful than Yahweh. In the New Testament miracles are prominent in the ministry of Jesus. God's extraordinary actions are an exception to his maintaining the regularity and predictability of the universe. In fact, the biblical writers often emphasize the regularity of nature in contrast to the chaotic concepts of their pagan neighbors (Jer 31:35).

Second, biblical miracles serve a variety of purposes, from mighty acts of deliverance and healing to specific events designed to accredit a prophet and his message. Third, the biblical writers are no more concerned about *how* miracles occur than about the mechanism of natural events. All are attributed to the activity of God.

Finally, we need to emphasize that the natural/supernatural distinction of medieval theology is unbiblical whenever it draws a line between "laws of nature" and "acts of God." Rather, the biblical distinction is between ordinary, *recurring events,* which are predictable, and *miracles,* which are not. God is just as active in the former as in the latter. We have already pointed out that the Hebrew vocabulary has no equivalent to our Western term *nature,* which connotes a universe running independently on its own power. "In the biblical view 'natural event' such as rainfall, and 'supernatural event' such as quailfall (Ex 16) are *both* the action of God."[18]

To summarize, a miracle may be defined as an extraordinary event produced by God at a specific time as a sign of his activity and purpose in human history.

"The same Creator may act within the world and he may act upon the world. In both cases there is a resultant order. . . . The kinds of miracles that Christians believe in are not pure random manifestations. . . . They are manifestations of a divine ordering of nature."[19]

Miracles and Modern Science

Several observations can now be made on the relationship between miracles and scientific laws. First, the term *natural laws* as usually understood is a misnomer. In a strict sense nature does not have mathematical laws, but rather what we may call forces.[20] At present they may be generally categorized as gravitational, electromagnetic, and weak and strong field forces, although these categories are open to question. The point is that modern scientists bring such distinctions (along with constructs like velocity, energy, mass and acceleration) *to* their study of nature, whose activity they choose to describe in mathematical terms. Hence we have used the term *scientific laws* to connote the fact that, although as maps or models they do tell us something about nature, they are not laws in any absolute sense, much less the only true way of describing nature's working. Thus it is hardly "scientific" to rule out miracles because they supposedly break or violate the "laws of nature." According to the Bible, God does not "intervene" in a semi-independent order of nature; nor is he a God-of-the-gaps working only in cracks and crevices of the universe. In what we call miracles he is simply choosing to work in an unprecedented rather than a customary way. If the powerful, transcendent God of the Bible exists, he is quite likely to have at his disposal forces as yet unknown to us. He is free to produce extraordinary events we cannot explain to serve his saving purposes in human history.

Our scientific laws and theories do not *prescribe* (legislate) what must have happened in the past or will happen in the future. They *describe* (explain in mathematical terms) some repeated events we have been able to observe so far. At best, scientific laws predict what will *probably* happen in the future—since we believe in the orderliness of God's creation. All they prescribe is our expectations, so that we can make predictions and act accordingly. Therefore, it makes no sense to complain about a miracle breaking the laws of nature as if they, like criminal and civil law, prohibited certain kinds of activity.

In this connection C. S. Lewis observes that the laws of nature no more cause events than the rules of arithmetic produce money. They simply present patterns with which events or transactions are consistent, unless some new factor is added. "If God annihilates or creates or deflects a unit of matter, He has created a new situation at that point. Immediately all Nature domiciles this new situation. . . . The moment it enters her realm it obeys all her laws."[21] Miraculous bread nourishes the body just like any other bread; a miraculous conception produces a natural pregnancy and birth. A miracle is not an event without a cause or without results. Its cause is God's activity; its results follow according to normal patterns. Far from breaking them, miracles depend on those patterns in two ways. First, without regularity and consistency in nature there cannot be a remarkably significant exception. Second, after the exceptional event occurs, the resulting situation follows the familiar, predictable pattern.

In the last analysis, the question of miracles is primarily an issue for philosophy and history. A miracle is a unique, nonrecurring event; as such it is beyond the purview of scientific inquiry, which looks for patterns of repeated, observable events. A pattern requires more than a single point. Two points determine a straight line and three confirm it. Many more data points are needed to establish a significantly different curve for phenomena where a straight line has always been expected. Scientists, *as scientists,* cannot say that a given extraordinary event is a miracle, or is impossible—only that it is foreign to their experience and highly improbable on the basis of accepted empirical scientific theory.

Regrettably, scientists sometimes fail to take off their professional laboratory attire when they make religious or philosophical pronouncements. For example, Carl Sagan's pronouncement "The cosmos is all there is, all there was, and all there ever will be" is likely to be taken by the public as a scientific truth. In reality it is a philosophical assertion, his article of faith.

Miracles are a problem for the philosophy of *naturalism,* which assumes that the natural world is the whole of reality. It was from that nontheistic perspective that Hume defined the uniformity of nature in such a way as to exclude the possibility of miracles.[22] Within that framework they cannot even be discussed. In that respect one who accepts naturalism is, ironically, more like a Greek philosopher than a modern scientist, since the matter is decided deductively on the basis of first principles before considering the evidence. Such an attitude resembles that of the professor at Pisa who refused to look through Galileo's telescope at the reported moons of Jupiter, since Aristotle had taught that such a phenomenon couldn't exist.

For anyone willing to consider empirical evidence, miracles are essentially a question of history. With regard to miracles the theist is more "scientific" than the philosophical naturalist, being open-minded about their possibility. The issue is one of historical record: Were reliable witnesses present? Have their reports been accurately preserved? The criteria are the same as those for determining the historicity of any reported event, yet even the best evidence fails to convince those who choose not to believe. Miracles are signs bearing witness to God's call for repentance, faith and obedience. They ultimately become an issue in our individual history, our values and purpose in life. James Houston concludes:

> The real issue is the nature of transcendence—of God's rule over creation. In the biblical world this is affirmed; in the Greek world it is denied. To the Greeks, the *kosmos* was an orderly structure, based on cause and effect, linked to the innate power of things in themselves, to nature. To the Hebrews, creation was expressive of the will and Word of God, whose consistency did not depend on the Greek idea of *physis* (form), but upon the moral character of God. The Old Testament Israelites never questioned the reality of God. They simply questioned what God was doing, and why He was doing it.[23]

To ask that question ourselves we turn to Genesis 1, which recounts the creation of the universe by the will and word of God.

10
GENESIS ONE: ORIGIN OF THE UNIVERSE

Moses wrote in a popular style
things which, without instruction,
all ordinary persons endued with
common sense are liable to understand.
JOHN CALVIN

ROM TIME IMMEMORIAL PEOPLE HAVE SPECULATED ABOUT HOW the world began. Many fascinating myths and legends date from the dawn of civilization in the Middle East. Reflecting polytheistic religion, they feature violent struggles by a variety of deities for supremacy over the world.

For example, Sumerian tablets around 2500 B.C. present a pantheon of four prominent gods, among them Enki who leads a host of the gods against Nammu, the primeval sea. In one Egyptian myth the sun god Re emerges from the deep to create all other things. The best-known of the creation myths is the Babylonian national epic *Enuma Elish*, which was composed primarily to glorify the god Marduk and the city of Babylon. Amid such a mythological environment Israel fled from Egypt, wandered in the wilderness and took possession of Canaan.

The biblical creation accounts in Genesis have some similarities with those of Israel's pagan neighbors as well as several radical differences. The relative importance of those elements has been a focal point of theological controversy for more than a century. Some issues have been resolved, but considerable confusion persists over the nature and purpose of Genesis 1.

Genesis is a book of beginnings: the origin of the universe, birth of the human race and founding of the Hebrew family. Yet the book is more than an account of origins. It provides a foundation for many themes prominent throughout the Old and New Testaments. Here one learns about God, humanity and nature in their mutual relationships. The Creator and Controller of the universe reveals himself as the Lord and Judge of history, which has both a purpose and goal. Such great doctrines as creation, sin and salvation trace their beginnings to this remarkable book. Concepts of covenant, grace, election and redemption permeate God's saving activity to overcome the consequences of evil and sin. It should not surprise us that Genesis, more than any other part of the Bible, has been a scene of historical, literary, theological and scientific battles. Some of those battles have made their way out of church and seminary into the schools and courts.

Much of the controversy arises from a misunderstanding of what the Genesis account of creation intends to teach. What message was it meant to convey to ancient Israel in their struggle against the pagan mythologies of the surrounding countries? How does that meaning apply in a post-Christian culture whose gods and values infiltrate even the church?

Approach to Genesis

An interpretation of Genesis 1 must deal with three elements: historical context, literary genre and textual content. Many commentaries skip lightly over the first two in an eagerness to grasp the meaning for today. As a result their interpretations at critical points would hardly have been intelligible to ancient Israel, much less equip God's people to resist the influence of pagan mythologies. Therefore, we will adhere to a principle outlined in chapter eight: What the author *meant then* determines what the message *means now.*

1. *Historical context.* What was the situation of the Israelites who received the message of Genesis, especially their cultural and religious environment? The answer to that question depends to a large extent on certain assumptions about the authorship and date of the document. Two main approaches have dominated the interpretation of Genesis during the last century.

One position rejects the Mosaic authorship and early date of the Pentateuch along with its divine inspiration and trustworthiness. The *developmental* view of the nineteenth century treated those five books as the culmination of a long process of social growth. It assumed that, culturally and religiously, humankind has moved through evolving states from savagery to civilization. But as new data provided by archeology tended to discredit that view, the *comparative religion* model became increasingly popular. It holds Genesis 1—11 to be a Jewish borrowing and adaptation of the religions of neighboring nations. Both views consider the Pentateuch to be writing of unknown authors or redactors (editors) long after Moses, probably late in the period of the Hebrew monarchy.

A contrasting position holds that Moses wrote most of the Pentateuch (though he may have used earlier sources) and that some editing took place after his death. The *historical-cultural* model used in this chapter assumes that the Genesis creation narratives were given to the Israelites in the wilderness, after the exodus from Egypt but before the conquest of Canaan. This view considers the Pentateuch to be a revelation from God, through his prophet Moses, to Israel en route to the Promised Land. An understanding of the historical context and primary purpose of that revelation lays the foundation for our interpretation.

For more than four hundred years the Hebrews had languished in Egypt far from the land promised to Abraham. Those centuries took a spiritual as well as physical toll. The people had no Scriptures, only a few oral traditions of the patriarchs. Devotion to the God of their forefather Joseph had largely been supplanted by worship of the gods of other nations. The incident of the golden calf suggests that fertility cults may have been part of Hebrew religious life in Egypt (Ex 32:1-6). Even though they were miraculously delivered from slavery and led toward Canaan, many of the people may have had a minimal understanding of the God of Abraham, Isaac and Jacob.

When the wanderers arrived at Horeb, their world view and lifestyle differed little from that of the surrounding nations. Their culture was essentially pagan. Now God was calling them to keep his covenant, to become "a kingdom of priests and a holy nation" (Ex 19:6). Although the people responded, their yes was just the beginning of a long, painful process by which God would create a new culture.

Although trained by God in Pharaoh's house and then in the hills forty years, Moses faced a formidable task. His people needed a radically different theology for a knowledge of God and his purposes; a new cosmogony to restructure their attitudes toward the created order; a new religious institution to guide their worship; a new anthropology to understand the human condition; and a different lifestyle for moral and ethical living. The five books of Moses were designed to make the Hebrews a people of God through a divinely instituted culture.

The location of God's people at that point is significant. In each pagan nation the gods, of which there were hundreds, permeated and dominated every aspect of life. A people and their gods formed an organic whole with their land. Religion existed for the welfare of society, not primarily for the individual. Religious change was not possible; it occurred only when one nation conquered another. Even then the defeated gods were usually absorbed into the victorious pantheon. In Egypt, for example, only Egyptian gods were worshiped. Hence Moses had initially asked Pharaoh to permit the Hebrews to go three days' journey into the wilderness to worship their God; there the Egyptian gods had no power and need not be feared. Now God had created for the Hebrews a religious crisis that opened them to the new order he desired to institute. The events of Sinai could never have taken place in Goshen.

Although Israel had left Egypt behind, they still retained its world view. Paganism is more than polytheism; it is a way of looking at the whole of life. So a complete break with Israel's past required the strong antipagan teaching provided in the Pentateuch, beginning with Genesis.

2. *Literary genre.* What kind of literature are we dealing with? Is it prose or poetry, history or parable? Only after that question is answered can the appropriate interpretive guidelines be applied.

The style of Genesis 1 is remarkable for its simplicity, its economy of language. Yet to ask whether it is prose or poetry is a serious oversimplification. Although we do not find here the synonymous parallelism and rhythms of Hebrew poetry, the passage has a number of alliterations. The prominence of repetition and of its corollary, silence, brings the writing close to poetry; its movement toward a climax places it in the order of prose. Sometimes called a "hymn," it appears to be a unique blend of prose and poetry.[1]

Although it has no trace of rhetoric, the passage does use figurative language for describing God's activity: anthropomorphisms which represent God as if he were a human being—speaking and seeing, working and resting. Yet a conclusion that Genesis 1 is semipoetic and has figurative language by no means determines the main question: the connection of the narrative with actual events.

Once for all we need to get rid of the deep-seated feeling that figurative speech is inferior to literal language, as if it were somewhat less worthy of God. The Hebrew language is rich in figures of speech. Scripture abounds with symbols and metaphors which the Holy Spirit has used to convey powerfully and clearly the message he intended. What would be left of Psalm 23, for example, if it were stripped of its figurative language? Further, we must give up the false antithesis that prose is fact while poetry is fiction (prose = literal fact, and poetry = figurative = fiction). Indeed, prose writing often has figures of speech and can recount a legend or parable as well as history; by the same token, poetry may have little if any figurative language and narrate actual events. The prophets, for example, recalled past facts and predicted future events with a welter of symbols and images as well as literal description. (See Ezekiel 16 and 22 for two versions of the same events.) Jesus summarized centuries of Hebrew history in his parable of the wicked tenants (Mt 21:33-41). Good biblical interpretation recognizes and appreciates this marvelous and effective variety of literary expression.

Genesis 1 appears to be a narrative of past events, an account of God's creative words and acts. Its figurative language is largely limited to anthropomorphisms. (For a highly imaginative and figurative account of creation, read Job 38:4-11.) The text does not have the earmarks of a parable, a short allegorical story designed to teach a truth or moral lesson. That genre generally deals with human events and often starts with a formula like "There was a man who had two sons" in Jesus' parable of the prodigal son (Lk 15:11-31). Genesis 1 is "historical" in the sense of relating events that actually occurred. Modern historians distinguish between "history," which began with the invention of writing or the advent of city life, and "prehistory."[2] According to that definition, the events in Genesis 1 are prehistorical. Nevertheless the writing can be called historical narrative, or primeval history, to distinguish it from legend or myth, in which ideas are simply expressed in the form of a story.

Our interpretation of a passage should also be guided by its structure. Narrators have the freedom to tell a story in their own way, including its perspective, purpose, development and relevant content. The importance of this principle comes to focus in the Genesis 1 treatment of time. The dominating concepts and concerns of our century are dramatically different from those of ancient Israel. For example, our scientific approach to the natural world seeks to quantify and measure, calculate and theorize, about the mechanism of those events. For us time is as important a dimension as space, so we automatically tend to assume that a historical account must present a strict chronological sequence. But the biblical writers are not bound by such concerns and constrictions. Even within an overall chronological development they have freedom to cluster certain events by topic. For example, Matthew's Gospel has alternating sections of narrative and teaching grouped according to subject matter, a sort of literary club sandwich. Since Matthew did not intend to provide a strict chronological sequence for the events in Jesus' ministry, to search for it there would be futile.

By the same token our approach to Genesis 1 should not assume that the events are necessarily in strict chronological order. An examination of the phrases used by the author reveals his emphasis on the creative word: "And God said" appears eight times, in each case to begin a four-line poem (figure 9).[3] These poems form the basic structure of the narrative. (The third and seventh poems do not have the final line, "And there was evening, and there was morning," since they are combined with the fourth and eighth creative words, respectively, to link with the third and sixth days.) Although the eight poems vary in length and minor details, they have the same basic format.

It also becomes evident that the *eight words* are linked with the *six days* in an overall symmetrical structure (figure 10). The second half

Word	Day	Poem	Verse
1	1	(a) And God said, "Let . . ."	3
		(b) and there was . . .	
		(c) God saw that . . . was good.	4
		(d) And there was evening, and there was morning—the first day.	5
2	2	(a) And God said, "Let . . ."	6
		(b) And it was so.	7
		(c)	
		(d) And there was evening, and there was morning—the second day.	8
3	3	(a) And God said, "Let . . ."	9
		(b) And it was so.	
		(c) And God saw that it was good.	10
		(d)	
4		(a) Then God said, "Let . . ."	11
		(b) And it was so.	
		(c) And God saw that it was good.	12
		(d) And there was evening, and there was morning—the third day.	13
5	4	(a) And God said, "Let . . ."	14
		(b) And it was so.	15
		(c) And God saw that it was good.	18
		(d) And there was evening, and there was morning—the fourth day.	19
6	5	(a) And God said, "Let . . ."	20
		(b)	
		(c) And God saw that it was good.	21
		(d) And there was evening, and there was morning—the fifth day.	23
7	6	(a) And God said, "Let . . ."	24
		(b) And it was so.	
		(c) And God saw that it was good.	25
		(d)	
8		(a) Then God said, "Let . . ."	26
		(b) And it was so.	30
		(c) God saw . . . it was very good.	31
		(d) And there was evening, and there was morning—the sixth day.	

Figure 9. Eight Poems of Genesis 1

Creative Words	Day	Elements	Creative Words	Day	Elements
1 (verse 3)	1	light	5 (verse 14)	4	luminaries
2 (verse 6)	2	firmament	6 (verse 20)	5	birds
3 (verse 9)	3	seas	7 (verse 24)	6	fishes
4 (verse 11)		land & vegetation	8 (verse 26)		animals & humankind

Figure 10.   Literary Structure of Genesis 1

of the week (fourth to sixth days) parallels the first half. Augustine noted this literary framework early in the church's history. He believed that everything had been created at once and that the structure of the days is intended to teach the *order* in creation. Two centuries ago J. G. von Herder recognized the powerful symmetry between the two triads of days. The two have been contrasted in several ways: creation of *spaces* and then their *inhabitants; forming* of the world followed by its *filling.*[4] Such a sequence is indicated by the conclusion of the narrative in Genesis 2:1 (RSV): "Thus the *heavens and the earth* were completed [days 1-3] and *all the host of them* [the crowds of living organisms, days 4-6]."

The writer's use of the significant numbers *3, 7* and *10* also highlights the careful construction of the creation account. It starts with three problem elements (formless earth, darkness and watery deep) which are dealt with in two sets of three days; the verb "create" is used at three points in the narrative, the third time thrice. Both the completion formula "and it was so" and the divine approval "God saw that it was good" appear seven times. The phrase "God said," the verb "make" and the formula "according to its/their kind" appear ten times.

In both its overall structure and use of numbers the writer paid as much attention to the form as to the content of the narrative, a fact which suggests mature meditation. The *historico-artistic* interpretation of Genesis 1 does justice to its literary craftsmanship, the general biblical perspective on natural events and the view of creation expressed by other writers in both Old and New Testaments.

Interpretation of Genesis 1

The third step, after determining the historical context and literary genre, is to discover what this account of creation meant to the first readers. Although a thorough exegesis cannot be done in a few pages, we can note the narrative's development and the meaning of several key words.

1. *In the beginning God created the heavens and the earth.*

God is not only the subject of the first sentence, he is central to the entire narrative. It mentions him thirty-four times. The phrase "God created" can also be translated "When God began to create," but the latter translation is linguistically cumbersome; it also seems to connote a dualism incompatible with the rest of the chapter.[5]

The meaning of the word "create" *(bara)* in this context is determined in the light of its meanings elsewhere in the Old Testament. Its subject is always God; its object may be things (Is 40:26) or situations (Is 45:7-8). Companion words are mainly "form" *(yatsar)* and "make" *(asah)*, which appear several times in Genesis (for example, 1:26-27; 2:7, 19) and can have more than one meaning. (A concept can be expressed by several words or synonyms.)[6] In Isaiah 43:7 all three occur: "Everyone who is called by my name, whom I created for my glory, whom I formed and made" (see also Is 45:18). The specific context determines whether the creation is an initial bringing into existence (Is 48:3, 7) or a process leading to completion (Gen 2:1-4; Is 65:18).

The Bible's opening statement may be taken as either the beginning of God's creative activity or a summary of the account that follows. Either way, the "beginning" includes not only the material universe but also time itself. Since all of our thought and action occurs within a timescale of past/present/future, we find it difficult if not impossible to conceive of timelessness. Yet as Augustine observed many centuries ago, God created not *in* time but *with* time.[7]

2. *Now the earth was formless and empty, darkness was over the surface of the deep.*

The writer expands on his initial statement, making the earth his vantage point (compare Ps 115:16). He uses two rhyming words, *tohu* and *bohu*,[8] to describe a somber scene: a trackless waste, formless and empty in the utter darkness. Those two words signifying a lack of *form* and *content* provide a key to the chapter's literary structure.

The word for "deep" *(tehom)*, a focal point of controversy, is particularly significant for the antipagan teaching function of the narrative. A hundred years ago, publication of Babylonian versions of the creation and flood spawned a school of scholarship that considered Israel's faith a pale reflection of a superior Babylonian religion. Genesis 1 was thought to be borrowed from the latter's mythical epic. It was argued that the Hebrew *tehom* was directly related to *Tiamat*, the female monster of the Babylonian epic.

In recent years that view has been refuted (although it continues to be advanced).[9] First, *tehom* does not derive from *Tiamat*, although both words come from a common Semitic root. Second, a study of the thirty-five occurrences of *tehom* and its derivatives in the Old Testament shows it to be a poetic term for a large body of water used in an inanimate sense. Gerhard Hasel concludes, "The author of the Hebrew creation account uses the term *tehom* in a 'depersonalized' and 'non-mythical' sense. Tehom is nothing else but a passive, powerless, inanimate element in God's creation."[10] In fact the term may have been deliberately chosen to contrast with its cognates in the pagan religions, as an antimythical polemic.

3-5. *And God said, "Let there be light," and there was light. . . . And there was evening, and there was morning—the first day.*
Here is the first of eight creative commands distributed over six days. A major focus of the narrative is the word of God: God "speaks" and it is done. The Hebrew *amar* has a variety of meanings.[11] Its use in Genesis 1 emphasizes God's creative command, his pledge to sustain the creation and his revelation as the Creator (this theme is echoed in Ps 148:5 and Heb 11:3). The words leave no room for the divine emanation and struggle so prominent in pagan religions. Nevertheless, there has been too much emphasis on God's creating simply by command. Only verses 3 and 9 report creation by word alone; the other six occurrences include both a word and an act of some kind, indicated by verbs such as *make, separate* and *set.*

The creation of light marks the first step from primeval formlessness to order. "God saw that the light was good" (v. 4). There is no hint of ethical dualism, good and evil coexisting from eternity. To some of the pagans day and night were warring powers. Not so here. The Creator assigns to everything its value (4a), place (4b) and meaning (5a).

6-8. And God said, "Let there be an expanse between the waters to separate water from water." . . . *And there was evening, and there was morning— the second day.*

An expanse or firmament separates the waters below (the seas and underground springs) from those above in the clouds which provide rain. Unlike the first day, the creative command here is followed by an action: "So God *made* the expanse and separated the water under the expanse from the water above it. And it was so" (v. 7). That combination of word and act also occurs on the fourth day: "God *made* two great lights . . . *made* the stars . . . *set* them in the expanse of the sky" (vv. 16-17); and on the fifth day, "God *created* the great creatures of the sea . . ." (v. 21). The wording for the sixth day is unusual in that God commands himself, so to speak, and then does it: "Then God said, 'Let us make man.' . . . So God created man . . ." (vv. 26-27). This variety of wording for the eight creative events/processes should caution against an attempt to formulate one basic procedure or mechanism for the creation.

9-10. And God said, "Let the water under the sky be gathered to one place, and let dry ground appear." And it was so.

11-13. Then God said, "Let the land produce vegetation: seed-bearing plants and trees." . . . *And it was so.* . . . *And there was evening, and there was morning—the third day.*

Two events are linked to the third day. In the first, a creative command continues to give form to the world through differentiation, the land from the sea. In the second, a procreative action of the land, empowered by God, brings forth vegetation in an orderly fashion "according to their various kinds." That phrase, also used for the reproduction of the animals (v. 24), would be especially meaningful to the Hebrews, since pagan mythologies featured grotesque human-beast hybrids. (The concept *fixity of species*, often read into this phrase, would have been unintelligible to the original hearers.) Here God commands *the earth* to produce something, and it does so.

The emphasis has begun to shift from *form* toward *fullness*, which becomes prominent in the remaining creative words. Originally formless and empty, the earth is now structured (through the division of light from darkness, upper from lower waters, dry land from the seas) and clothed with green, ready for its inhabitants. What God has formed he now fills. The second half of the week generally parallels the events of the first.

14-19. *And God said, "Let there be lights in the expanse of the sky to separate the day from the night." . . . God made two great lights . . . to govern the day and . . . the night. . . . And there was evening, and there was morning—the fourth day.*

The expanse of the sky is now filled with the stars, sun and moon "to give light on the earth." (*Our* problem of how the earth could be lighted (v. 4) before the sun appeared comes when *we* require the narrative to be a strict chronological account.) It is significant that the sun and moon are not mentioned by name—because those common Semitic terms were also the names of deities. This description may be seen as a protest against every kind of astral worship, so prevalent in the surrounding nations.[12] Here the heavenly bodies do not reign as gods but serve as signs (see Ps 121:6). They "govern" (vv. 16, 18) only as bearers of light, not as wielders of power. These few sentences undercut a superstition as old as Egypt and as modern as today's newspaper horoscope.

20-23. *And God said, "Let the water teem with living creatures, and let birds fly above the earth across the expanse of the sky." . . . And there was evening, and there was morning—the fifth day.*

The sea and sky are now filled with their inhabitants. The word for birds literally means "flying things" and includes insects (compare Deut 14:19-20). The special reference to great creatures (*tanninim*, "sea monsters") also serves a polemic purpose. To the Canaanites the word was an ominous term for the powers of chaos confronting the god Baal in the beginning. In the Old Testament the word appears without any mythological overtones; it is simply a generic term for a large water animal. Here the writer makes a special point of putting these fearsome creatures in their proper place, *in* the water just like their smaller companions. Further, the term *bara* is employed for the first time since verse 1 to emphasize that they were *created* by God; the sea creatures are not the pre-existent rivals of the Creator as they appear in Canaanite mythology. In fact the *tanninim* in Psalm 148:7 are called, along with other created beings, to praise the Lord.

24-25. *And God said, "Let the land produce living creatures according to their kinds." . . . And it was so. God made the wild animals according to their kinds.*

26-31. *Then God said, "Let us make man in our image, in our like-*

ness."... So God created man in his own image, ... male and female he created them. ... God saw all that he had made, and it was very good. And there was evening, and there was morning—the sixth day.

The seventh and eighth creative acts are linked to the sixth day. The former populates the land with three representative groups of animals: "livestock, creatures that move along the ground, and wild animals." The creative action here parallels that in verses 20-23, but is unique in one respect: God commands the earth to do something, yet he himself makes it. Here as elsewhere in the Bible, what we call "natural" reproduction and God's creative activity are two sides of the same coin.

The eighth act produces man and woman both *in* nature and *over* it. They share the sixth day with other land creatures, and also God's blessing to be fruitful and increase; yet their superiority is evident in the words *Let us make* (instead of "Let the land produce") and in the mandate to "fill the earth and subdue it." Human uniqueness lies in the relationship to God: "Let us make man in our image"—that of a rational, morally responsible and social being. The words *male and female* at this juncture have profound implications. To define humanity as bisexual makes the partners complementary and anticipates the New Testament teaching of their equality ("There is neither Jew nor Greek, slave nor free, male nor female, for you are all one in Christ Jesus"—Gal 3:28).

The culmination of creation in man and woman who are to rule over the earth and its inhabitants is especially significant to Israel. In pagan mythology the creation of mankind was an afterthought to provide the gods with food and satisfy other physical needs. But in Genesis 1 the situation is reversed. The plants and trees are a divine provision for human needs (v. 29). From start to finish the creation narrative challenges and opposes the essential tenets of the pagan religions of Egypt, where the Hebrews stayed so long, and of Canaan, where they would soon be living.

At each stage of creation, six times, God has pronounced his work to be good. "Thus the heavens and the earth were completed in all their vast array" (Gen 2:1). The creation narrative then concludes with a seventh day.

2:2-3. By the seventh day God had finished the work he had been doing; so on the seventh day he rested from all his work. And God blessed the seventh day and made it holy, because on it he rested from all the work of creating that he had done.

The word *rested* means "ceased" (from *sabat*, the root of "sabbath"). It is a rest of achievement or pleasure, not of weariness or inactivity, since God constantly nurtures what he has created. Nature is not self-existent but is constantly upheld by his providential power.

This part of the narrative has an immediate application embodied in the Ten Commandments. The seven-day format is given as a model for Israel's work week and sabbath rest:

Remember the Sabbath day by keeping it holy. Six days you shall labor and do all your work, but the seventh day is a Sabbath to the LORD your God. . . . For in six days the LORD made the heavens and the earth, the sea, and all that is in them, but he rested on the seventh day. (Ex 20:8-11)

2:4a *This is the account of the heavens and the earth when they were created.*

The narrative finally ends with a *colophon,* a statement that identifies a document's contents, which we generally put at the beginning of a book.

The Creation Days

Much controversy over the interpretation of Genesis 1 focuses on the meaning of the word *day.* Many commentaries wade into that question first and soon bog down in a hermeneutical quagmire. First one's perspective on the chapter should be defined. Since no one is completely objective, it is not a question of *whether* we have an interpretive model but *which one* we are using.

The *comparative religion* approach views Genesis 1 as the work of an unknown author long after Moses, and considers its creation account similar to the primitive stories in other Semitic religions. The *concordist* model assumes a harmony between the Genesis 1 and scientific accounts of creation, and seeks to demonstrate the Bible's scientific accuracy. In this book the *historical-cultural* approach views the narrative as given by Moses to Israel in the wilderness, and tries to discover what the message *meant then* without any attempt to harmonize it with either past or present scientific theories (see chapter 13).

Throughout the Old Testament the word "day" *(yom)* is used in a variety of ways. Usually meaning a "day" of the week, the word can also mean "time" (Gen 4:3), a specific "period" or "era" (Is 2:12; 4:2), or a "season" (Josh 24:7). We have already noted the literary symmetry of eight creative words linked to six days, which occur in two parallel sets of three. The six days mark the development from a dark, formless, empty and lifeless earth to one that is lighted, shaped and filled with teeming varieties of life, culminating in the creation of man and woman. What, then, is the significance of *day* in this chapter?

Before 1750 it was generally held that God created the world in six twenty-four-hour days, although some early church fathers like Augustine viewed them allegorically.[13] Archbishop Ussher around 1650 even calculated the date of creation to be 4004 B.C. But as the science of geology matured in the 1800s, many were shocked to discover that the earth was millions of years old. Since modern science had gained so much prestige, many interpreters strove to retain credibility for the Bible by attempting to demonstrate its scientific accuracy. Therefore, a variety of concordistic (harmonizing) views were proposed to correlate biblical teaching with current scientific theories.

For example, "flood geology" attempted to account for fossil discoveries through the catastrophe of a universal flood.[14] When new geological discoveries questioned that view, it was replaced by the "restitution" or "gap" theory popularized by a Scottish clergyman, Thomas Chalmers, in 1804. According to that view a catastrophe occurred between Genesis 1:1 and 1:2 to allow the necessary time for the geological formations to develop. Eventually it became necessary to assume a series of catastrophies or floods to account for newer scientific findings.

Although such theories accounted for the time that science required, they could not explain the sequence of the geological record. The "day-age" interpretation considered the Genesis days to be metaphorical for geological ages. That view was advocated by influential North American geologists J. W. Dawson and James Dana as well as many theologians. The Genesis days were then correlated, more or less accurately, with the proposed epochs. Another version retained literal twenty-four-hour days of creative activity, but separated them by geological epochs.

The above views, with varying degrees of credibility, have in common three major problems. First, they attempt to find answers to questions the text does not address, about the *how* or the mechanism of natural forces. (To see how inappropriate such an approach is, consider its opposite: suppose one tried to derive information about the meaning and purpose of life from a technical treatise on astronomy in which the author had no intention of revealing his philosophy.) The biblical accounts of creation do not provide scientific data or descriptions. John Calvin emphasized that point: "The Holy Spirit had no intention to teach astronomy. . . . He made use by Moses and the other prophets of the popular language that none might shelter himself under the pretext of obscurity."[15] Adapting Calvin's principle to the present we can affirm, "The Holy Spirit had no intention of teaching geology and biology."

Second, not only do the concordistic views strain Genesis by importing concepts foreign to the text, but any apparent success in harmonizing the message with "modern science" guarantees a failure when current scientific theory is revised or discarded. During the last two centuries, that pattern has been evident in the continual efforts of harmonizers to keep abreast of rapidly changing scientific views. The credibility of the Bible is not enhanced by thrusting it into the scramble of catch-up in a game it was never intended to play. What is the point of trying to correlate the ultimate truths of Scripture with the ever-changing theories of science? No wonder that when those theories go out of date, in the minds of many people the Bible joins them in gathering dust on the shelf.

Third, any extent to which Genesis teaches modern scientific concepts would have made its message unintelligible to its first readers, and to most of the people who have lived during the last three thousand years. Even in our own century, what per cent of the people understand the abstract language of science? And of those who do, how many use it in the communications of daily life with which the biblical writers are primarily concerned?

The *historical-cultural* approach avoids those problems by explaining the creation days in light of the author's purpose, the literary genre of his message and what it meant to Israel at Mount Sinai.

The author's purpose—teaching about God and his creation in order to counteract the pagan myths of neighboring countries—has become clear in our exposition of Genesis 1. Israel's God is the all-powerful Creator of heaven and earth. His world is orderly and consistent. Man and woman are the culmination of creation, made in the image of God, to enjoy and be responsible for their stewardship of the earth.

The literary genre is a semipoetic narrative cast in a historico-artistic framework consisting of two parallel triads. On this interpretation, it is no problem that the creation of the sun, necessary for an earth clothed with vegetation on the third day, should be linked with the fourth day. Instead of turning hermeneutical handsprings to explain that supposed difficulty, we simply note that in view of the author's purpose the question is irrelevant. The account does not follow the chronological sequence assumed by concordist views.[16]

The meaning of the word *day* must be determined (like any other word with several meanings) by the context and usage of the author. A plain reading of the text, with its recurring phrase of evening and morning, indicates a solar day of twenty-four hours. That would have been clear to Moses and his first readers. The context gives no connotation of an era or geological age. Creation is pictured in six familiar periods followed by a seventh for rest, corresponding to the days of the week as Israel knew them. But the question still remains whether the format is figurative or literal, that is, an *analogy* of God's creative activity or a chronological *account* of how many hours he worked.

Chapter eight of our discussion noted that God is a spirit whom no one can see, whose thoughts and ways are higher than ours. So (apart from the Incarnation) we can know him only through analogy, "a partial similarity between like features of two things, on which a comparison may be based."[17] In the Bible the human person is the central model used to reveal God's relationship and actions in history. God is pictured as seeing, speaking and hearing like a person even though he doesn't have eyes, lips or ears. Those figures of speech (anthropomorphisms) assure us that God is at least personal and can be known in an intimate relationship. (Science also uses analogies; for example, a billiard-ball model in physics helps us understand the behavior of gas molecules which we cannot see.)

The human model appears throughout Genesis 1. The writer also links God's creative activity to six days, marked by evening and morning, and followed by a day of rest. In the light of the other analogies, why should it be considered necessary to take this part of the account literally, as if God actually worked for six days (or epochs) and then rested? Biblical interpretation should not suddenly change hermeneutical horses in the middle of the exegetical stream.

A stringent literalism disregards the analogical medium of revelation about creation, raising meaningless questions about God's working schedule. For example, did he labor around the clock or intermittently on twelve-hour days? If God created light instantaneously, was the first day then mostly one of rest like the seventh? How did the plant and animal reproductive processes he constituted on succeeding days fit so neatly into that schedule?

The fact that the text speaks of twenty-four-hour days does not require that they be considered the actual duration of God's creative activity. Even on a human level, when we report the significant achievements of someone in a position of power, the length of the working day is generally irrelevant. For example, a historian might write, "President Roosevelt decided to build the atomic bomb and President Truman ordered its use to destroy Hiroshima and Nagasaki to end the war with Japan. Two days radically changed the entire character of modern warfare." The exact details of *how* and *when* the commands were implemented over years or weeks are unimportant to the main concern of *who* and *why*, and what resulted.

Preoccupation with *how long* it took God to create the world, in days or epochs, deflects attention from the main point of Genesis 1. Such "scientific" concerns run interpretation onto a siding, away from the main track of God's revelation. Once we get past arguments over the length of the days, we can see the intended meaning of these days for Israel. First, their significance lies not in *identity*, a one-to-one correlation with God's creative activity, but in an *analogy* that provides a model for human work. The pattern of six plus one, work plus rest on the seventh day, highlights the sabbath. In doing so, it emphasizes the uniqueness of humanity. Made in the image of God, and given rule over the world, man and woman are the crown of creation. They rest from their labor on the sabbath, which is grounded in the creation (Gen 2:2; Ex 20:11).

A metaphor uses the commonplace (or commonly understood, if you wish) meaning of a word in a figurative manner. When, for example, Jesus calls Herod "that fox" (Lk 13:32), the word does not refer vaguely to any animal but to that one whose characteristics are well known; yet Jesus doesn't mean that Herod is literally a fox. Likewise, when David in Psalm 23 says "The Lord is my shepherd," he refers not to just any kind of animal keeper but to one who cares for sheep. It is the commonplace meaning of fox and shepherd that makes the metaphor understandable. So the fact that the day in Genesis 1 has its ordinary workaday meaning, and not an epoch of some kind, makes possible the metaphor of God's creative activity as a model for human work of six days followed by sabbath rest.

Linking God's creative activity to days of the week serves as another element in the antipagan polemic. "By stretching the creation events over the course of a series of days the sharpest possible line has been drawn between this account and every form of mythical thinking. It is history that is here reported—once-for-all and of irrevocable finality in its results."[18] Genesis 1 contrasts sharply with the cyclical, recurring creations described by Israel's pagan neighbors.

Two other interpretations of the days have been advanced. Archeologist P. J. Wiseman considers them days of revelation with the narrative given over a period of six days, each on its own tablet.[19] He notes a precedent for that literary form in other ancient literature. It has also been suggested that Genesis 1 was used liturgically somewhat like the narratives in other religions.[20] Whatever the merits of those views, they at least use the historical-cultural model to focus on what the narrative could have meant to the first hearers.

The Significance of Genesis 1

During the last century, Genesis 1 has suffered much from Western interpreters. Liberal literary criticism removes the divine authority of its message through Moses; conservative concentration on implications for science misses its intended meaning. Scholars from the theological left, armed with scissors and paste, have rearranged supposed authors and dates into a variety of configurations. Commentators from the right, scientific texts in hand, have repeatedly adjusted their interpretations to harmonize with the latest theories. In the process, the message of Genesis 1 has been so muffled that the average reader wonders what it means and whether it can be trusted. Hence we conclude by summarizing the significance of its account for ancient Israel, biblical theology, modern science and the church's life today.

1. *Israel at Mount Sinai.* Genesis 1 achieves a radical and comprehensive affirmation of monotheism versus every kind of false religion (polytheism, idolatry, animism, pantheism and syncretism); supersti-

tion (astrology and magic); and philosophy (materialism, ethical dualism, naturalism and nihilism). That is a remarkable achievement for so short an account (about 900 words) written in everyday language and understood by people in a variety of cultures for more than three thousand years. Each day of creation aims at two kinds of gods in the pantheons of the time: gods of light and darkness; sky and sea; earth and vegetation; sun, moon and stars; creatures in sea and air; domestic and wild animals; and finally human rulers. Though no human beings are divine, *all*—from pharaohs to slaves—are made in the image of God and share in the commission to be stewards of the earth.

For Israel those were life-and-death issues of daily existence. God's people do not need to know the *how* of creation; but they desperately need to know the *Creator*. Their God, who has brought them into covenant relationship with himself, is no less than the Creator and Controller of the world. He is not like the many pagan gods who must struggle for a period of time in their creative activity. He is stronger than all the powers that stand between his people and the Promised Land, the only One worthy of their worship and total commitment. Creation is the ground of Israel's hope for preservation as God's chosen people. For them the doctrine of creation is not so much a cosmogony as a confession of faith repeatedly expressed in psalms and prophecies throughout the Old Testament.

2. *Biblical theology.* Both Old and New Testaments connect God's creative power with his redeeming love.

Blessed is he whose help is the God of Jacob,
　whose hope is in the LORD his God,
the Maker of heaven and earth,
　the sea, and everything in them—
the LORD, who remains faithful forever. (Ps 146:5-6)

In these last days he has spoken to us by his Son . . . through whom he made the universe, . . . sustaining all things by his powerful word. After he had provided purification for sins, he sat down at the right hand of the Majesty in heaven. (Heb 1:2-3)

God the Creator of the universe is the Lord and Judge of history who comes in Jesus Christ to demonstrate his saving love and power. Three great creeds emerging from the church's early theological controversies—the Apostles', Nicene and Chalcedonian—affirm that fundamental connection. It has provided the basis for creativity and meaning in human life, and for Christian confidence in ultimate victory over all forms of evil. Thus creation is also closely connected with *eschatology*, the doctrine of the end-times in which God ultimately vindicates his own creativity.

Eschatology is more than futurology, despite prevalent fascination about timetables of future events. It deals with the fulfillment of what God initiated in creation. God creates through his eternal Word; he also redeems and brings to completion through the incarnation and glorification of the same Word in Jesus of Nazareth. "Creation, as the going forth from God, is simultaneously the first step of the return to God; and the return is the completion of the journey begun in creation. God creates for a purpose which becomes known as the future of the world in the resurrection of Jesus, the Christ."[21] Even though creation has scientific and philosophical implications, its central significance is theological.

3. *The scientific enterprise.* We have already noted in chapter nine the positive contribution of biblical teaching about God and the world to the development of modern science. Yet a certain kind of modern theology has considered the biblical description of nature a liability, requiring "demythologizing" to make it acceptable to a scientific age. Actually, Genesis 1 prepared the way for our age by its own program of demythologizing. By purging the cosmic order of all gods and goddesses, the Genesis creation account "de-divinized" nature. The universe has no divine regions or beings who need to be feared or placated. Israel's intensely monotheistic faith thoroughly demythologized the natural world, making way for a science that can probe and study every part of the universe without fearing either trespass or retribution.

That does not mean that nature is secular and no longer sacred. It is still God's creation, declared to be good, preserved by his power and intended for his glory. The disappearance of mythical scenes and polytheistic intrigues clears the stage for the great drama of redemption and the new creation in Christ.

4. *The contemporary church.* Meanwhile, the doctrine of creation has profound implications for contemporary Christian thought and life. Study of Genesis 1 illuminates two major questions that should concern Christians in modern culture. First, what false gods command a

following in our society and even in our churches? Although they differ radically from the false deities of ancient Israel's neighbors, their worship can produce similar results. In order to escape the influence of current unbiblical philosophies, religious ideas and superstitions, the message of Genesis 1 is urgently needed.

Second, in a day of increasing environmental concerns, what actions should Christians take as stewards of the earth? Environmental problems have scientific and technological, political and economic, social and legal aspects. Important moral and ethical concerns derive from the biblical doctrines of creation and human responsibility for the earth. Basic to such concerns is our understanding of nature. Most other religions view the world as spiritual in itself or as irrelevant to spiritual concerns. But in the biblical view, the natural world is created, material and significant in God's purposes. From that teaching come basic principles which are belatedly receiving attention from Christian writers.[22] Surely the church needs a solid contemporary theology of creation to help define our human relationship to the natural world.

The doctrine of creation is foundational for God's providential care of his creation, for his redemption of humanity and for his re-creation of a new heaven and earth. Its teaching of God's transcendent sovereignty and power is embodied in a hymn in the last book of the Bible:

You are worthy, our Lord and God,
   to receive glory and honor and power,
for you created all things,
   and by your will they were created
   and have their being. (Rev 4:11)

III
CONFLICTS
AND RECONCILIATION

11
A CHANGING WORLD:
GEOLOGY
AND BIOLOGY

I have called this principle,
by which each slight variation,
if useful, is preserved,
by the term Natural Selection.
CHARLES DARWIN

FTER NEWTON THE NEW OUTLOOK MOVED BEYOND ASTRONOMY and physics into other physical sciences. During the eighteenth century the natural world was generally viewed as a "law-abiding machine," self-sufficient and impersonal. The mechanistic view became a prevailing philosophy, identifying a scientific model for explaining nature with the whole of reality.

For many, Christian theism was replaced by *deism,* which rejected biblical revelation in favor of "natural theology." According to that view, the "Divine Clockmaker" had created a universe that ran by itself. Arguments for God's existence were primarily based on the orderliness and intelligibility of nature, the evidence of design and purpose, and gaps in scientific explanation requiring divine attention.

The God of the Bible seemed increasingly irrelevant to a world in which the methods of science apparently supplied the answers to life.

The nineteenth century produced a scientific revolution of its own. Before 1800, most people believed that the world had been created within the brief period of one week during 4004 B.C. and that it had continued much the same ever since. Astronomy and physics had broken away from tradition, but a revolution in geology and biology was just beginning, generating heated controversies over creation. Certain concepts of biological science, such as the immutability of species, had become dogma; now they were challenged by new views of probability and progress. The key figure in the debates was Charles Darwin.

Evolution's Family Tree

Ideas of organic evolution were conceived by a number of early Greek philosophers. Anaximander (611-547 B.C.) proposed a theory of the spontaneous generation of life from primordial fluid. Aristotle (384-322 B.C.) believed in a perfecting principle that continually operated to improve the living world. Those seminal ideas had never been developed to a degree that gained them widespread acceptance.

Until the early 1800s the prevailing geological theory was *catastrophism*. It held that the earth had passed through a number of great cataclysms of which Noah's flood was the most recent. Each was thought to have destroyed most living things, entombing their remains in strata deposited by the catastrophe, after which God created new species. Naturalist Georges Cuvier produced a monumental study of vertebrates; by 1801 he had reconstructed from fossil bones twenty-three species then extinct, including the giant mastodon. He believed that such creatures were produced by divine activity amid great world upheavals.

Catastrophism fit the nineteenth-century concept of miracle: divine intervention in the regular processes of nature at various stages in the past. Since such a series of divine acts bore some resemblance to the account in Genesis 1, the scientific theory of catastrophism came to be regarded as the orthodox Christian position. The "God-of-the-gaps" now found employment, although it turned out to be as temporary as Newton's role for divine intervention to adjust irregularities in the solar system.

The supremacy of catastrophism was soon challenged by a new scientific view. In 1788 geologist James Hutton published his *Theory of the Earth,* which argued that the earth's history should be interpreted in the light of presently known processes. That principle, *uniformitarianism,* was advanced as the key to unlocking the secrets of the past. Charles Lyell produced a mass of evidence to support the adequacy of present processes acting over a long period of time "within the existing order of nature" to account for past changes. His three-volume *Principles of Geology* (1830-1833) marked the birth of modern geology. On the basis of the continuity and uniformity seen in the earth's inorganic history, Lyell concluded that the origin of new species might have been a "natural, in contradistinction to a miraculous, process."[1] His portrayal of such a long, natural process had a formative influence on Darwin's thought.

At a time when geology was struggling to establish its place in the scientific sun, Lyell's book integrated the professional domain and provided masterful expression to a growing consensus about geological method. In order to define and protect geological expertise, Lyell rewrote the history of geology "as though every path of inquiry in the science had been blocked repeatedly with Noah's Ark, every thread of induction had routinely been snapped with a divine creative fiat."[2] His polemical account (in the introductory chapter of *Principles*) treated with disdain those who tried to make Genesis teach geology, especially the "scriptural geologists" who were not competent in the field.

The principle of uniformitarianism itself was not considered irreligious. For Hutton, who preceded Lyell, that approach was inspired by his recognition of divine design in nature. The new geology did not alter the prevailing assumption of biologists concerning the fixity of species. In the mid-1700s botanist Carolus Linnaeus had formulated the first comprehensive binomial system for classifying plants and animals. The usefulness of Linnaeus's classification perpetuated the conviction of permanent differences between species. When French naturalists Buffon and Lamarck proposed natural variability and organic change of species, at first they found few supporters. Nevertheless, such ideas prepared the climate and soil into which Darwin eventually dropped his seed: an effective mechanism for change.

Belief in the stability of biological forms, so long dominant in Western thought, had two primary roots. First, Aristotle taught that individual beings are embodiments of eternal forms (unchanging essences). The primary explanation of an organism's structure was found in its *final* cause (its purpose or goal); hence, a search for explanations of its *efficient* cause (the way it works) was considered relatively unimportant. Second, Genesis 1 had long been interpreted to teach that God created each species in its present form.

Before Darwin, the rise of modern geology had produced no serious conflict between the scientific and biblical views of nature. The six days of Genesis 1 could readily be interpreted as figurative expressions or as geological epochs. Basic biblical affirmations were not challenged. As long as human beings were a special creation by God, human uniqueness was protected. Geology did not undermine the argument from design, which still enjoyed popularity.[3] During that period many volumes traced the providential adaptation of creatures to their goals. William Paley's widely read *Natural Theology* (1802) gave numerous examples. He reasoned that whenever a means seemed adapted to some purpose, it could be taken as evidence that God designed it so. The existence of lower forms of life was explained by their usefulness to humankind, for whose benefit nature was established in a hierarchy of life—an immutable "chain of being." That form of natural theology proved particularly vulnerable to the concept of evolution.

A mode for the origination of new species was proposed by Robert Chambers in *Vestiges of the Natural History of Creation* (1844). He suggested as a key to understanding the organic world a process of development in which adaptive evolutionary changes gave rise to new species: "The simplest and most primitive type . . . gave birth to the type next above it, this again produced the next higher, and so on." Although Chambers remained vague concerning the mechanism of such development, he suggested a law of nature in the organic arena as fundamental and comprehensive as the law of gravitation in the inorganic realm. Anticipating that he would be treading on theological toes, Chambers wrote, "The idea of an almighty author becomes irresistible, for the creation of a law for an endless series of phenomena . . . could have no other imaginable source."[4] Published anonymously, *Vestiges* provoked a high pitch of popular excitement as well as scientific and theological opposition. For the scientists, Thomas H.

Huxley and Charles Lyell led the attack on the book's thesis.

Charles Darwin

In 1832 Charles Darwin went to sea on the "Beagle" as the ship's naturalist. A five-year voyage took him around the world. The second volume of Lyell's *Principles of Geology* reached him as he was observing flora and fauna in South America. Lyell's uniformitarian openness to a natural origin for new species was probably on Darwin's mind during his studies of slight variations among species, especially the finches in the remote Galapagos chain of islands.

Six years later, in economist T. R. Malthus's comments on the role of human population pressure and competition, Darwin found the clue for a theory to interpret his extensive data:

Being well prepared to appreciate the struggle for existence which everywhere goes on, from long-continued observation of the habits of animals and plants, it at once struck me that under these circumstances favorable variations would tend to be preserved and unfavorable ones to be destroyed. The result of this would be the formation of new species. Here, then, I had at last got a theory by which to work.[5]

Darwin had his theory essentially complete by 1844, but he took another fifteen years to mature it. In 1859 he published *On the Origin of Species by Means of Natural Selection, or the Preservation of Favoured Races in the Struggle for Life*. By that time he had spent twenty-five years amassing an array of observations from a variety of biological species.

Although Darwin was not the first to suggest the *possibility* of evolution, he presented a wealth of evidence to support a possible *mechanism*, the concept of *natural selection*. His work illustrates the basic scientific method of interaction between observation and theory. No amount of data constitutes or produces a scientific theory until it is given creative coherence. And as can be seen in the Greek precursors of Copernicus and Darwin, theory alone is insufficient unless it can be tested by observations and can guide the collection of additional data.

Darwin's theory of the origin of species by natural selection combined several concepts: (1) *random variations* among the individual members of a species; (2) the *struggle for survival* in which a slight variation gives an advantage in the intense competition for existence;

(3) the *natural selection* of individuals with that advantage as, on the average, they live longer and have more progeny. (The phrase "survival of the fittest" was coined by sociologist Herbert Spencer and adopted by Darwin in his 1866 edition.) Darwin argued that over a long period of time a reduction and eventual elimination of the less favorable variations effect a gradual transformation of a species.

In his first book Darwin avoided a discussion of human origins. But in 1871 he presented a thorough treatment in *The Descent of Man*. He attempted to show how all human characteristics could be accounted for by a gradual modification of anthropoid ancestors through the process of natural selection. Not only physical elements but also human mental and moral faculties differed only in degree, and not in kind, from the capacities of animals. Our own human existence, formerly considered sacrosanct, thus came within the sphere of natural law to be analyzed by the same methods used for other forms of life.

The publication of the *Origin of Species* initiated a period of intense excitement. Correspondence during the years following 1859 shows that talk of conversion to scientific Darwinism was on everyone's tongue. Some scientists resisted to their death; others went partway scientifically but stopped short of complete conversion. A third group enthusiastically embraced the new model of evolution. Although many subsidiary points such as the mechanism of natural selection have been debated for more than a century, the change in outlook associated with 1859 is one of the rare major shifts in the whole of intellectual history.[6]

The Impact of Evolution

Darwin's theory of evolution eventually altered the prevailing view of nature in three major respects.[7]

1. The idea of the world was transformed from that of a fixed hierarchical order into a dynamic process. The importance of change had already been suggested in specific areas by the nebular hypothesis in astronomy and by uniformitarianism in geology. Now Darwin's work convinced the scientific community that all living things were in a state of change. The traditional concept of the world was challenged by this revolutionary idea of a dynamic process of development.

2. Nature could be considered a complex of interacting forces in organic interdependence. The relationship between the individual

and the environment assumed greater significance. Following Darwin, the interactive character of the "web of life" and the importance of the environmental context became prominent in the study of nature.

3. The idea of evolution extended the rule of natural law into other areas of nature. In fact, a new kind of statistical law incorporated the element of chance. In the following decades determinism gained ground, although after the turn of the century some philosophers viewed chance as allowing for novelty.

Further, evolution stimulated the interest of social scientists in the processes of change. The biological model was applied to such an extent that some writers tried to deduce from it the laws of every field from astronomy to ethics. That historical and genetic approach viewed all ideas, institutions, religions and cultures as evolving. Evolution as a scientific theory became the springboard to a full-blown philosophy of evolutionary naturalism and even a religion of moral and ethical evolutionism. With Darwin, as we saw earlier with Newton, a method was made into metaphysics, a theory into a comprehensive world view.

The crosscurrents of thought and controversies of the last part of the nineteenth century were far more complex than the popular view perpetuated into our own century. The scholarly writings of the period 1870-1900, despite the celebrated confrontation between Bishop Wilberforce and Thomas Huxley in 1869, do not support the picture of a simple polarity between Christianity and evolution.[8] For one thing, the scientists themselves were divided in their opinions; many had doubts about both the method and metaphysics of evolution. Further, a significant number of leading scientists were Christians well grounded in theology, and many clergymen were competent in science.

The "Galileo myth" of Christianity and science as implacable enemies was reinforced by two books, even though they made no significant contribution to the issues raised by Darwin: *History of the Conflict between Religion and Science* by John Draper (1874); and *A History of the Warfare of Science with Theology in Christendom* by Andrew White (1896). Draper said little if anything about evolution and religion, and White used only twenty of his nine hundred pages to settle the question of origins. Yet the "military metaphor" of their titles became standard for historians describing the controversy over evolution. The warfare imagery tells more about Draper and White than it does about the debates over evolution. Instead of violent antagonism, the record indicates honest disagreements among colleagues who for the most part stayed friendly: "In each of its major implications the military metaphor perverts understanding with violence and inhumanity. . . . Henceforth, interpretations of the post-Darwinian controversies must be non-violent and humane."[9]

The decade following publication of the *Origin of Species* witnessed a gradual acceptance of the theory of evolution, although in some quarters natural selection was rejected as its mechanism. Yet the debates over evolution became much more divisive than those following the innovations of Copernicus and Galileo. Although the earlier theories also contradicted widely accepted interpretations of the Bible, they could be argued at the largely abstract level of astronomy and physics. But Chambers had moved scientific explanation from the inorganic to the organic realm, and Darwin had carried it into the domain of humanity itself—with profound religious implications.

Christian Reactions to Darwin

Roman Catholic theology was largely able to see evolution as God's *modus operandi,* at least below the human level. Protestant theologians had three major reactions to Darwin's teaching during the final decades of the nineteenth century. Their concerns centered on the theory of evolution itself, its relationship to the Genesis account of creation, and the implications of evolutionary theory for the nature of human beings. The theological reactions varied according to the degree that they met head-on the theory of natural selection. Darwin did not claim that natural selection was the exclusive mechanism of evolution, but it came to represent a rigorous naturalism in which no external divine agency was conceived as directing the course of evolutionary development according to a plan and purpose.[10]

1. *Conservative anti-Darwinians.* One group of traditional Christians considered the observed design in nature to be a crucial argument for the existence of God. Now they were confronted by the claim that natural selection could account for design in the organic world without recourse to divine activity. At stake in that issue, they believed, were the existence of God, his relationship to nature, the integrity of

the Bible and the authority of religious truth. Here we note two scientists and a theologian.

William Dawson, an eminent Canadian geologist, poured much of his life into developing McGill University, where he made the sciences the bulwark of his educational philosophy. He became one of the last great spokesmen for the tradition of two theologies—one natural and one revealed. Dawson's commitment to that view led him to persist in his uncompromising anti-Darwinian stand. Louis Agassiz came to the Harvard University faculty with a major reputation in geology and zoology. From Europe he brought a full-blown philosophy of natural history based on discrete creations separated by catastrophes. He based his anti-Darwinian position on scientific reasons. Agassiz used his power as a writer and lecturer to carry on a broadly publicized and persistent campaign against Darwin's ideas.[11]

Another leading spokesman against Darwinism was Charles Hodge of Princeton Seminary, the most influential Presbyterian theologian of his day. In *What Is Darwinism?* he identified the main elements of the *Origin:* evolution, natural selection and natural selection without design. He asserted that the first two had been taught much earlier and only the last was distinctive to Darwin's theory and its most important element.[12] Hodge provided documentation to show how the theory held that all the organs of plants and animals, as well as instincts and mental capabilities, could be accounted for without reference to divine purpose and guidance. He could not accept the idea of God's acting through a secondary cause like evolution by natural selection. Hodge accorded to his belief in the argument from design the status of an absolute truth: "To any ordinarily constituted mind, it is absolutely impossible to believe that the eye is not a work of design. . . . [God] has given to the human mind intuitions which are infallible, laws of belief which men cannot disregard any more than laws of nature."[13]

Hodge's dynamic and devastating critique of Darwinism exerted widespread influence. His argument clearly implied that either Darwin was wrong or God did not exist; no middle ground was defensible. The opposition of this group to Darwinism was also based on two philosophical views lurking below the surface of the theological debate: the fixity of species and the certainty of science.[14] In many of the debates those philosophical assumptions were much more prominent than the biblical arguments against the theory of evolution.

2. *Conservative Darwinians.* One group of conservative scholars did stake out a "middle ground" on which they firmly stood with confidence in both biblical theology and evolutionary theory. James McCosh, a theologian and president of what is now Princeton University, suggested that the scriptural and scientific views of nature could be reconciled as parallel revelations. He believed that natural selection was only one of several means by which evolution took place, and that even that mechanism is consistent with divine design. Since "supernatural design produces natural selection,"[15] McCosh wrote that Darwin had wrongly contrasted the two as opposites. Understood in this light, evolution as God's method "is in no way inconsistent with Scripture."[16] McCosh noted that the Bible is not concerned with the question of the absolute immutability of species, a scientific concept associated with Linnaeus.

Asa Gray, professor of natural history at Harvard, was one of the great botanists of his time. As the most persuasive advocate of biological evolution in America, he demonstrated that an eminent scientist could coordinate the theory with a vital Christian faith. In a lecture at the Yale Divinity School, published in 1880, Gray rejected the view that Holy Scripture teaches natural science. He noted that attempts to demonstrate agreement between biblical and scientific statements rely on "extraneous suppositions and forced constructions of language." Gray affirmed that "the teachings of the two, properly understood, are not incompatible. We may take it to be the accepted idea that the Mosaic books were not handed down to us for our instruction in scientific knowledge, and that it is our duty to ground our scientific beliefs upon observation and inference, unmixed with considerations of a different order."[17]

Gray and other Christian Darwinians grounded the process of evolution in the sovereignty of God. For them, Darwinism posed no *new* problem for Reformed theology. Providence and chance, primary and secondary causes, might be difficult to reconcile, but no more than predestination and free will. Gray stated that the true issue regarding design is not between creationism and Darwinism but between design and chance, purpose and no intention. He also rejected the prevalent "God-of-the-gaps" approach: "I do not approve either the divinity [theology] or science of those who are prompt to invoke the supernatural to cover our ignorance of natural causes, and equally so to discard this aid whenever natural causes are found sufficient."[18]

For twenty years Gray and Darwin corresponded concerning the relationship between Christian theism and natural selection. Despite their differences, they agreed that the theory of evolution itself deals only with efficient causes, the observable events of nature and their mechanism. As a biblical Christian, Gray was convinced that final causes, God's ultimate purposes, remained untouched by evolution.

George Wright, a friend and collaborator of Gray for fourteen years, published many articles explaining the theory of evolution. He opposed the Baconian philosophy of science to which Christian anti-Darwinians had wedded their theology. Wright showed that in a changing world modern science offers approximations and not certainties. The Christian Darwinians affirmed that evolutionary theory, with its implications of probability and development, was not only better science but also more in harmony with biblical theology than was the philosophical concept of the fixity of species. They reaffirmed the age-old biblical conviction that God's superintendence of his creation is immediate and continuous, not limited to special creative acts and miracles.

3. *Liberal Darwinians.* Already involved in reformulating Christian doctrines to harmonize with the tune of the times, liberal Darwinians vested nothing of religious importance in the historical accuracy of the Bible, including Genesis. Liberalism viewed Jesus as one of many religious teachers, human nature as essentially good, progress as inevitable and morality as the heart of religion. Some even went as far as to make evolution the cornerstone of their theological perspective.

Anglican theologian Frederick Temple, a moderate, located the divine governance of nature in an original decree rather than in God's subsequent activity. He asserted that the doctrine of evolution left the argument for an intelligent creator and governor even stronger, although the execution of his purpose was inherent in the original creation.[19] Temple believed that Darwinian evolution could not explain how life or morality originated. Nevertheless, he stood to the left of McCosh in looking on evolution as providing a positive insight into new theological foundations, including the nature of God's relationship to the world.

Other scholars further to the left expressed enthusiasm for the new life they saw evolution breathing into Christian doctrine. In America the prosperity of the 1880s encouraged theologians to make evolution consistent with the prevailing atmosphere of progress and optimism, producing an amalgam of Darwinism and romanticism.[20] By the early years of the twentieth century such "Darwinists" had reinterpreted the gospel along the lines of evolutionary thought. Some attempted to harmonize Christianity and evolution by showing that Christianity itself, including the Incarnation, was simply a phase of evolutionary law.[21] Their full-blown evolutionism went far beyond the competence of science and the content of biblical teaching. As a philosophical flight of fancy it was brought to earth by the carnage of World War 1, which shattered the dream of inevitable peace and progress.

A New World View

In every age theology has two major tasks, (1) to provide a coherent understanding of the biblical faith for the Christian community; and (2) to mediate the values and meaning of biblical faith to the culture at large. The two concerns are closely related since the experience of believers is conditioned by the thought-categories of their culture. Theological communication is a two-way street. As the Christian message is related to contemporary thought, elements of that world view work their way into the structure of theology. In theology also, all data are "theory-laden"; what we look for in the Bible and how we interpret it is influenced by our point of view.

Such interaction has been evident in the emergence of modern science. We have seen that the theological vision of the world offered by medieval theologians reflected the geocentric universe of Aristotle and Ptolemy. The change to a heliocentric view advocated by Copernicus and Galileo challenged the entire world view in which that theology had been framed. No wonder that the new science appeared to be an enemy of Christianity. Much of the opposition to Copernicanism was an effort to defend biblical doctrines and theological methods that had become wedded to Aristotle's system.

In retrospect, we can see the same pattern in the nineteenth-century conflict between science and theology. The rise of evolutionary theory was one feature of an emerging scientific world view radically different from the Newtonian model popularized by the Baconians. The latter, in the tradition of Aristotle, placed primary emphasis on *stability* and explained *change* within a philosophy of *being*. The new view, like the ancient philosophy of Heraclitus, emphasized *change* and accounted for *stability* within a philosophy of *becoming*. The old finished and stable universe was giving way to one in constant change and flux.

Bacon believed that scientific knowledge arises from the accumulation of perceived facts obtained directly by objective observers. His scientific method was reinforced by the Scottish "philosophers of common sense" who appealed to the universal, down-to-earth perceptions of humankind for the validity of cause and effect, God's existence and God's moral standards for life. The scientific method shaped by Bacon and the Scottish realists has been termed Baconianism. Its explanation of both science and theology prevailed in America during the early nineteenth century. It insisted that science stick to the facts and reject "hypotheses" that could not be confirmed by direct observation.

Many Christian apologists based their proofs for the existence of God, including the argument from design in nature, on the Newtonian world view. By uniting Christianity and Baconianism, evangelical scholars could champion morality as both biblical and scientific. But in doing so they overlooked three crucial questions:[22] (1) Is the Baconian idea of truth biblical, much less the only adequate form for Christian explanation? (2) What are the implications of letting one currently fashionable scientific world view influence, if not determine, biblical interpretation? (3) Should belief in the existence of God, the accuracy of the Bible and the validity of Christianity be based on our ability to confirm it by scientific methods?

While many American evangelicals had their theology and science firmly hitched to the wagon of Baconianism, a new form of scientific explanation loomed on the horizon. Its broader perspective included creative views of the whole picture (which in geology and biology took in the historicity of the earth and its life), not just the isolated "facts" of the Baconian ideal. A science of the *forest* had begun to replace the science of the *trees*. The question was not so much whether specific formulas or laws would be preserved, but rather what kind of meaning they took on in the new theory as a whole (chapter 9).

Regrettably, the newer scientific outlook came to the attention of American evangelicals through Darwin's evolutionary theory, which was being used by liberal Darwinists to oppose Christian doctrines and to foster agnosticism and materialism. The biological theory of evolution became a lightning rod for evangelical concern about those philosophies. Evolution became a misplaced focus of opposition to the new scientific currents and to Darwinist teaching, which were seen to be linked together. Again, as in Galileo's time, conservative Christians fought against new science in the name of a biblical interpretation they had linked to an older science and philosophy.

Yet in one respect the situation was exactly the opposite. In the sixteenth century, when Christian theism was the prevailing philosophy, the church was the recognized authority; in order to have his science accepted, Galileo had to prove that it was biblically accurate. In the nineteenth century, however, the philosophy of naturalism had become dominant, and science occupied the position of influence; in order to have their theology accepted, many conservative Christian scholars thought they had to harmonize the Bible with science.

Many of the same issues still underlie twentieth-century debates over creation and evolution. Some scholars advocating organic evolution have gone beyond their scientific authority to make philosophical and theological pronouncements. The opposition of some evangelical Christians to the theory of evolution seems to reflect a strong commitment to Baconianism. Those attitudes lie at the heart of the current creation-science controversy—to which we now turn.

12
THE
CREATION-SCIENCE
CONTROVERSY

I do not approve either the theology
or the science of those who are
prompt to invoke the supernatural
to cover our ignorance of natural causes.
ASA GRAY

THE 1925 SCOPES TRIAL IN DAYTON, TENNESSEE, BROUGHT NATION-
wide publicity to the creation-evolution controversy. News-
papers carried a blow-by-blow account of the confrontation
between prosecution assistant William Jennings Bryan and
defense attorney Clarence Darrow in the case of a high-school
teacher indicted for breaking the state's new anti-evolution law.
Scopes was convicted, but two years later the Tennessee Supreme
Court reversed the decision on technical grounds.

During the following years the anti-evolutionists focused their attention on local school boards. Publishers of high-school texts tended
to avoid the issue, although teachers could present aspects of evolu-

tion they deemed appropriate. A 1942 survey showed that fewer than half of the high-school biology teachers mentioned evolution in their courses. By 1964 one historian was predicting that a renaissance of the creationist movement would not be likely.[1]

Nevertheless (to paraphrase Mark Twain) the reports of its death were greatly exaggerated. During the 1970s and '80s the creation-evolution controversy returned to public school classrooms and to the courts. It came to a head in a 1982 trial in Arkansas. A number of issues emerged in that confrontation. How should they be evaluated in the light of our discussion of the biblical and scientific views of nature?

The importance of this question lies mainly in its impact on the general public, since in twentieth-century science the most revolutionary developments have again occurred in astronomy and physics. Although Darwin's idea of natural selection, revolutionary in the nineteenth century, has already to some extent become "classical biology" in the twentieth, few if any practicing biologists see biology moving away from evolution. Yet many Christians hope that it will. Why? Because in their view evolution undermines the basic biblical doctrine of creation and reduces human beings to products of blind chance.

Definition of Terms
Every field of study has a special language of technical terms with precise definitions. Since the same word can have different meanings in different disciplines, and still another meaning in popular language, definitions are the first order of business for clear thinking and accurate communication. This step is even more important today than a century ago. Increasing specialization has left us with relatively few scholars distinguished in both science and theology. Many prominent scientific supporters of organic evolution demonstrate little if any understanding of biblical theology. By the same token, few of evolution's opponents have a grasp of the historical development and philosophy of modern science. As a result, communication is crippled while controversy runs rampant.

1. *Evolution.* "Evolution" has a variety of common meanings, including (a) an unfolding, working out; process of development; (b) result of this process; thing evolved; (c) the development of a species, organism or organ from its original to its present state; and (d) a

theory that all species of plants and animals developed from earlier forms. Here we focus primarily on the last two definitions, or what may be called *microevolution* and *macroevolution;* we are concerned also with a philosophical and social concept that might better be called *evolutionism.*

Biologist G. A. Kerkut defines the *special theory of evolution* (microevolution), as the proposition that "many living animals can be observed over the course of time to undergo changes so that new species are formed."[2] In certain cases this type of evolution can be demonstrated by experiments. Phenomena of genetic change that can be observed in the laboratory and in nature, together with logical deductions made regarding speciation, compose the major elements of this kind of limited evolution. In this sense it is possible to call evolution a fact. Current literature shows that most biologists are giving their attention to microevolution.

The *general theory of evolution* (macroevolution) is defined by Kerkut as the theory that "all the living forms in the world have arisen from a single source which itself came from an inorganic form."[3] This is the classical evolution taught in textbooks and courses in zoology. The amount of time and space required for general or macroevolution precludes the possibility of laboratory experiment or observation of the entire process in nature. Therefore, evidence comes from such areas as comparative anatomy and embryology, the fossil record, zoogeography, vestigial organs and comparative physiology and biochemistry. Sometimes such evidences are taken as proofs when in reality, except for the fossil record, they are simply examples of reasoning on the basis of assumptions and analogy. For example, it is assumed that because small changes occur in a brief time, large changes will take place during a longer time. Like other scientific generalizations, macroevolution includes gaps and extrapolations.

On what, then, is the general theory of evolution based? Kerkut identifies seven assumptions, including the following five: that spontaneous generation occurred, but only once; that viruses, bacteria, plants and animals are all interrelated; that protozoa give rise to metazoa; that invertebrates give rise to vertebrates; and that fish progressed to amphibia to reptiles to birds and mammals.[4] By their very nature these assumptions cannot be proved (or disproved). Yet many biologists have become so taken with the "fact" of evolution that they fail to recognize or identify the assumptions behind the general theory of evolution. For example, Julian Huxley, one of the world's leading evolutionists, participated in the Darwin Centennial, declaring, "Evolution of life is no longer a theory; it is a fact and the basis of all our thinking. . . . We do not intend to get bogged down in semantics and definitions."[5] (It seems strange that, of all scholars, a scientist should want to dispense with the question of what his words mean.)

At present, no one evolutionary sequence, with an explanation of its mechanism, is widely accepted. Leading biologists advance significantly different proposals. Nevertheless, macroevolution with its assumptions, like other scientific theories, can be accepted as a *working hypothesis* that attempts to correlate the data and guide further research. To be scientifically accurate, however, textbooks and lecturers should refrain from according to the general theory the status of factuality enjoyed by the special theory, microevolution.

Failure to recognize the distinction between the two theories of evolution confuses many issues and fosters unnecessary misunderstanding. Although most attacks on evolution focus on the general theory, they are usually understood by evolutionists to be a repudiation of the special theory—for which empirical evidence exists. Some anti-evolutionists will not concede that data supporting special evolution are relevant to the general theory; on the other hand, many ardent evolutionists overrate such evidence as validating the latter.

A third concept, one which we call *evolutionism*, is not really a scientific theory but an evolutionary philosophy. Assuming that general biological evolution is an established law of nature, adherents of evolutionism extrapolate that concept into the realms of history and sociology, ethics and religion (see chapter 11). All life is viewed as one grand development from lower to higher forms, leading to continuing human improvement as people now become conscious of evolution and complete for themselves the age-long process. For some, evolutionism can become a pseudoreligion, with a faith system competing with Christianity for people's allegiance.[6]

Recognizing those three distinct meanings of evolution, one sees that each concept must stand or fall on its own merits: special evolution based on empirical evidence; general evolution as a comprehensive theory; evolutionism as a philosophy of life. Some scientists accept the first but not the second; others accept both of the scientific theories but not the philosophy of evolutionism.[6]

2. *Creation.* Definition is equally important in discussing the word *creation,* whose meanings include (a) bringing into being; origination; design; invention; (b) bringing about; causing; (c) investing with a new rank or function; (d) in theater, being the first to portray a role. In popular language we speak about creating a new fashion in clothes or an arrangement of flowers—obviously using pre-existing materials. Or we may create a controversy, new administrative post or character in a play.

The biblical use of the word *create* (chapter 10) is also varied. God's creative activity "in the beginning" (Gen 1:1) has been understood by the church from its earliest centuries as *ex nihilo* ("out of nothing"), a creation of matter and energy and time itself. Unlike the pagan gods who worked with pre-existing materials, God spoke and creation occurred. It appears in Genesis that some creation was instantaneous: " 'Let there be light,' and there was light" (1:3). Some creative acts apparently took time: " 'Let the water under the sky be gathered to one place, and let dry ground appear.' And it was so" (1:9). Others initiated a creative process: " 'Let the land produce living creatures according to their kinds. . . .' And it was so" (1:24). In observing such distinctions, though, we must remember that our Western analytical approach (which divides into components and exploits small differences) is radically different from the Hebrew synthetic view (which saw life and events as a whole). Psalmists and prophets did not sharply divide God's creative activity into theological and philosophical compartments of creation and providence, supernatural and natural, primary and secondary causes. Unconcerned with scientific mechanisms, the biblical writers ascribed everything in nature, from beginning through to the end, to God the Creator and Sustainer of the world, who is also the Lord and Judge of history, Israel's redeemer and preserver.

Since both creation and evolution have varied meanings, it is a mistake to use the terms *creationist* and *evolutionist* as if each represented only one concept, or as if they were mutually exclusive positions. Many competent scholars accept both biblical creation and biological evolution. Yet people are surprised to hear that one can have full confidence in the reliability of the Genesis accounts of creation and also use macroevolution as a scientific theory to correlate known data and guide future research. That set of views, held by the Christian Darwinists of the late nineteenth century, is common among evangelical Christians in science today.

We should not only recognize the essential difference between the biblical and scientific views of nature, but we should also maintain their integrity. In other words, macroevolution, like any other scientific theory, must be judged on its own merits; its validity is not determined by theological or philosophical convictions. Likewise, a proposed interpretation of the Genesis creation accounts, like other biblical doctrines, must satisfy recognized hermeneutical criteria and not be determined by scientific theories.

Nevertheless, recent decades have seen the development of the "creation-science" movement, which endeavors to combine theology and science in a certain way. The movement has attracted national attention through its political activities and several courtroom controversies.

Creation-Science

The Russian launching of sputnik in 1957 precipitated a scrutiny of American science education. In the early 1960s the federally funded Biological Sciences Curriculum Study introduced a series of texts that included the origin of life and evolution of major types of organisms. In 1968 the United States Supreme Court ruled the 1928 Arkansas anti-evolution law unconstitutional; two years later Mississippi repealed the last of the state laws forbidding the teaching of evolution. In many states some form of evolutionary theory became the sole explanation given for origins and was often taught in public schools as a "scientific fact."

A group of creationists in California reacted against those developments with a petition to the State Board of Education, which unanimously passed the following:

1. Special divine creation is not just a theistic belief but can also be explained as a scholarly and scientifically valid doctrine by the Creation Research Society. Therefore, it deserves equal status with other scientific explanations concerning the origin of man.

2. The current science framework presents an unbalanced philosophical approach, i.e., atheistic humanism. Such an unbalanced approach is prohibited by law.[7]

A year later news of that action in the March 1970 issue of *Bioscience* attracted nationwide attention and produced a variety of reactions. The kind of creationism that had been offered as an alternative to evolutionary theory taught that the universe is about ten thousand years old; the major species were created in six twenty-four-hour days; and the geological data can be explained by the worldwide flood of Noah which lasted about a year.[8]

The "young-earth" creationists had obviously made a major tactical shift. Instead of trying to outlaw evolution, as they had done in the 1920s, they now attempted to gain equal time for their view of creation. Rather than appealing to the authority of the Bible, they downplayed the Genesis account in favor of what they termed creation-science. Since the U.S. Supreme Court had declared the 1928 Arkansas anti-evolution law unconstitutional, they feared that legislation requiring the teaching of *biblical* creationism might suffer the same fate. The door would also be opened to other interpretations of Genesis, to say nothing of non-Christian versions of creation. So they pressed only for teaching the scientific aspects of creationism—arguments for a recent worldwide catastrophe and against evolution—leaving out reference to the Genesis days and Noah's ark.

That approach is reflected in the 1981 legislation entitled Arkansas Act 590, which defined creation-science as follows:

"Creation-science" means the scientific evidences and related inferences that indicate: (1) Sudden creation of the universe, energy, and life from nothing; (2) The insufficiency of mutation and natural selection in bringing about development of all living kinds from a single organism; (3) Changes only within fixed limits of originally created kinds of plants and animals; (4) Separate ancestry for man and apes; (5) Explanation of the earth's geology by catastrophism, including the occurrence of a worldwide flood, and (6) A relatively recent inception of the earth and living kinds.[9]

In 1982 that "balanced treatment" act, which had become law in Arkansas, was challenged in federal district court and ruled unconstitutional. Judge William Overton concluded that the law was an attempt by creationists to characterize what is essentially a religious statement as science, when in fact it is not accepted by a credible portion of the scientific community. He stated that religion should remain outside the schoolroom.[10]

That evaluation of creation-science focuses on the central issue of our discussion. Quite apart from any strengths or weaknesses of the position as defined in Act 590, is it science? Our answer must be based on clear definitions, which regrettably are often absent from such discussions.

Modern science works with observations of repeated or repeatable events, quantifying and calculating, in an attempt to devise a model that not only explains the current data but also leads to productive predictions. Scientists look for patterns of events and their mechanisms. When investigators advance a theory, they generally devise problem-solving strategies to test it.

To what extent does creation-science follow that procedure and satisfy those criteria? To support its view of a "young earth" (10,000 years), it advances a "flood geology" to account for the geological record and the observed fossil sequence. The existence of basic "kinds" of organisms is attributed to the special creative events of one "calendar" week. In other words, scientific explanation is based on both empirical data and revealed truths of the Bible. Adherents appeal to miraculous divine action outside the realm of scientific investigation to substantiate their theory.

The above procedure is significantly different from the "God-of-the-gaps" approach, which begins with the consensus of current scientific explanation but calls for divine intervention in phenomena not yet understood. Creation-science has a "God-the-scientist" view; it discovers its scientific explanation (in this case, a catastrophism linked with the fixity of species) in biblical teaching, into which empirical data are expected to fit. The theological basis of creation-science has been expressed by Morris and Whitcomb: "The real issue is not the correctness of the interpretation of various details of the geological data, but simply what God has revealed in His Word concerning these matters."[11]

In the Arkansas case, Judge Overton observed that the creation-scientists had characterized an essentially religious statement as science. If their approach were genuine science, it would offer mechanisms, propose problem-solving strategies and test hypotheses without recourse to theology. Equally important, conclusions would be accepted on their *scientific* merits by many scholars of differing theological persuasions. As it has been defined by its proponents, the term *creation-science* is an anomaly, an attempt to amalgamate two essentially different views of nature (see chapter 13).

The creation-science legislation of Arkansas Act 590 offered a false choice between two packages, based on an oversimplification of "creation" versus "evolution." For example, many evangelical Christians hold *both* one of the creation-science items listed in the act ("sudden creation of the universe, energy and life from nothing") *and* one of the evolution-science items ("explanation of the earth's geology and the evolutionary sequence by uniformitarianism"). The act's either-or formulation ignored the different kinds of creation and evolution, and various possible combinations such as the one just noted.

Origins

Three major questions continue to capture the imagination and stimulate the research of scientists: How did the universe originate? How did life begin? Did humans have nonhuman ancestors?

1. *Origin of the universe.* Astronomer Owen Gingerich has traced the recent development of scientific thought concerning the age of the universe. In the 1920s Einstein's theory of general relativity led to an entirely new method of calculation.[12] It had been discovered that the galaxies are receding at high velocities. Moreover, those farthest away from us are traveling the fastest. Calculations based on their speeds and distances suggest the following scenario. The galaxies were all together at their origin about thirteen billion years ago. Because the distances to remote galaxies cannot be accurately determined, the calculated "age of the universe" lies between nine and seventeen billion years. According to the *big bang* theory, the universe was originally compressed into one comprehensive "primeval atom." Assuming that the laws of nature were the same, physicist George Gamow concluded that the matter in our universe was originally pure energy, which within a few minutes changed into hydrogen. Subsequent collisions built up heavier atoms, and the expansion of the universe was under way.

Understandably, Gamow's theory fails to explain where the original energy came from. Since science generalizes from the continuous and repeatable, the unique creation of a primeval atom or energy-ball constituting the entire universe lies outside the limits of scientific explanation. Further, scientists are interested in the material conditions that are connected to (or "cause") a pattern of events. But creation must have been a "conditionless" event; a theist would say that only God existed. Creation was unconditioned; it occurred by God's free choice. Therefore, we have no way by theory or experience to duplicate the "original conditions." Where that cannot be done, we cannot predict events and see whether they recur under the same conditions—and therefore we are no longer doing science. Nevertheless, most astronomers now favor this "evolutionary" view of the universe expanding from an initial, highly compressed state. The widespread interest in the theory is due mainly to its essential contribution to understanding the present structure of the universe.

Because the big bang theory views the formation of atoms within minutes or even seconds, yet leaves the prior origin of the energy unaccounted for, many Christians have seized on it as a "scientific proof" for creation. Evidently they have not learned from the Copernican conflict the consequences of linking biblical teaching to a particular scientific hypothesis. The Genesis 1 account of creation was not intended to teach *how* or *when* God created the universe—or to become linked to *any* transitory scientific theory. The Bible clearly affirms, "By faith we understand that the universe was formed at God's command" (Heb 11:3).

2. *Origin of life.* The question of how life began is one of life's oldest puzzles. Is it possible for nonliving material simply to become living? Or is some outside "vital" force necessary? The question of *abiogenesis* (living organisms from nonliving matter) seems accessible to scientific research, since investigation begins with materials already in existence. Although some progress has been made, biologist Thomas Emmel offers a note of caution: "Probably more words have been written on the origin of life by scientists with fewer facts and direct evidence at hand than any other topic in biology."[13]

In recent decades a variety of methods have indicated that the earth is about five billion years old, give or take a few million. That figure was confirmed to a remarkable degree by analyses of rocks and dust brought back from the moon by Apollo 11. Obviously such a great age provides at least the *time* necessary for evolution, which the creation-science figure of a few thousand years would not.

Since the mid-1950s, systems have been devised to irradiate mixtures of simple gases (such as methane, ammonia and water vapor) to form amino acids, simple peptides and carbohydrates. The more complex proteins and nucleoproteins, which are important in the development and maintenance of life, have not yet been synthesized under such conditions. Two different approaches are possible to produce such compounds. One procedure tries to duplicate the conditions in which we imagine that living organisms first occurred; it irradiates simple solutions and hopes for random combinations. The second procedure uses regular laboratory methods to synthesize proteins and nucleoproteins, and then tries to place them in their correct structural relationship. A combination of such compounds with nucleic acids, lipids and carbohydrates might lead to the formation of a simple viruslike compound that could reproduce, if an artificial solution could be devised to maintain the artificial virus. Although an experimental success might show much about life processes, one could not say from such carefully contrived experiments by intelligent scientists that "chemical evolution," the spontaneous appearance of living organisms in the universe, had actually occurred in that way.

Kerkut has examined the evidence for the assumption that life arose only once and that hence all living things are interrelated. Although that is a useful working hypothesis to provide a simple basis for experimentation, the evidence is not as conclusive as many textbooks claim. Kerkut has also considered the evidence for the view that life has arisen many times through spontaneous generation. A variety of other possibilities has also been suggested in recent years, including the arrival of living material on meteorites. Kerkut concludes: "There is no evidence to show that when life was formed on this earth it was a unique event."[14]

A recent study has evaluated current experimental procedures to effect chemical evolution and the probable existence of the "prebiotic soup" on which most proposals depend.[15] It identifies several critical weaknesses intrinsic to the theory itself, not simply state-of-the-art problems which one can expect to be solved in time. The problem is not so much what we do not know but what we *do* know from three decades of experimental inquiry into life's beginnings. Thus a boundary has slowly emerged between what can be expected from matter and energy left to themselves, and what can be accomplished only through the crucial intervention of an intelligent investigator. Since chemical evolution is a speculative reconstruction of a unique past event, it cannot be tested against nature; that is, it cannot be falsified. No matter how fruitful in suggesting experiments, such a hypothesis at best shows only *one* of the ways life *might* have arisen.

Chemist Charles Thaxton makes a distinction between two kinds of science. *Operation science* deals with recurring phenomena, so its hypotheses can be checked against observations in nature and falsified if they are wrong; *origin science* deals with unique, nonrecurring, nonobservable events of the past. Although a hypothesis for the latter may be considered plausible or implausible on the basis of recurring events, it cannot be tested against the unique event itself. Thaxton repudiates any "God-of-the-gaps" explanations in operation science, yet he regards the special creation of life by an intelligence external to the cosmos as the most plausible of five alternative hypotheses to chemical evolution—which seems increasingly implausible.

After answering several cogent scientific objections to divine creation, Thaxton shows that the problem cannot be solved at the scientific level. It inevitably depends, for everyone, on certain metaphysical presuppositions of one kind or another. The theistic belief that God created life, regardless of the means he used, is ultimately based not on scientific explanation but on confidence in the Bible as God's revelation. Similarly, a strong conviction that divine intelligence had nothing to do with the origin of life is another kind of faith.

3. *Origin of human life.* Although the third question is even closer in time and seems more readily answered, it also faces a radical discontinuity. From the Christian perspective, human beings, whatever their physical similarities to the animals, are uniquely different, created in the image of God with a mandate to govern the earth and with an eternal destiny. The Bible has relatively little to say about God's creation of the universe and life after the account in Genesis 1, but in Genesis 2 and 3 it focuses on the creation and moral responsibility of humankind, followed by the entry of sin and its consequences. The remainder of the Bible develops the drama of God's redemptive activity in the arena of history, his mighty acts of judgment and mercy that lead to the mission of Christ and culminate in the re-creation of a new heaven and earth. Consequently the origin and nature of humanity have been a crucial issue in controversies over biblical theology and biological evolution.

The scientific evidence advanced for the evolution of *Homo sapiens* over a long period of time lies in an incomplete fossil record. Human-like groupings range from Cro-Magnon (50,000 years ago) and Neanderthal (80,000) to Zinjanthropus (1,750,000). Geologist Donald Eckelmann concludes that humanity has a long, continuous history going back several million years.[16] Such a statement raises a question: What do we mean by human? In that regard the role of investigators and their presuppositions are crucial. Unlike the origin of the universe and life, this question has immediate consequences for the meaning, values and purpose of an individual's life. Much is at stake for our lifestyle and destiny. Here the relationship between the knower and knowledge is particularly intimate; an investigator's view of what is human cannot help but affect his or her conclusions about when human life began.

Biologist Jan Lever has reviewed the evidence for human evolution and the questions it raises for the interpretation of Genesis. After considering alternative ways of relating the scientific and biblical approaches to the origin of human life, he concludes: "How the operation of the origin of man took place is not revealed to us in Scripture. Also science is not able to answer the question."[17] The problem is more complicated than initially imagined since neither the book of Scripture nor the book of nature yields the answers we seek. Nevertheless, that ambiguity should not obscure the fact that man and woman were created by God with the purpose and implications for human life clearly taught in the Bible. To that point science cannot speak, even though so eminent a paleontologist as George Gaylord Simpson has declared, "Man is the result of a purposeless and materialistic process that did not have him in mind. He was not planned."[18] Such statements should be recognized for what they are—not science but a philosophy of evolutionism expressing its kind of faith.

Our continuing study of this problem will be made more fruitful by using clearly defined terms and by avoiding as much as possible three commonly used phrases that combine theological and scientific concepts. First, as already noted, "creation-science" attempts to make the scientific data fit a model derived from one particular interpretation of Genesis 1.[19] A second approach, "progressive creation," reverses the procedure by trying to make an interpretation of the biblical narrative harmonize with a developmental scientific theory. (The adjective *progressive* is added because the word *creation* has picked up such a strong "young earth" connotation.) These two views assume a jigsaw-puzzle model in which theology and science contribute pieces to the same picture.

A third view, "theistic evolution," adds an adjective to negate any atheistic connotations of the word *evolution*. This designation implies acceptance of the theory of evolution as a mechanism that God may have used in the development of life. Although somewhat less a hybrid of theological and scientific concepts, the term still has the disadvantage of appearing to mix the two. To some ears it sounds as meaningless as theistic relativity or theistic gravitation.

The fact is that informed theists disagree on scientific questions and informed scientists disagree on theism. We have already examined a conflict between theistic scientists on opposite sides of the Copernican fence. Today many biblical Christians—like many nontheistic scientists—accept the theory of evolution, but others do not. The issues seem to remain in clearer focus when scientific and theological terms are not mixed. It should suffice to say, "I accept the biblical accounts of creation and the scientific theory of evolution." (The only problem with such a position is that extremists on *both* sides of the so-called creation-evolution controversy will argue that it is impossible. Sometimes that seems to be the one point on which they can agree.)[20]

Genesis 1 and 2

So far our theological discussion of creation has centered on Genesis 1, where most attempts to correlate the Bible with modern science concentrate. Rare is the conservative scholar who attempts to harmonize the first two chapters, much less bring Genesis 2 into line with the latest geological explanations of the earth's history. Yet if a sequence of creation events must be taken as strictly chronological, how does Genesis 2 (earth and heavens [vv. 4-6], man [v. 7], plants [v. 10], living creatures [v. 19] and finally woman [vv. 20-23]) harmonize with the sequence in Genesis 1? Some commentators do try to explain how all the events of the last half of chapter 2 fit into the sixth day of chapter 1, but at considerable cost to exegetical credibility.

At a more basic level, why should the second account be subordinated to the first any more than John's Gospel to the chronology of Mark? Sound biblical interpretation must take the passages on their own merits in light of their literary style and teaching purpose, however different they may be.

A study of the two accounts shows several significant differences.[21] (1) Without exception, Genesis 1 uses the word *God* while Genesis 2 refers to the Creator as *the LORD God.* (2) A clear, strictly symmetrical structure marks the first account; the story in the second has no such divisions in its warmer and more lively style. (3) As noted above, the two report significantly different sequences of events. (4) The two accounts distinctly differ in the way they describe creation: Genesis 1 highlights the *word* with frequent use of the phrase "and God said, 'Let . . .' "; Genesis 2 reports creation through God's *acts,* using words such as "formed . . . planted . . . made to grow." (5) The first account deals with the creation of the heavens and the earth; the second is concerned only with the earth and especially a certain garden. (6) In Genesis 1 man and woman are created at the same time; in Genesis 2 man is created first, then other creatures and finally woman. (7) In the first account man and woman are the finale, the apex of the pyramid, but in the second man is the center of a circle as each item is related to him.

What are we to conclude from such differences? In putting the two accounts side by side the writer must have had a purpose in mind other than describing exactly how God created heaven and earth with its inhabitants, including human beings. Therefore it is both futile and misguided for us to try to determine one precise method of creation from these accounts.

Genesis 2 and 3

In both style and content Genesis 2 and 3 form a unit. God's command in 2:17 not to eat from the tree of the knowledge of good and evil introduces an element of moral responsibility and sets the stage for the temptation events of Genesis 3. Adam and Eve take their destiny into their own hands, eat the forbidden fruit and suffer disastrous consequences. From then on, the biblical narratives highlight human sin in its variety and virulence, coupled with God's redeeming actions of judgment and mercy.

What can we say about the "historicity" of the account of the creation of Adam and Eve as founders of the human race? Two comments are in order. First, the popular idea that modern science and evolutionary theory render such a belief untenable is erroneous. Even a thoroughgoing demonstration of the validity of macroevolution would not preclude the possibility of that unique event, any more than our "scientific laws" of physiology rule out Jesus' miraculous conception or resurrection. The most accurate biological description of human development in accordance with evolutionary theory can neither account for nor discount the meaning of human beings made in the image of God, much less our origin. A belief that Adam and Eve existed is not jeopardized by the current dogma that "scientific man" can no longer accept that ancestry.

Equally important is a comment on the theological significance of creation and the Fall. Since *Adam* simply means "the man," to what extent is Adam's sin merely symbolic of all human rebellion against God? Although the Old Testament uses that account very little, New Testament teaching both assumes it and argues from it. Jesus' lineage is traced back to Adam; Jesus uses the principle of Genesis 2:24 as a basis for his teaching on the unity and permanence of marriage. The classic passage, however, is Romans 5:12-21, in which Paul draws a rigorous parallel between Adam and Christ to compare the influence of each and to contrast the results of their actions.[22] In fact, Paul even calls Christ the "last Adam" in his major chapter on the resurrection: "For as in Adam all die, so in Christ all will be made alive. . . . So it is written: 'The first man Adam became a living being'; the last Adam, a life-giving spirit" (1 Cor 15:22, 45). Adam's life, sin and death were as much events to Paul as the life, death and resurrection of Christ.

In the biblical record God's self-revelation appears in historical acts as well as prophetic words. Biblical religion differs from all others as much in the significance of its history as in the uniqueness of its teachings. Any attempt to escape the supposed scientific obsolescence of the Genesis 1—3 events by making them imaginary or mythical at the expense of their actual occurrence undermines the foundation of the biblical revelation within history.

This review of the theological and scientific issues in the current creation-science controversy now brings us to a consideration of how those two perspectives on the natural world can properly be related.

13
CONNECTIONS: THEOLOGY AND SCIENCE

*Happy is the man who can
recognize in the work of today
a connected portion of the work of life,
and an embodiment of the work of Eternity.*
CLERK MAXWELL

I N HIS 1880 ADDRESS TO THE STUDENTS AT YALE DIVINITY SCHOOL, Professor Asa Gray, the eminent Harvard botanist, concluded: "We students of natural science and of theology have very similar tasks. Nature is a complex, of which the human race through investigation is learning more and more the meaning and the uses. The Scriptures are a complex, an accumulation of a long series of records, which are to be well understood only by investigation."[1]

So far in our study we have emphasized the differences that exist between the biblical and scientific perspectives on the natural world. The book of Scripture and the book of nature each have their own languages. Their explanations of the universe serve different though complementary purposes. But in some ways they are also similar. How should the two perspectives be related?

Personal Knowledge

Until recently the popular picture of the objective scientist has prevailed: a researcher, detached and unemotional, methodically solves scientific problems and makes discoveries through cold logic and observation. In reality the situation is radically different. Michael Polanyi—distinguished professor of physical chemistry and philosopher of science—has convincingly argued that all knowledge is personal. All human knowing takes place within a framework (a faith structure) of unprovable commitments that motivate and guide the knower in acquiring knowledge.[2] A person's faith structure includes a wide range of beliefs, from ultimate presuppositions (the universe is orderly) to a mundane confidence (the sun will rise tomorrow). The former must be assumed; the latter is based on sense perception. Also important is one's "tacit knowledge," unseen and inexpressible, which forms a kind of foundation for all other knowledge. A lack of formal proof (certainty) does not mean that faith has no evidence, in either theology or science. Whether ultimate or mundane, faith is not blind; it arises from and is embedded in evidence assimilated from our experience.[3] The main point is that for everyone, in all fields of study—including science—faith is a motivating and unifying component in knowing.

Further, such knowing is not merely a function of the mind focusing on ideas; it is a function of a whole person encountering the totality of human experience. In other words, not just the intellectual but also the emotional, volitional, spiritual and physical dimensions of our being are part of the process. Our knowledge includes events of history and relationships with others as well as observations of physical reality. In this respect scientific knowledge is intensely personal; research is far from being detached and unemotional. The "love of science" is a recurring phrase in Polanyi's writings. From his own experience he affirms that scientists work conscientiously, responsibly and ardently. "Scientists who would suddenly all lose their passion for science and take up instead an interest in [breeding] greyhounds would instantly cease to form a scientific society."[4]

A scientist's faith structure is operative at every stage of research. No one can do science without believing that the scientific method and its presuppositions are fundamentally valid and can be unquestioningly accepted. Polanyi concludes: "We have here an instance of the process described epigrammatically by the Christian Church Fathers in the words: *fides quaerens intellectum,* faith in search of understanding."[5]

For example, a scientist is perplexed by a problem or puzzle as yet unsolved. Belief that a solution can be discovered leads to research. Such faith provides the motivation and courage for long months, even years, of fruitless efforts and frustrating dead ends, as with Kepler wrestling with the orbit of Mars or Galileo perplexed by the problem of acceleration. At last, "certain visions of the truth, having made their appearance, continue to gain strength both by further reflection and additional evidence."[6] Polanyi identifies four phases present in all fields of creative activity: preparation, incubation, illumination and verification. With Copernicus and Newton the illumination came relatively early, but many years passed before verification was achieved.

Scientists persevere in the belief that ultimately the scientific community will recognize what is true in their work. Although each discovery is personal, the validity of a hypothesis is not an individual decision but one made by the community to which scientists are committed.

Commitment in Community

Throughout their careers scientists as well as theologians are personally associated with a community that requires commitment to its tradition and authority. At the outset they become apprentices in order to be trained in the scientific tradition. Polanyi observes that although rules can guide scientific discovery, they are merely *rules of art:* their application requires the exercise of creativity. A precise prescription can manufacture a product, but it does not create a work of art. "Since an art cannot be precisely defined, it can be transmitted only by examples of the practice which embodies it. He who would learn from a master by watching him must trust his example. He must recognize as authoritative the art which he wishes to learn and those of whom he would learn it."[7]

So novices enter the scientific community, where they are given a long, painstaking initiation into its methods and standards. They must claim the ground on which their mentors stand before they can achieve their own independence. At every stage of that process the apprentices are sustained by their faith that nature can be understood and that certain things as yet beyond their understanding are true and valuable. The two legs on which scientific training progresses are *faith* in the whole enterprise and *commitment* to the authority of its leaders.

Not even the last stage takes place in individual isolation. Even when a new discovery initially meets resistance inside (and outside) the scientific community, the researcher recognizes the community's ultimate judgment. From start to finish, scientists' work is characterized by commitment to the community. Eventually they become senior members engaged in evaluating the work of others.

Polanyi draws parallels in law and Christianity. In both there is a community of consciences jointly rooted in the same ideals recognized by all. The community becomes an embodiment of those ideals and a living demonstration of their reality. Those principles and steps are evident in the astronomy of Copernicus and in the leadership of both Moses and Saul of Tarsus.[8] Each was characterized by a "conversion" and lifelong commitment.

Finally, if a scientist's work is valid, it will contain within it the seeds of new truths to be discovered. The theory or law is in touch with reality, and it also points the way to further research. Most complex theories need correction. For example, Copernicus's new model of the solar system retained the ancient, ideal circular orbits until they were replaced by Kepler's ellipses and laws of motion, preparing the way for Newton's discovery of universal gravitation. Likewise, the visions of both Moses in the desert and Saul on the road to Damascus not only brought them into the reality of God's purpose for his people, but also led to new discoveries by those who followed them.

Similarities and Differences
Figure 11 summarizes major ways in which the biblical and scientific approaches to the natural world are similar and different. This chart and the current discussion consider only the physical and biological sciences, not the social sciences; they look at only biblical theology, and not natural theology.

In light of the differences and similarities between the scientific and biblical views of nature, how should they be related? Two models for relating them have been most prominent: the "two-realm" and the

Item	Theology	Natural Science
Subject matter	God, humankind, nature	Forces of nature
Source of information	God's revelation (the Bible, inner experience)	Natural events (observations, experiments)
Purpose of study	Who and why (formal and final causes) (plan and purpose)	How (efficient causes) (mechanisms)
Basic language	Words—everyday speech	Mathematics—technical terms
Method	Hermeneutics (literary interpretation)	Measurement analysis (observation, experiment)
Results	Moral imperative—what *ought* to be	Explanation of what *is*
Validation	Biblical principles, personal experience	Internal consistency, empirical testing
Limitations	Mechanisms not explained	Goals and values not provided
Community of function	Church	Scientific establishment

Figure 11. Theology and Natural Science

"concordist" views, each of which has several varieties.

1. *Two realms.* Most discussions view theology and science as having radically different spheres, jurisdictions or arenas. Although the realms are defined in different ways, they inevitably raise the problem of territorial disputes.

In the thirteenth century, Thomas Aquinas related Aristotle's natural science to reason and Christian theology to faith. According to Aquinas, the scientist uses reason to study the natural world and explain the way it works—which can also provide proofs for the existence of God. By faith the theologian accepts the revealed truths of Christianity, such as the Trinity and Incarnation, which cannot be discovered through reasoning. Unfortunately, in later centuries the Thomistic model was used to support an unwarranted antithesis between reason and faith, which still prevails in current discussion. For example, "science and faith" is commonly used as a label for the difference between science and theology—though both require "reasoning faith" or "trusting reason." Each relies on a method of interaction between hypothesis and observations, whether scientific theory and experimental data or theological doctrine and biblical statements. The Thomistic formulation also led to the "God-of-the-gaps," functioning only in unexplained natural events and eventually restricted largely to the arena of human relationships.

During the nineteenth century, liberal theologians, following Friedrich Schleiermacher and Albrecht Ritschl, defined the two realms as entirely separate spheres. No conflict or encroachment was possible since the supernatural and natural planes of being and acting did not intersect. Such theologians rejected reconciliations like that of James McCosh, who insisted that theology has the right to make metaphysical assertions about nature. They viewed Christianity as essentially an ethical and social teaching arising from and acting on feeling, not knowledge.[9] Some did recognize that since science cannot discover God and his purposes, its strictly causative explanation of nature must be subordinated to religion. However, their redefinition of Christianity bore little resemblance to the biblical teaching that moral and ethical principles are firmly grounded in God's self-revelation through historical and natural events.

Twentieth-century neo-orthodoxy, led by Karl Barth and Emil Brunner, emphasized the transcendence of God and the gulf between divine revelation and the results of human inquiry of any sort, including science. According to that view, theology deals with the infinite God who can be known only through special revelation, in which he takes the initiative. Science makes statements about observable phenomena, deals with the finite and uses a human methodology. Theology and science deal with different realms and so are incommensurate. Although neo-orthodoxy appeared in a variety of versions, several basic beliefs laid the foundation for its wall between theology and science.[10] First, a desire for religious certainty required that theological doctrine not be dependent on the changing results of higher criticism, whether historical or scientific. Second, revelation was thought to provide a different source of knowledge from that of reason and/or sensory experience; therefore it produces different *kinds* of knowledge. Third, neo-orthodoxy supposed that revelation is non-propositional, so that its content escapes rational scrutiny. Fourth, the radical distinction between God and his creation contributed further to an intellectual mapping that placed theology and science in different hemispheres. This approach also tended to reinforce a false antithesis between faith and reason.

The two-realm model, in its various versions, fails to do justice to the biblical revelation and its teaching about the natural world. Theology and science need not be domiciled in adjacent territories with disputed boundaries, separated by a Berlin wall. They should not be assigned to unrelated realms. Theology and science do live in the same world and observe some of the same phenomena.

2. *Concordism.* A second approach, also with various versions, attempts to harmonize the biblical and scientific explanations of nature on the same plane. It assumes that both produce pieces of a jigsaw puzzle that presents a picture of the natural world. For example, the Genesis account of creation is thought by some to provide historical-scientific information by divine revelation to supplement the data gained through geological study. Together the two sources of information are thought to provide an explanation of how the earth has developed since its creation. For example, a recent book interprets Genesis 1 verse by verse with words and phrases explained by and correlated with modern scientific information. A detailed chart and diagram show how neatly the two sources of data fit. The writers state, "It is hoped that this book will encourage Christians in believing that God has communicated basic (and even complex) scientific truths in the non-technical vocabulary of ancient Israel."[11] Theologian Bernard Ramm has described many earlier attempts, including some that endeavored to find "anticipations" of modern science hidden in odd texts and terms.[12]

The concordist approach has several significant flaws. From a hermeneutical standpoint it appears to be a new version of Origen's allegorical method of interpretation. To his literal, moral and spiritual senses of a text was later added an anagogical meaning (see chapter 8). Now we are supposed to look for a fifth, *scientific* sense as well. For example, in addition to other senses of the word *day* in Genesis 1 the concordist model adds a scientific meaning of "geological era," which would have been meaningless to the first hearers—and to everybody else until about two hundred years ago. In this approach biblical interpretation becomes increasingly complicated and potentially fanciful.

The concordist model has other weaknesses. Since scientific explanation is subject to change, it periodically replaces its pieces of the puzzle with others which form a new picture. As a result, the current biblical pieces no longer fit and must be reshaped if they are to contribute to that new picture. In other words, the theological contribution (as long as it may be needed) constantly depends for its validity on the scientific setting. However, despite the concordist assumption that science and theology provide pieces designed for the same puzzle, in reality they belong to different pictures: the impersonal, mathematical mechanism of science contrasts with the biblical portrait of a personal God with plan and purpose for his world.

To change the metaphor, how can two people play a single game of Scrabble with different kinds of language—the numbers of science and the words of the Bible? Since the language of natural science is mathematics (with an alphabet consisting of numbers), the words of biblical everyday language can hardly contribute to a scientific explanation of nature.

The concordist model endeavors to show that the Bible is scientifically accurate. But it fails to consider the question: Whose science? After a long defense of the Ptolemaic system, biblical interpretation was adjusted to accommodate Copernican astronomy. Eventually theology became wedded to Bacon's philosophy of science and the Newtonian world-machine. Then during the nineteenth century history repeated itself; many biblical scholars fought the new biology which challenged that view of science and the world.

George Santayana observed that if we do not learn from the lessons of history, we are doomed to repeat its errors. The concordist approach has yet to learn the self-defeating nature of its program. For many people, the church has never recovered the respect it forfeited by convicting Galileo. Nor has the Genesis account of creation regained the credibility it lost because literalist interpretations have been martialed against the theory of evolution. A theology that weds the science of one generation is likely to find itself a widow in the next.

Perspectives on Nature
The natural world, like the whole of reality, has many facets; it can

be viewed from a variety of perspectives. Among them the biblical and scientific descriptions can be regarded as two distinct but partial views. For example, imagine four individuals—Einstein, Gauguin, Beethoven and King David—standing on a hilltop surveying a magnificent valley bathed in late afternoon sunlight. They admire a pastoral panorama framed by gold-red clouds. Although all are *looking* at the same scene, each *perceives* something different. They agree to represent their perceptions, each in his own medium, then meet to share them with one another. Six months later the four reassemble. Einstein the scientist produces sheets of paper filled with mathematical formulas that scientifically explain the relative motions of the earth and sun, the color of the light and the composition of the clouds. Gauguin the artist holds up a canvas conveying the beauty of the sunset displayed in a variety of brilliant colors. Beethoven the musician passes around the score of his Pastoral Symphony, then asks his colleagues to close their eyes and listen to the recording he has brought along. Finally, David the psalmist sings out, "The heavens declare the glory of God; the skies proclaim the work of his hands" (the opening lines of Psalm 19).

Which is the *best* description? The answer depends on the purpose of the inquirer. If one wishes to go to the moon or launch a space shuttle, Einstein's formulas will prove most helpful. But over the mantle of a fireplace many would rather hang Gauguin's painting. After a very busy day we might prefer to close our eyes and listen to Beethoven's music. To express appreciation and praise of the Creator we would choose the words of David's psalm. Not only does nature have varied facets, but people have many dimensions of experience. Whole-person encounter with a complex environment neither compartmentalizes life nor reduces explanations of nature to one perspective.[13]

In such a *partial-view* model, the biblical and scientific descriptions are complementary perspectives—different kinds of maps for the same terrain (see chapter 9). Their respective limitations are not a matter of territory (as in the two-realm model) but of purpose and methodology. The limits are not boundaries, marked by fences with "No Trespassing" signs, where theologians and scientists stake out and protect their turf. Rather, the self-imposed limitations are inherently required by the kind of description and the language used. (See figure 12. This chart does not show the knowledge of God through inner experience or natural theology.)

Donald MacKay gives the illustration of an electric advertising sign with a running sequence of words.[14] Perched high above the street, hundreds of light bulbs flash on and off to inform viewers that "Things go better with Bongo." Ask an electrician to tell us in technical language what's on the board, and we will hear words like volts, amperes, resistances and switches that explain exactly *how* each lamp flashes at the prescribed time and in sequence. His thorough account of every item and event on the board cannot be considered incomplete—though it does not mention the words of the message and their meaning. For that we must turn to the advertiser who can account for the sign as a whole, the *who* and *why* behind it.

MacKay warns against the prevalent practice of *reductionism,* which attempts to explain a phenomenon on the basis of a single component. Such "nothing-buttery" explains away whatever is not apparent in that component. For example, some say a human being is nothing but a collection of atoms (physics) or a combination of compounds (chemistry) or an animal (biology)—as if the sign in MacKay's illustration were nothing but an electric circuit.

Let us return to our pastoral scene and its observers. Beethoven should not say to Einstein, "You cannot analyze my symphony." In fact, a physicist can give an excellent analysis of the sound produced by each instrument and the whole orchestra in terms of wave lengths, frequencies and decibels. But such a scientific explanation no more gives the meaning of the music than the electrician communicates the message of the sign. In each case the limitation is not territorial but methodological. Each partial view of nature serves its intended purpose and should be appreciated for the specific contribution it makes to our lives. The biblical and scientific perspectives on nature can mutually benefit from interacting with each other as allies with complementary approaches.[15]

The two perspectives often overlap and interact with each other. Their mutual stimulation can be highly productive in the life and research of a scientist. The distinguished nineteenth-century physicist James Clerk Maxwell, for example, combined devout Christian faith and rigorous scientific activity.[16] For him, personal faith in God and commitment to the biblical revelation were profoundly integrated

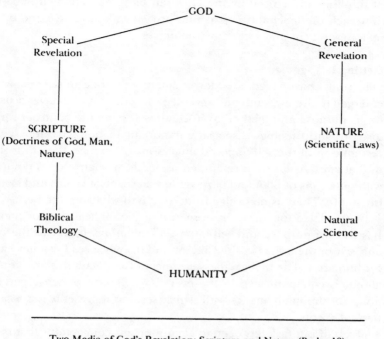

Two Media of God's Revelation: Scripture and Nature (Psalm 19)

Scripture reveals truth about God, man and nature
(main focus of theology: relationship between God and humanity in history)

Nature reveals patterns of events
(main focus of science: discovery of nature's mechanisms)

Figure 12. Connections between Theology and Science

with his scientific understanding. His discovery of the relationship between electricity, magnetism and light, his expression of it in partial differential equations and his concept of the field of electromagnetic force were among the most significant breakthroughs of the period. Maxwell's theological and philosophical concept of *relational thinking* had inspired his scientific imagination, which prepared the way for Einstein, who said of Maxwell's equations, "The formulation of these equations is the most important event in physics since Newton's time, not only because of their wealth of content, but also because they form a pattern for a new type of law."[17] A ruggedly independent way of thinking, influenced by his Christian faith, had enabled Maxwell to breach the mechanistic structure of Newtonian science and open up a new way of understanding the universe.

Getting It Together

Our study has traced the development of modern science as it emerged in the sixteenth and seventeenth centuries. We have focused on its purpose and method as it freed itself from the control of philosophy and theology. Especially important in our scientific age is recognition of the self-imposed limitations of science, the other side of that coin. As Einstein reminded us, modern science does not deal with questions of plan and purpose in nature, or of values and meaning in life. There is no bridge from what *is* to what *ought* to be.

By the same token, we have seen that the biblical view of nature has its own purpose and self-imposed limitations. It reveals the *who* and *why* of the universe, the Creator and his purposes for nature and for humanity. The biblical message, meant for all cultures and generations, is communicated in the everyday language of sense perception, not the mathematics with which science represents the *how* of natural events.

Much of our task has been to clear away misconceptions that complicate the issues, generate unnecessary misunderstanding and waste energy in futile efforts. Our study of how to relate the biblical and scientific views of nature has brought us only to the bottom rung—but at least to a rung on the right ladder. There remains a world of work for philosophers and theologians to do, though they can no longer dictate which scientific theories are acceptable.

Science may have thrown off the yoke of philosophy, but by no means is it free from philosophical presuppositions or analysis of its method and the meaning of its theories and laws. Further, the relationship of natural science to other perspectives on the world, to disciplines in the social sciences, humanities and fine arts, is of continuing concern.

Likewise, theology must provide an evaluation of both science and technology in light of God's command to be stewards of the earth. Biblical studies freed from futile attempts at *doing* science can focus on the broader issues of *using* science (and technology) for the good of humanity and our environment. We also need a full-fledged theology of nature, including not only special revelation in the Bible but general revelation to human senses and reason. Genesis is not the last word on creation but the first statement of a theme carried through Old and New Testaments. To understand creation fully, besides looking back to the beginning we must also look forward to the created world's relationship to Jesus Christ and the new creation he effects. Creation and covenant are integrally related (though traditionally separated); God creates with purposes that gradually become known in historical dealings with his people.

Much Christian theology of nature too long has been a satellite of science. Modern society has placed a scientism with great prestige and power at the center of its intellectual universe. All other disciplines are expected to revolve around it, basking in any light it sheds on them. Theology (once called the "queen of sciences") thus becomes another planet circling the scientific sun. Concordism, constantly trying to harmonize the Bible with the latest scientific theories, surrenders to this scientism. But no amount of adjusting its orbit with hermeneutical epicycles, eccentrics or deferents will make biblical teaching fit a scientific framework. Something like an intellectual "Copernican revolution" is needed to reinstate the biblical view, along with other perspectives, as an independently valid way of representing the natural world.

A Christian cosmogony should not be based on any specific astronomy, ancient or modern, or on some other scientific model of the world. The unique position of humanity depends neither on our home being the center of the universe, nor our origin having occurred in a specific manner, but on the revelation in Scripture that we are created in the image of God and given authority over the earth. When we start with the biblical view of nature—God's creation and preservation of the world—all other perspectives can be appreciated in its light.

Formidable challenges face Christian theology. Yet the ultimate relationship of science and theology, philosophy, the humanities and the arts should be demonstrated not so much in a comprehensive system of thought as in human life. God's self-revelation has taken place in history through acts and words, and it needs to manifest itself in our personal histories. In the last parable of the Sermon on the Mount (Mt 7:24-27), Jesus compared everyone who hears his words and obeys them to the wise person who built a house on a rock so that it could withstand the most violent storms. Biblical theology arises from life situations and speaks to them.

Of the four scientists we have studied, Johannes Kepler reflected most clearly in his research and writing a connection between theology and science that permeated his daily life. He concluded the *Harmonies of the World*, his favorite work, on a note of thanksgiving and praise to God.

I give thanks to Thee, O Lord Creator, who has delighted me with Thy creation. I rejoice in Thy handiwork. Behold! I have now completed the work of my profession. . . . I have demonstrated the glory of Thy works. . . .

My soul, praise the Lord thy Creator, as long as I shall live. . . . To Him be praise, honor and glory, world without end. Amen.[18]

Epilog
BLAISE PASCAL: CHRISTIAN AND SCIENTIST

God of Abraham,
God of Isaac, God of Jacob,
not of the philosophers
and scholars.
BLAISE PASCAL

T HE NEW SCIENCE EMERGED THROUGH THE DISCOVERIES OF MANY brilliant scholars who were committed Christians. In part one we looked at four: Copernicus, Kepler, Galileo and Newton. These men are understandably acclaimed primarily for their pivotal scientific achievements. We turn now to view a historical figure who is remembered as much for his contribution to theology as to science.

Blaise Pascal was born the same year Galileo began writing on his *Dialogue on the Two Principal World Systems*. A man of scientific genius, devout faith and literary skill, Pascal made a unique contribution to modern thought in the way he contrasted the roles of authority in science and theology. His example and teaching, coupled with deep devotion to God and active concern for the poor, provide a model for Christians today who are members of the scientific community.

Early Life

Auvergne in central France is a land of opposites in both climate and texture of life. In a cold country under a southern sky, its people exhibit "a combination of tartness and ardor."[1] Their formal decorum and personal warmth also characterized the personality of Blaise Pascal. For many centuries the provincial capital was Clermont, where in 1095 Peter the Hermit began preaching the First Crusade. After the Reformation a number of Clermont citizens, including the Pascal family, were threatened with persecution because of Protestant leanings.

In 1616, Etienne Pascal and Antoinette Begon were married. Their first child Anthonia died shortly after her baptism. Gilberte was born in January 1620, Blaise in June 1623, Jacqueline in October 1625. Blaise began life as a sickly child who barely survived his infant years. As with Kepler, physical suffering also marked his mature years, bringing periods of painful incapacity interspersed with bursts of strenuous activity.

Antoinette Pascal died in 1625, leaving her husband to raise the three young children. Etienne personally undertook the education of his son in a manner radically different from the scholastic formalism of the day. He encouraged Blaise's natural inquisitiveness and focused his instruction on problems to be solved rather than on blocks of material to be memorized. The father's high standards and flexibility fostered in the son a love of learning, a passion for truth and a habit of careful observation with step-by-step reasoning to reach conclusions.

Scientific Achievements

At the age of eleven Pascal noticed that when a knife struck a dish, it made a noise until touched by his hand. Pascal then conceived and carried out several experiments on sound which he reported in a short essay. That approach was characteristic of his later research on more complicated scientific problems. A respect for all the facts to be accounted for led him to search persistently for the cause by experimenting under a variety of conditions. He always endeavored to formulate a clearly defined, comprehensive principle that could be tested.

At the age of twelve, before any formal study of geometry, Pascal independently discovered and demonstrated Euclid's thirty-two propositions. Four years later he wrote an *Essay on Conic Sections*. His novel use of projection in what became known as the Pascal Theorem opened up a new branch of mathematical investigation. In the essay's conclusions, Pascal's religious faith asserted itself: "If this matter be deemed worthy of further consideration, we shall attempt to push it to whatever point God shall give us strength to carry it."[2]

Pascal's genius moved in very practical directions. At seventeen he conceived and started constructing a calculating machine to lighten his father's burden as a provincial bureaucrat. He persevered for five years and succeeded after trying fifty models. This practical bent may have kept him from becoming overly abstract in either science or theology.

Pascal's mathematical achievements included important work on the calculus of probability. He was able to reconcile the rigor of scientific logic and the uncertainty of probability (which seem contrary) in a mathematics of chance which prepared the way for Newton's binomial theorem and Leibniz's integral calculus.

Pascal also worked out the equation for the cycloid—the curve described by a point on the circumference of a wheel rolling in a straight line.[3] Others before him, including Galileo, had investigated the properties of that figure. In 1658, after a long period of withdrawal from mathematics because of his pressing religious concerns, Pascal returned to that problem, submitting his solution to a competition. He published his conclusions in the form of letters, one of which stimulated Leibniz to invent the calculus. According to science historian Alexandre Koyré, "the subtlety, ingenuity and virtuosity displayed by Pascal in these writings is dazzling."[4]

As an experimental physicist, Pascal is best known for his research on the vacuum. The axiom of Aristotle that a vacuum anywhere in nature is impossible persisted through the Middle Ages and was prevalent among seventeenth-century scientists. Galileo's pupil Torricelli had performed experiments with mercury in a tube that reopened the question of a possible vacuum. When news of the experiment reached Pascal, he began a series of experiments with tubes and siphons of different sizes, filled with other liquids, at various altitudes. Pascal's experiments of 1648, carried out by others because of his illness, demonstrated that the liquids were held up by atmospheric pressure from the outside. His conclusion, based on research documented with precise procedures, exact measurements and carefully organized data, was accompanied by logical arguments and suggestions for further experiments and practical applications.

In the lucid, vivacious style of Bacon and Galileo, Pascal took his opponents to task. He urged the disciples of Aristotle to collect the profoundest writings of their master to try to attribute Pascal's results to nature's abhorrence of a vacuum: "If they cannot, let them learn that experiment is the true master to be followed in physics. . . . No matter what influence this antiquity has had, the truth must always prevail even though it is newly discovered."[5] Pascal was never able to finish his *Treatise on the Vacuum,* but his preface clearly shows how much he valued experimental knowledge. He was also intensely interested in such practical applications of his discoveries as the barometer and weather forecasting. He conceived the idea of a hydraulic press, though he had no chance to build it.

Theological Concerns
In January 1646 Etienne Pascal fell on the frozen ground and dislocated his hip. The Deschamps brothers, doctor and surgeon, attended him. They were recent converts to Jansenism, an evangelical theology derived from the teaching of Augustine and adapted to the seventeenth century. At age twenty-three and in poor health himself, Blaise Pascal was deeply impressed with their concern for both physical and spiritual suffering. In a "first conversion" Pascal resolved to turn from a worldly life to one of piety. That did not mean giving up his scientific studies, but only a pursuit of them merely for his own enjoyment.

Pascal developed a growing interest in books, including the Bible, with which the Jansenist doctrinal views were closely bound. As a Catholic, he came to the Scripture through the teaching of Augustine and used the Latin Vulgate edition, which he often quoted from memory. Soon the Bible became his most important reading as he resolved to give first place in his life to the God of Jesus Christ. The laboratory became an upper room in which the Bible held the place of honor.

The authority of the Bible was confirmed to Pascal by the harmony between the Jansenist interpretation and his scientific activity. His experimental science was based on the uniformity of nature and the possibility of prediction. Pascal recognized that such a conviction was grounded in the immutability of God. From that time on, Pascal was filled with both enthusiasm for science and zeal for religion. He set to work with determined energy.

The published results of Pascal's research on the vacuum were attacked by Jesuit Father Noel, who appealed to the authority of Descartes in science and Aristotle in philosophy. Pascal replied with an explanation of correct scientific method. The truth of a hypothesis, he said, depends not on deductive reasoning but on the facts of nature obtained through observation and experiment. At the same time Pascal reaffirmed the authority of a theology based on the teaching of the Bible against those who were launching a naturalistic method in theology. In later years he vigorously opposed innovations imported into theology by the Jesuits. Pascal was a lay Christian who considered theology his business when the cause of Christianity was at stake.

As Pascal's health turned worse, he traveled to Paris to consult the best physicians. For a while he was paralyzed from the waist down; pains in his head and abdomen were almost unbearable. In January 1648 he rarely had an hour without pain, and from March to September his doctors ordered him to give up research. During these trials Pascal searched his conscience in the light of Scripture. In the process he came to see clearly the line between religious and secular truths. One difference he had found in his own experience: "Physical science will not console me for the ignorance of morality in the day of affliction. But the science of ethics will always console me for the ignorance of the physical sciences."[6]

Early in 1656 Port-Royal, the home of Jansenism, came under attack by the Jesuits, who were influential at the Vatican. Pascal entered the controversy on the side of the Jansenists with a series of anonymous letter-pamphlets "to a friend in the provinces." Written with verve, humor and irony, the *Provinciales* ("Provincial Letters") displayed a wealth of imagery drawn from life. Their superb literary style had a lasting effect on French literature. Pascal's realism produced a new type of apologetic that began with a reader's situation and persuasively led him or her to the desired conclusions. Whether his subject was miracles or the vacuum, God's grace or the cycloid, he wrote as one human being talking good sense to another.

Pascal realized that authority plays different roles in religion and science. His remarkable scientific manifesto, the preface to the unpublished *Treatise on the Vacuum,* states that in theology the sole source of truth is the Scriptures and the Fathers, so that we must "confound the insolence of those foolhardy souls who produce novelties in theology." But in matters of the reason and the senses, authority is useless, and we should "pity the blindness of those who rely on authority alone in the proof of physical matters."[7] This striking division of authority helps make sense of many supposed inconsistencies in Pascal's thought.

In the eighteenth *Provincial Letter* Pascal defined his position as a Christian man of science:

> If it relates to a supernatural truth, we must judge of it neither by the senses nor by reason, but by Scripture and the decisions of the Church. If it concerns an unrevealed truth, something within the reach of natural reason, reason must be its proper judge. If it is a question of a point of fact, we must yield to the testimony of the senses, which are the natural judges of such matters.[8]

If a passage of Scripture seems to contradict the senses or reason (scientific explanation), "we must interpret the Scripture, and seek therein another meaning which will be in agreement with the testimony of the senses." Since the Word of God is infallible, and our observations provide reliable information, the two must be in agreement when properly understood. To confirm that principle Pascal quoted both Augustine and Aquinas.

Pascal's view of natural theology was complex. He believed that nature expresses the handiwork of the Creator; God has represented the invisible in the visible. "Nature has some perfections to show that she is the image of God, and some defects to show that it is only His image."[9] But Pascal also believed that God has hidden his truth behind a veil that the study of nature cannot lift. The road to God is not a walk in his garden but a pilgrimage through Scripture and grace. In the *Provincial Letters* and other polemical writing, the Bible plays the primary role since it presents the facts on which Christianity rests. Pascal's authority became the Holy Scriptures interpreted according to the best tradition of the church.

Christian Commitment

In early 1654 Pascal went to Port-Royal for study and spiritual direction. The biblical character of that institution was striking, as prayer and meditation constantly interacted with Scripture. Members of the community tested all teaching and practice by a study of its pages. There Pascal developed his method of exegesis: Explain the Bible by using the Bible; anchor theology in the statement of Scripture. Pascal's devotion to the Bible was inseparable from his love of Christ: "The Scripture has Jesus Christ alone for its object."[10] He both read the Scripture and prayed through it. Pascal summarized wisdom in three words: *listening to God.* Psalm 119 was his favorite, and he knew it by heart.

On the night of November 23, 1654, Pascal had an intense, two-hour religious experience which he recorded on parchment and kept secret. For eight years he took care to sew and unsew it in the lining each time he changed his coat. His *Memorial* was discovered a few days after his death:

FIRE

God of Abraham, God of Isaac, God of Jacob, not of
the philosophers and scholars.
Certitude. Certitude. Feeling. Joy. Peace.
God of Jesus Christ,
  My God and thy God.
  "Thy God shall be my God."
Forgetfulness of the world and of everything, except God.
  He is to be found only by the ways taught in the Gospel.
  Greatness of the soul of man.
  "Righteous Father, the world hath not known Thee,
  but I have known Thee."
  Joy, joy, joy, tears of joy.
                                    .   .   .

Jesus Christ.
I have fallen away: I have fled from Him,
denied Him, crucified Him.
May I not fall away forever.
We keep hold of Him only by the ways taught
in the Gospel.
Renunciation, total and sweet.

Total submission to Jesus Christ and to my director.

Eternally in joy for a day's exercise on earth.

I will not forget Thy word. Amen.[11]

After that experience, Pascal's viewpoint became essentially evangelical and Christocentric, his language that of a prophet and Christian mystic.

Encouraged by the success of the *Provincial Letters,* Pascal determined to write a comprehensive *Apology for the Christian Religion* on a new, entirely biblical basis. Henceforth his greatest desire was to plant the love of Christ in people's hearts. From 1656 until late winter 1658, when he again became seriously ill, Pascal put together a large body of material. Although his *Apology* was never completed, that collection of almost one thousand notes and fragments as well as finished pieces was published as *Pensées* ("Thoughts") in 1670, eight years after his death. Their rich imagery drawn from daily life mirrors the many facets of Pascal's thought. Both the theological themes and style are fashioned by the Bible.

During the last few years of his life Pascal drafted other works into practically finished shape. When in good health, he was capable of producing a prodigious amount of work. In addition to *Writings on Grace,* his *Abrege,* a short life of Christ, was a pioneering attempt to harmonize the different accounts of the four Gospels. He also wrote two pamphlets designed as textbooks for teaching reading and mathematics at Port-Royal.

Although Pascal's piety was intensely personal, it was not selfish or individualistic; it had a strong social as well as sacramental dimension. His love of God was matched by compassion for the poor, in whom he saw Jesus. "I love poverty, because He loved it. I like wealth because it gives the means whereby to assist the needy."[12] Increasingly Pascal deprived himself in order to give more. He sold his coach and horses, fine furniture and silverware, even his library. In the last months of his life he kept only his Bible, Augustine and a few devotional books.

One day Pascal noticed a crowd of people hurrying in the same direction toward their work and wondered why they should not be transported together by groups. He conceived the idea of the omnibus and helped to form the first bus company. On March 18, 1662, vehicles carrying passengers at five sous a ride started their runs in the streets of Paris. Pascal asked for an advance of one thousand francs, which he sent to the poor of Blois who had suffered severely from the bitter winter. He then signed over his interest in the company to the hospitals of Paris and Clermont.

Pascal integrated his biblical and scientific views of nature—along with his philosophy, inventions and literary works—in a life of increasing devotion to God, whom he loved with all his heart, soul, mind and ebbing strength, and to his neighbors, whom he loved more than himself.

In June 1662, his health deteriorating, Pascal welcomed into his home a family of poor people. Since one of the children had smallpox, the host decided that he, instead of the little boy, should go elsewhere and had himself taken to the home of his brother-in-law.

In mid-August Pascal's strength rapidly waned. On the night of the eighteenth he was seized by convulsions. The priest who attended him administered the holy sacrament and extreme unction. On August 19, 1662, around one o'clock in the morning, Pascal breathed his last. He was only thirty-nine years old.

The funeral rites were celebrated in the Church of Saint-Etienne-du-Mont on August 21. Gathered around the family were friends, scientific colleagues, worldly companions, converts, writers and Christian laymen he had helped. The back of the church was thronged with the poor; hiding among them, risking arrest, were the members of Port-Royal.

Notes

Prolog: The Trial

[1]Jerome J. Langford, *Galileo, Science and the Church* (Ann Arbor: University of Michigan Press, 1971), p. 138.

[2]Giorgio de Santillana, *The Crime of Galileo* (Chicago: University of Chicago Press, 1955), p. 262.

[3]Ibid.

[4]Ibid., p. 241.

[5]Ibid., p. 303.

[6]Ibid., p. 310.

[7]Colin A. Ronan, *Galileo* (New York: G. P. Putnam's Sons, 1974), p. 253.

[8]William R. Shea, *Galileo's Intellectual Revolution: The Middle Period* (New York: Science History Publications, 1971), p. i.

[9]Thomas S. Kuhn, *The Structure of Scientific Revolutions*, 2d ed. (Chicago: University of Chicago Press, 1970), chap. 7, "Crisis and the Emergence of Scientific Theories."

[10]See chapter 5. Galileo was fond of citing the saying of Cardinal Baronius quoted at the head of this chapter—Stillman Drake, *Galileo* (New York: Hill and Wang, 1980), p. 29.

[11]Thomas S. Kuhn, *The Copernican Revolution: Planetary Astronomy in the Development of Western Thought* (Cambridge, Mass.: Harvard University Press, 1957), p. 3.

Chapter 1: Greek Science: Aristotle and Archimedes

[1]Frederick Copleston, *A History of Philosophy*, vol. 1, *Greece and Rome* (London: Burns and Oates, 1961), pp. 22-24.

[2]Ibid., pp. 29-37.

[3]Ibid., p. 266.

[4]G. E. R. Lloyd, *Early Greek Science: Thales to Aristotle* (New York: Norton, 1971), pp. 123-24.

[5]Aristotle, *De Caelo*, trans. J. L. Stocks, vol. 2 of the Oxford translation of Aristotle's works, ed. W. D. Ross (Oxford: Oxford University Press, 1922), chap. 14, p. 179.

[6]D. B. Balme, "Aristotle," in *Dictionary of Scientific Biography*, ed. Charles C. Gillispie (New York: Charles Scribner's Sons, 1981), vol. 1, p. 250. "Aristotle's explicitly stated methodical doubt as a condition for the discovery of truth and his exhaustive accumulation of 'difficulties' *(aporiai)* have trained generation after generation in the art of

testing statements, of analyzing formulations, of trying to avoid sophistry."
[7]Marshall Claggett, "Archimedes," in Gillispie, *Dictionary of Scientific Biography*, vol. 1, p. 213.
[8]R. Hooykaas, *Religion and the Rise of Modern Science* (Grand Rapids: Wm. B. Eerdmans, 1978), p. 76. Even for scientific purposes, manual work, except for medicine, was generally considered beneath the dignity of philosophers.
[9]William Stahl, "Aristarchus of Samos," in Gillispie, *Dictionary of Scientific Biography*, vol. 1. See Owen Gingerich, "Did Copernicus Owe a Debt to Aristarchus?" *Journal for the History of Astronomy* 16 (1985):36-42.
[10]Kuhn, *Copernican Revolution*, p. 80.
[11]Owen Gingerich, "Ptolemy, Copernicus, and Kepler," in *The Great Ideas Today: 1983*, ed. Mortimer J. Adler and John van Doren (Chicago: Encyclopaedia Britannica, Inc., 1983), pp. 142-43.
[12]This precession is caused by the gradual westward movement of the equinoctial points as the earth's axis changes direction to describe a complete cone in about 26,000 years—a motion like the wobble of a top.
[13]G. J. Toomer, "Apollonius of Perga," in Gillispie, *Dictionary of Scientific Biography*, vol. 1.
[14]Rene Taton, "Ptolemy," in Gillispie, *Dictionary of Scientific Biography*, vol. 2.
[15]Gingerich, "Ptolemy, Copernicus, and Kepler," p. 141.
[16]Ibid., p. 139.

Chapter 2: Copernicus: Sun and Earth
[1]Paul W. Knoll, "The Arts Faculty at the University of Cracow at the End of the Fifteenth Century," in *The Copernican Achievement*, ed. Robert S. Westman (Berkeley: University of California Press, 1975), p. 140.
[2]Stephen P. Mizwa, *Nicholas Copernicus* (Port Washington, N.Y.: Kinnikat Press, 1943), pp. 37-38. The family name was spelled in different ways: Koperek, Koprnik, Copernik, and so on. Watzenrode had almost as many variations: Wacqenrod, Wacelrod, Wazelrod.
[3]Ibid., pp. 11, 34. Originally Nikolaj Kopernik, he later used the simplified Latin version Copernicus.
[4]Edward Rosen, trans., *Three Copernican Treatises*, 3d. ed. (New York: Octagon Books, 1971), p. 315.
[5]Alexandre Koyré, *The Astronomical Revolution* (Ithaca, N.Y.: Cornell University Press, 1973), p. 85. The full title was *De hypothesibus motuum coelestium a se constitutis commentariolus;* the date of its writing has been debated. An early date is indicated by the discovery of a catalog of Matthew of Miechow dated 1514 with a reference to this work.
[6]Rosen, *Three Copernican Treatises*, p. 58.
[7]Quoted in Gingerich, "Ptolemy, Copernicus, and Kepler," p. 160.
[8]Rosen, *Three Copernican Treatises*, p. 352.
[9]Ibid., p. 359.
[10]Quoted in Koyré, *Astronomical Revolution*, p. 35.
[11]Quoted in Bruce Wrightsman, "Andreas Osiander's Contribution to the Copernican Achievement," in Westman, *The Copernican Achievement*, pp. 233-43. The full title of the letter was *Ad lectorem de hypothesibus huis operis.*
[12]Ibid., p. 41. Since Osiander was a well-known zealous reformer, the use of his name would have risked the security and acceptance of the work both he and Copernicus desired. The phrasing of *To the Reader* clearly indicates that it was written by someone

other than Copernicus, whose dedication to Pope Paul is labeled "Author's Preface" at the top of each page (but not on the page on which the letter is printed). If anything, Osiander's letter protected *On the Revolutions* from critical scrutiny during a period of intense ideological conflict and permitted its use as a practical manual in the way astronomers were accustomed to treat such hypotheses.

[13]Quoted in Gingerich, "Ptolemy, Copernicus, and Kepler," p. 138.

[14]Kuhn, *Copernican Revolution*, pp. 73-77.

[15]Charles Glenn Wallis, trans., "On the Revolutions of the Heavenly Spheres," in *Great Books of the Western World*, vol. 16, *Ptolemy, Copernicus, Kepler*, ed. Robert Maynard Hutchins (Chicago: Encyclopaedia Britannica, Inc., 1952), pp. 506, 509.

[16]Gingerich, *Did Copernicus Owe a Debt to Aristarchus?* p. 11.

[17]Wallis, "On the Revolutions," p. 509.

[18]Georg Joachim Rheticus, *Narratio Prima*, quoted in Koyré, *Astronomical Revolutions*, p. 31.

[19]Edward Rosen, "Copernicus," in Gillispie, *Dictionary of Scientific Biography*, vol. 3, p. 410.

[20]Owen Gingerich, " 'Crisis' versus Aesthetic in the Copernican Revolution," in *Vistas in Astronomy*, ed. Arthur Beer and Peter Beer (New York: Pergamon Press, 1975), vol. 17, p. 150.

[21]Wallis, "On the Revolutions," pp. 526, 528.

[22]Ibid., pp. 508, 506, 526.

[23]Mizwa, *Nicholas Copernicus*, p. 11.

[24]Quoted in David C. Knight, *Copernicus* (New York: Franklin Watts, 1965), p. 110.

Chapter 3: Kepler: Planetary Orbits

[1]Alfred North Whitehead, *Science and the Modern World* (New York: New American Library, 1949), p. 40.

[2]Kuhn, *Copernican Revolution*, p. 187.

[3]Robert S. Westman, "The Copernicans and the Churches," in *God and Nature: Historical Essays on the Encounter between Christianity and Science*, ed. David C. Lindberg and Ronald L. Numbers (Berkeley: University of California Press, forthcoming).

[4]Kepler, *Mysterium cosmographicum*, quoted in Owen Gingerich, "Johannes Kepler," in Gillispie, *Dictionary of Scientific Biography*, vol. 7, p. 290.

[5]Kepler, *Opera*, bk. 6, quoted in Edwin Arthur Burtt, *The Metaphysical Foundations of Modern Science* (London: Routledge and Kegan Paul, 1959), p. 47.

[6]Kepler, *Mysterium cosmographicum*, quoted in Gingerich, "Johannes Kepler," p. 290.

[7]Doris Hellman, "Tycho Brahe," in Gillispie, *Dictionary of Scientific Biography*, vol. 1, pp. 405-12. Kuhn, *Copernican Revolution*, pp. 201-6.

[8]Kepler, quoted in Gingerich, "Johannes Kepler," p. 295.

[9]Ibid.

[10]Curtis Wilson, "How Kepler Discovered His First Two Laws," *Scientific American* 226 (March 1972), pp. 93-99.

[11]Alexandre Koyré, *Astronomical Revolution*, pp. 263-64.

[12]Kepler, quoted in Gingerich, "Ptolemy, Copernicus, and Kepler," p. 175.

[13]Ibid., p. 299.

[14]Wallis, trans., "The Harmonies of the World," *Great Books*, vol. 5, p. 1009.

[15]Max Caspar, *Kepler*, trans. Doris Hellman (New York: Abelard-Schuman, 1959), p. 26.

[16]Kepler, *Opera*, bk. 8, quoted in Burtt, *Metaphysical Foundations*, p. 57.

[17]Ibid., p. 50.

[18]Gingerich, "Johannes Kepler," p. 307.

[19]Edward Rosen, *Johannes Kepler: Werk und Leistung,* quoted in Gingerich, "Johannes Kepler," p. 293.
[20]Gingerich, "Ptolemy, Copernicus, and Kepler," p. 180.
[21]Caspar, *Kepler,* p. 358.

Chapter 4: Galileo: Physics and Astronomy

[1]Stillman Drake, *Galileo Studies: Personality, Tradition, and Revolution* (Ann Arbor: University of Michigan Press, 1970), pp. 55-59.
[2]Drake, *Galileo,* p. 15.
[3]William R. Shea, *Galileo's Intellectual Revolution* (London: Macmillan, 1972), p. 2.
[4]Stillman Drake, "Galileo Galilei," in Gillispie, *Dictionary of Scientific Biography,* vol. 5, p. 238.
[5]Stillman Drake, *Galileo at Work: His Scientific Biography* (Chicago: University of Chicago Press, 1978), chap. 3.
[6]Ibid., pp. 104-10.
[7]Paul Tannery, "Galileo and the Principles of Dynamics," in *Galileo: Man of Science,* ed. Ernan McMullin (New York: Basic Books, 1967), p. 170.
[8]Drake, *Galileo Studies,* chap. 6, "Galileo, Kepler and Their Intermediaries."
[9]Ibid., "Galileo and the Telescope," chap. 7.
[10]Kuhn, *Copernican Revolution,* pp. 224-25.
[11]Galileo, *The Sidereal Messenger,* trans. E. Carlos (London: Dawson's, 1959), p. 11.
[12]Santillana, *Crime of Galileo,* p. 6.
[13]Drake, *Galileo Studies,* chap. 4, "The Accademia dei Lincei."
[14]Olaf Pedersen, "Galileo and the Council of Trent: The Galileo Affair Revisited," *Journal for the History of Astronomy* 14 (1983), pp. 6-7.
[15]Jerome J. Langford, *Galileo, Science and the Church* (Ann Arbor: University of Michigan Press, 1971), pp. 54-58.
[16]Quoted in Drake, *Galileo at Work,* pp. 224-25. See A. R. Peacocke, *Creation and the World of Science* (Oxford: Clarendon Press, 1979), pp. 3-7.
[17]Quoted in Langford, *Galileo, Science and the Church,* p. 57.
[18]McMullin, *Galileo,* pp. 11-13.
[19]Galileo, *Discourses Concerning Two New Sciences,* quoted in McMullin, *Galileo,* p. 11.
[20]Galileo, *The Assayer,* quoted in Drake, *Galileo,* p. 70.
[21]Dominique Dubarle, "Galileo's Methodology of Natural Science," in McMullin, *Galileo,* pp. 308-10.
[22]A. Rupert Hall, "The Significance of Galileo's Thought for the History of Science," in McMullin, *Galileo,* pp. 73-74.
[23]Galileo, *Opere* 8, quoted in Ernan McMullin, "The Conception of Science in Galileo's Work," in Robert E. Butts and Joseph C. Pitt, eds., *New Perspectives on Galileo* (Dordrecht: D. Reidel Pub., 1978), p. 217.
[24]Ibid., pp. 213-17.
[25]Ibid., pp. 251-52.

Chapter 5: Galileo: Science and Theology

[1]William R. Shea, "Galileo and the Church," in Lindberg and Numbers, *God and Nature,* chap. 4.
[2]Pedersen, "Galileo and the Council of Trent," pp. 16-17.
[3]This quotation from *Letter to Christina* and the others which follow are from Pedersen, "Galileo and the Council of Trent," pp. 17-20.

[4]McMullin, "Introduction," in *Galileo*, pp. 33-35.

[5]Galileo, *Letter to Christina*, Drake, p. 182.

[6]Ibid., p. 185.

[7]Pedersen, "Galileo and the Council of Trent," pp. 2-3.

[8]Bellarmine, *Letter to Foscarini*, trans. Owen Gingerich in "The Galileo Affair," *The Scientific American* (August 1982), p. 137.

[9]*Discorso del flusso e reflusso del mare* ("Discussion Concerning the Flux and Reflux of the Sea"). In his struggle for acceptance of a moving earth Galileo was a better theologian than scientist. For a detailed discussion of this ill-fated theory ("a skeleton in the cupboard of the scientific revolution") see Shea, *Galileo's Intellectual Revolution*, pp. 172-87.

[10]Pedersen, "Galileo and the Council of Trent," pp. 8-11.

[11]Leonardo Olschki, "Galileo's Literary Formation," in Ernan McMullin, *Galileo*, chap. 7.

[12]Stillman Drake, "The Scientific Personality of Galileo," in *Galileo Studies*, chap. 3.

[13]R. Morris, *Dismantling the Universe: The Nature of Scientific Discovery* (New York: Simon and Schuster, 1983), pp. 94-98.

[14]Santillana, *Crime of Galileo*, p. 174.

[15]Drake, *Galileo*, p. 19.

[16]The problem of the "false injunction," how and when it was inserted into the files, has been vigorously debated. For differing views see Santillana, *Crime of Galileo*, chap. 8, and Ludovico Geymonat, *Galileo Galilei*, trans. Stillman Drake (New York: McGraw Hill, 1965), app. A.

[17]Quoted in Santillana, *Crime of Galileo*, pp. 292-93.

[18]Ibid., p. 312.

[19]Ibid., p. 324, n. 3.

[20]Ronan, *Galileo*, p. 213.

[21]Santillana, *Crime of Galileo*, pp. xii-xiii.

[22]Quoted in Drake, *Galileo*, p. 92.

[23]Quoted in Geymonat, *Galileo Galilei*, p. 201.

Chapter 6: Newton: Universal Gravitation

[1]The main sources for the details of Newton's biography are Richard S. Westfall, *Never at Rest: A Biography of Isaac Newton* (Cambridge: At the University Press, 1981); I. B. Cohen, "Isaac Newton," in Gillispie, *Dictionary of Scientific Biography*, vol. 9; and Alexandre Koyré, *Newtonian Studies* (Cambridge, Mass.: Harvard University Press, 1965).

[2]I. Bernard Cohen, "Newton's Discovery of Gravity," *Scientific American* 244:3 (March 1981), pp. 167-79.

[3]Quoted in Koyré, *Newtonian Studies*, p. 224. Chapter 5 traces the controversies between the two men from 1672-1680 with excerpts from their correspondence. Page numbers inserted after quoted material on pages 134 to 135 refer to Koyré.

[4]Cohen, "Isaac Newton," pp. 81-83.

[5]Hooke, quoted in Koyré, *Newtonian Studies*, pp. 229-30.

[6]Cohen, "Newton's Discovery of Gravity," p. 169.

[7]Kuhn, *Copernican Revolution*, p. 256.

[8]Westfall, *Never at Rest*, pp. 202-4.

[9]Newton, *Correspondence 2*, quoted in Westfall, *Never at Rest*, p. 205, n. 11.

[10]Cohen, "Isaac Newton," pp. 68-69.

[11]Newton, "Principia," in *Newton's Philosophy of Nature: Selections from His Writings*, ed.

H. S. Thayer (New York: Hafner Press, 1953), p. 10.

[12]Newton, *Opticks*, Query 31, "The Method of Analysis," quoted in Robert Palter, "Newton and the Inductive Method," in *The Annus Mirabilis of Sir Isaac Newton 1666-1966*, ed. Robert Palter (Cambridge, Mass.: The M. I. T. Press, 1967), p. 246.

[13]Palter, *Annus Mirabilis*, p. 244. This method was stated explicitly by Huyghens in the preface to his *Treatise on Light* (1690). Newton and Huyghens used both methods, sometimes in a single investigation.

[14]Newton, *Letter to Cotes*, quoted in Koyré, *Newtonian Studies*, pp. 37-38. Chap. 2, "Concept and Experience in Newton's Thought," has an excellent discussion of "hypothesis" in its varied usage.

[15]Newton, *Mathematical Principles of Natural Philosophy*, book 3, "General Scholium," trans. Andrew Motte, revised, Florian Cajori, in Hutchins, *Great Books*, vol. 34, p. 371.

[16]Newton, *Letter to Bentley*, Thayer, p. 53.

[17]Frank E. Manuel, *The Religion of Isaac Newton* (Oxford: At the Clarendon Press, 1974), pp. 9-10.

[18]Newton, *Observations upon the Prophecies of Daniel, and the Apocalypse of St. John* (London, 1733), quoted in Cohen, "Isaac Newton," p. 81.

[19]Newton, *Keynes MS*, "The First Book Concerning the Language of the Prophets," quoted in Cohen, "Isaac Newton," p. 82.

[20]Newton, *Yahuda MS*, quoted in Manuel, *Religion of Isaac Newton*, pp. 48-49.

[21]Westfall, *Never at Rest*, pp. 312-18.

[22]Newton, *Principles*, in Hutchins, *Great Books*, vol. 34, pp. 369-70.

[23]Newton, *Yahuda MS*, quoted in Manuel, *Religion of Isaac Newton*, p. 22. Newton, in the British voluntaristic tradition, tended to subordinate God's intellect to his will; above his wisdom and knowledge are his power and dominion. For Galileo, a perfect God had perfect knowledge; for Newton, perfection entailed the constant activity of the divine will.

[24]Newton, in *The Correspondence of Isaac Newton* (Cambridge: At the University Press, 1959-77), vol. 3, p. 233.

[25]Newton, *Keynes MS*, quoted in Manuel, *Religion of Isaac Newton*, p. 28.

[26]Cotes, preface to Newton, *Mathematical Principles of Natural Philosophy*, trans. Andrew Motte, revised, Florian Cajori (Berkeley: Univ. of Calif. Press, 1934), p. xxxii.

[27]Edward B. Davis, Jr., "Creation, Contingency, and Early Modern Science: The Impact of Voluntaristic Theology on Seventeenth Century Natural Philosophy" (Ph.D. diss., Indiana University, 1984), p. 234.

[28]Quoted in Westfall, *Never at Rest*, p. 863.

Chapter 7: Modern Science: A New Perspective

[1]Frederick Copleston, *A History of Philosophy*, vol. 2, *Medieval Philosophy* (London: Burns and Oates, 1964), pp. 324-35.

[2]Newton, *Principles*, Book 3: "System of the World," quoted in Burtt, *Metaphysical Foundations*, pp. 218-19.

[3]William C. Dampier, *A History of Science* (Cambridge: At the University Press, 1961), p. 125.

[4]Charles S. Peirce, *Collected Papers*, vol. 1, p. 171, quoted in Norwood Hanson, *Patterns of Discovery* (Cambridge: At the University Press, 1961), pp. 85-86: "Deduction proves that something *must be;* Induction shows that something *actually* is operative; Abduction merely suggests that something *may be*. . . . A man has a certain Insight. . . . Perceptive Judgment."

[5]Gerald Holton, "Mainsprings of Scientific Discovery," in *The Nature of Scientific Discovery*, ed. Owen Gingerich (Washington: Smithsonian Institution Press, 1975).

[6]Norwood Hanson, *Patterns of Discovery* (Cambridge: At the University Press, 1961), pp. 72-84.

[7]Kuhn, *Structure of Scientific Revolutions*, p. 10.

[8]Enrico Cantore, *Scientific Man* (New York: Institute for Scientificc Humanism, 1977), pp. 225-35.

[9]Koyré, *Newtonian Studies*, p. 7.

[10]Stanley L. Jaki, *Cosmos and Creator* (Edinburgh: Scottish Academic Press, 1980), pp. 54-55.

[11]Andrew Dickson White, *A History of the Warfare of Science with Theology in Christendom* (New York: Dover Publications, 1960), vol. 1, back cover.

[12]See Stanley L. Jaki, *The Road of Science and the Ways to God* (Chicago: University of Chicago Press, 1978).

[13]M. B. Foster, "The Christian Doctrine of Creation and the Rise of Modern Natural Science," *Mind* 43 (1934): 446-68.

[14]W. Jim Neidhardt, *The Open-Endedness of Scientific Truth* (Hatfield, Pa.: Interdisciplinary Biblical Research Institute, 1983).

[15]John Calvin, *Institutes of the Christian Religion*, ed. John T. McNeill (Philadelphia: Westminster Press, 1960), vol. 1, pp. 273-74.

[16]John Calvin, *Commentaries on the Book of Genesis*, ed. John King (Grand Rapids: Wm. B. Eerdmans, 1981), pp. 86-87.

[17]John Dillenburger, *Protestant Thought and Natural Science* (Garden City, N.Y.: Doubleday, 1960), pp. 37-38.

[18]Charles Webster, "Puritanism, Separatism, and Science," in Lindberg and Numbers, *God and Nature*, chap. 7.

[19]Margaret Jacob, "Christianity and the Newtonian World View," in Lindberg and Numbers, *God and Nature*, chap. 9.

Chapter 8: Interpreting the Bible

[1]Francis Bacon, *Essays, Advancement of Learning, New Atlantis, and Other Pieces*, ed. R. F. Jones (New York: Odyssey, 1937), p. 179.

[2]Bernard Ramm, *Special Revelation and the Word of God* (Grand Rapids: Wm. B. Eerdmans, 1961), pp. 77-83. "Only in the web of event and interpretation, history and meaning, meeting and conversation is there significant meaning" (p. 79).

[3]Bruce Milne, *Know the Truth* (Downers Grove, Ill.: InterVarsity Press, 1982), p. 28.

[4]Ian G. Barbour, *Issues in Science and Religion* (Englewood Cliffs, N.J.: Prentice-Hall, 1966), pp. 217-18. Cf. Barbour, *Myths, Models and Paradigms* (New York: Harper and Row, 1974), pp. 12-18, 49-70.

[5]Malcolm A. Jeeves, *The Scientific Enterprise and Christian Faith* (Downers Grove, Ill.: InterVarsity Press, 1969), pp. 74-78.

[6]See K. A. Kitchen, *The Bible in Its World: The Bible and Archaeology Today* (Downers Grove, Ill.: InterVarsity Press, 1977); F. F. Bruce, *The New Testament Documents: Are They Reliable?* (Downers Grove, Ill.: InterVarsity Press, 1960).

[7]IVCF *Constitution and By-laws*, Madison, Wisc.

[8]I. H. Marshall, *Biblical Inspiration* (Grand Rapids: Wm. B. Eerdmans, 1982), p. 91.

[9]Gordon D. Fee and Douglas Stuart, *How to Read the Bible for All Its Worth* (Grand Rapids: Zondervan, 1982), pp. 15-17.

[10]Ibid., p. 20. This book provides special guidelines for interpreting ten biblical literary

forms.

[11]J. I. Packer, "Infallible Scripture and the Role of Hermeneutics," in *Scripture and Truth*, ed. D. A. Carson and John D. Woodbridge (Grand Rapids: Zondervan, 1983), pp. 325-60. See A. Thiselton, *The Two Horizons* (Grand Rapids: Wm. B. Eerdmans, 1980).

[12]Origen, quoted in *The History of Christianity* (Tring, England: Lion Publishing, 1982), p. 102.

[13]The apostle Paul used allegorical interpretation sparingly (1 Cor 10:1-4; Gal 4:21-31), but Origen evidently got carried away and stressed the method.

[14]H. C. Blackman, *Biblical Interpretation* (Philadelphia: Westminster Press, 1951), p. 111.

[15]James W. Sire, *Scripture Twisting* (Downers Grove, Ill.: InterVarsity Press, 1980). The author presents twenty ways that cults misread the Bible.

[16]Hooykaas, *Religion and the Rise of Modern Science*, pp. 7-16.

[17]Bernard Ramm, *The Christian View of Science and Scripture* (Grand Rapids: Wm. B. Eerdmans, 1955), chap. 11.

[18]John Calvin, *Commentary on Psalms* (Grand Rapids: Wm. B. Eerdmans, 1981), vol. 5, pp. 184-85.

[19]J. W. Dawson, quoted in Ramm, *Christian View*, p. 70.

Chapter 9: Miracles and Scientific Laws

[1]Ernest Nagel, *The Structure of Science* (New York: Harcourt, Brace, 1961), pp. 20-26.

[2]Hanson, *Patterns of Discovery*, chap. 1.

[3]Henry Margenau, *The Nature of Physical Reality* (New York: McGraw-Hill, 1950), p. 28.

[4]Karl R. Popper, *The Logic of Scientific Discovery* (New York: Science Editions, 1959), chap. 4, "Falsifiability."

[5]Nagel, *Structure of Science*, pp. 75-78.

[6]Cohen, "Newton's Discovery of Gravity," p. 167.

[7]Einstein, quoted in Gerald Holton, "Einstein's Model for Constructing a Scientific Theory," in *Albert Einstein: His Influence on Physics, Philosophy and Politics*, ed. Peter C. Aichelburg and Roman U. Sexl (Wiesbaden: Friedr. Vieweg Sohn, 1979), pp. 121-25.

[8]E. L. Mascall, *Christian Theology and Natural Science* (London: Longmans, Green, 1957), p. 58.

[9]Karl R. Popper, *Conjectures and Refutations* (New York: Harper and Row, 1965), chap. 3, "Three Views Concerning Human Knowledge."

[10]William H. Watson, *Understanding Physics Today* (Cambridge: At the University Press, 1963), p. 32. See P. W. Bridgman, *The Logic of Modern Physics* (New York: Macmillan, 1961), "From the point of view of operations, light means nothing more than *things lighted*" (p. 51).

[11]Stephen Toulmin, *The Philosophy of Science* (New York: Harper and Row, 1953), chap. 3, "Theories and Maps."

[12]Barbour, *Issues in Science and Religion*, chap. 6, "The Methods of Science."

[13]Aristotle, quoted in Hooykaas, *Religion and the Rise of Modern Science*, p. 6. See chap. 1, "God and Nature."

[14]Johann H. Diemer, *Nature and Miracle* (Toronto: Wedge, 1977), pp. 12-16.

[15]This view of God's continuing creative activity should not be confused with the unbiblical philosophical view of "continuous creation" or with the extreme kind of process theology which teaches that God himself is evolving or developing with the world.

[16]See also Job 12:7-9; 39—41; Psalm 107:25-31.

[17]Donald M. MacKay, *The Clockwork Image* (Downers Grove, Ill.: InterVarsity Press, 1974),

p. 60; MacKay's emphases.

[18]Milne, *Know the Truth*, p. 74.

[19]Colin Brown, *Miracles and the Critical Mind* (Grand Rapids: Wm. B. Eerdmans, 1984), p. 292.

[20]The term *force* has different meanings in various fields. It is used here in a general sense to mean the manifestation of fundamental interactions.

[21]C. S. Lewis, *Miracles* (New York: Macmillan, 1947), p. 72.

[22]Malcolm A. Jeeves, *The Scientific Enterprise and Christian Faith* (Downers Grove, Ill.: InterVarsity Press, 1969), pp. 32-34.

[23]James M. Houston, *I Believe in the Creator* (Grand Rapids: Wm. B. Eerdmans, 1980), p. 102.

Chapter 10: Genesis One: Origin of the Universe

[1]Henri Blocher, *In the Beginning* (Downers Grove, Ill.: InterVarsity Press, 1984), pp. 31-33.

[2]N. H. Ridderbos, *Is There a Conflict between Genesis 1 and Natural Science?* (Grand Rapids: Wm. B. Eerdmans, 1957), p. 10.

[3]Adrio König, *New and Greater Things: A Believer's Reflection*, part 3, "On Creation," trans. D. Ray Briggs, unpublished ms., pp. 14-18.

[4]Conrad Hyers, *The Meaning of Creation: Genesis and Modern Science* (Atlanta: John Knox Press, 1984), "The Plan of Genesis 1," pp. 67-71. The author identifies three fundamental problems confronting the establishment of an orderly cosmos: darkness, watery abyss and formless earth, which find their solutions on days one to three, respectively, of *preparation* followed by days four to six of *population*.

[5]Gerhard von Rad, *Genesis* (Philadelphia: Westminster Press, 1961), p. 46.

[6]Since our Western approach is *analytical* (dividing into parts and exploiting small differences), we must recognize that Hebrew thought is *synthetic* (appreciating the whole with its facets). Hence the frequent use of synonyms and parallelism—saying the same thing in different ways. We should resist the temptation to make technical terms out of popular language.

[7]Milne, *Know the Truth*, p. 78.

[8]Compare Deuteronomy 32:10; Job 6:18; 26:7; Isaiah 24:10; 34:11; 45:18.

[9]A. Heidel, *The Babylonian Genesis*, 3d ed. (Chicago: University of Chicago Press, 1963), pp. 90, 100.

[10]Gerhard F. Hasel, "The Polemic Nature of the Genesis Cosmology," *The Evangelical Quarterly* 46 (1974), pp. 81-84. "No god rises out of *tehom* to proceed with creation nor is *tehom* a pre-existent, personified Ocean as Nun in Heliopolitan theology" (p. 85).

[11]See *Theological Dictionary of the Old Testament*, vol. 1, ed. G. J. Botterweck and Helmer Ringgren (Grand Rapids: Wm. B. Eerdmans, 1974), pp. 328-45.

[12]Hasel, "Polemic Nature," pp. 78-80. The author lists six characteristics of this passage as an antipapal polemic.

[13]Davis A. Young, *Christianity and the Age of the Earth* (Grand Rapids: Wm. B. Eerdmans, 1982). Part One, pp. 1-67, traces the history of thought regarding the age of the earth from the early Greeks through church history to the twentieth century.

[14]Ramm, *The Christian View of Science and Scripture*, chap. 4, pp. 171-79, presents a detailed historical account and critique of each theory.

[15]Calvin, *Commentary on Psalms*, vol. 5, pp. 184-85.

[16]J. D. Douglas, ed., *The New Bible Dictionary* (Grand Rapids: Wm. B. Eerdmans, 1979), p. 271.

[17]Laurence Urdang, ed., *The Random House Dictionary of the English Language*, college ed. (New York: Random House, 1968), p. 48.

[18]Von Rad, *Genesis*, p. 57.

[19]P. J. Wiseman, *Creation Revealed in Six Days* (London: Marshall, Morgan and Scott, 1948), pp. 33-37.

[20]D. F. Payne, *Genesis One Reconsidered* (London: Tyndale Press, 1964), pp. 18-19.

[21]Langdon Gilkey, *Maker of Heaven and Earth: The Christian Doctrine of Creation in the Light of Modern Knowledge* (Garden City, N.Y.: Doubleday, 1965), p. 178.

[22]Richard H. Bube, *The Human Quest: A New Look at Science and the Christian Faith* (Waco, Tex.: Word, 1971), pp. 230-33.

Chapter 11: A Changing World: Geology and Biology

[1]Charles Lyell, *Life, Letters and Journals of Sir Charles Lyell* (London, 1881), vol. 2, p. 5.

[2]James R. Moore, "Geologists and Interpreters of Genesis in the Nineteenth Century," in Lindberg and Numbers, *God and Nature*, chap. 13. See Charles C. Gillispie, *Genesis and Geology* (New York: Harper Torchbooks, 1951), chap. 5.

[3]Gavin DeBeer, "Charles R. Darwin," in Gillispie, *Dictionary of Scientific Biography*, vol. 3, p. 567.

[4]Robert Chambers, *Vestiges of the Natural History of Creation* (New York: Harper and Brothers, n.d.), p. 158.

[5]Charles Darwin, in *Life and Letters of Charles Darwin*, ed. Francis Darwin (New York: D. Appleton & Co., 1887), vol. 1, p. 68.

[6]A. Hunter Dupree, "Christianity and the Scientific Community in the Age of Darwin," in Lindberg and Numbers, *God and Nature*, chap. 14.

[7]Barbour, *Issues in Science and Religion*, pp. 86-90. See John C. Greene, *Science, Ideology and World View: Essays in the History of Evolutionary Ideas* (Berkeley: University of California Press, 1981), chap. 3, "The Kuhnian Paradigm and the Darwinian Revolution in Natural History."

[8]James R. Moore, *The Post-Darwinian Controversies: A Study of the Protestant Struggle to Come to Terms with Darwin in Great Britain and America* (Cambridge: At the University Press, 1979), p. 41.

[9]Ibid., pp. 99-125.

[10]Frederick Gregory, "The Impact of Darwinian Evolution on Protestant Theology in the Nineteenth Century," in Lindberg and Numbers, *God and Nature*, chap. 15.

[11]Dupree, in Lindberg and Numbers, *God and Nature*, chap. 14.

[12]Charles Hodge, *What Is Darwinism?* (New York: Scribner, Armstrong and Co., 1874), pp. 48-51.

[13]Ibid., pp. 60, 134.

[14]Moore, *Post-Darwinian Controversies*, chap. 9.

[15]James McCosh, *The Religious Aspect of Evolution*, 2d ed. (New York: Scribner's Sons, 1890), p. 7.

[16]James McCosh, "Autobiographical Statement," in *The Life of James McCosh*, ed. William Sloane (New York: Scribner's Sons, 1891), p. 234.

[17]Asa Gray, "Natural Science and Religion," in *Is God a Creationist?* ed. Roland Frye (New York: Scribner's Sons, 1983), p. 109.

[18]Ibid., p. 113.

[19]Frederick Temple, *The Relations between Religion and Science* (London: Macmillan and Co., 1885), pp. 122-23.

[20]Moore, *Post-Darwinian Controversies*, chap. 10.

[21]Samuel Phillips, *Agreement of Evolution and Christianity* (Washington, D.C.: The Phillips Co., 1904). See Green, *Science, Ideology, and World View*, chaps. 4, 6.

[22]Mark Noll, "Who Sets the Stage for Understanding Scripture?" *Christianity Today*, 23 May 1980, p. 15.

Chapter 12: The Creation-Science Controversy

[1]Ronald L. Numbers, "The Creationists," in Lindberg and Numbers, *God and Nature*, chap. 16.

[2]G. A. Kerkut, *Implications of Evolution* (New York: Pergamon Press, 1965), p. 157.

[3]Ibid.

[4]Ibid., p. 6.

[5]Quoted in "Panel Two: The Evolution of Life" in *Evolution after Darwin*, ed. Sol Tax (Chicago: University of Chicago Press, 1960), vol. 3, p. 111.

[6]Green, *Science, Ideology, and World View*, chap. 7.

[7]Richard A. Dodge, "Divine Creation: A Theory?" American Institute of Biological Sciences *Education Review* 2 (1973), pp. 29-30.

[8]J. C. Whitcomb, Jr., and H. M. Morris, *The Genesis Flood* (Philadelphia: Presbyterian and Reformed Publishing Co., 1961).

[9]Norman L. Geisler, "Creationism: A Case for Equal Time," *Christianity Today*, 19 March 1982, p. 27.

[10]In Ashley Montagu, ed., *Science and Creationism* (Oxford: At the University Press, 1984), pp. 365-97.

[11]J. C. Whitcomb, Jr., and H. M. Morris, *Journal of the American Scientific Affiliation* 16 (June 1964): 60.

[12]Owen Gingerich, "Let There Be Light: Modern Cosmogony and Biblical Creation," in Frye, *Is God a Creationist?* chap. 8.

[13]Thomas C. Emmel, *Worlds within Worlds: An Introduction to Biology* (New York: Harcourt, 1977), p. 210.

[14]Kerkut, *Implications of Evolution*, p. 17.

[15]Charles B. Thaxton, Walter L. Bradley, and Roger L. Olsen, *The Mystery of Life's Origin* (New York: Philosophical Library, 1984), pp. 202-16.

[16]F. Donald Eckelmann, "Geology," in Bube, *The Encounter*, pp. 146-56.

[17]Jan Lever, *Creation and Evolution* (Grand Rapids: Kregel's, 1958), chap. 5.

[18]G. G. Simpson, *The Meaning of Evolution*, 4th ed. (New Haven: Yale University Press, 1950), p. 262.

[19]Wayne Frair and Percival Davis, *A Case for Creation*, 3d ed. (Chicago: Moody Press, 1983). "We can infer that all changes take place only within boundaries set by the creative hand of God, because the Scriptures teach that organisms reproduce 'after their kind.' . . . There are many biblical reasons for rejecting an evolutionary account of man's origin" (p. 129).

[20]See D. G. Jones, "Issues and Dilemmas in the Creation-Evolution Debate," in *Creation and Evolution*, ed. Derek Burke (Leicester, England: Inter-Varsity Press, 1985), chap. 7.

[21]König, *New and Greater Things*, part 3, pp. 28-39.

[22]Charles E. Hummel, "The Relationship between Adam and Christ in Romans Five" (master's thesis, Wheaton College, 1962).

Chapter 13: Connections: Theology and Science

[1]Asa Gray, "Natural Science and Religion," in Frye, *Is God a Creationist?* p. 117.

[2]Michael Polanyi, *Personal Knowledge* (Chicago: University of Chicago Press, 1958).
[3]W. Jim Neidhardt, "Realistic Faith Seeking Understanding—A Structured Model of Human Knowing," *Journal of the American Scientific Affiliation* 35 (March 1984): 42-45.
[4]Michael Polanyi, *Science, Faith and Society* (Chicago: University of Chicago Press, 1964), p. 68.
[5]Ibid., pp. 45-50. See Thomas F. Torrance, "The Framework of Belief," in *Belief in Science and in Christian Life*, ed. T. F. Torrance (Edinburgh: Handsel Press, 1980), chap. 1. Polanyi's key concern is the creative process in scientific discovery.
[6]Polanyi, *Science, Faith and Society*, p. 30.
[7]Ibid., p. 56.
[8]John Barr, "Conversion and Penitence," in Torrance, *Belief in Science*, pp. 49-52.
[9]Frederick Gregory, "The Impact of Darwinian Evolution," in Lindberg and Numbers, *God and Nature*, chap. 15.
[10]Keith E. Yandell, "Protestant Theology and Natural Science in the Twentieth Century," in Lindberg and Numbers, *God and Nature*, chap. 18.
[11]Robert C. Newman and Herman J. Eckelmann, Jr., *Genesis One and the Origin of the Earth* (Downers Grove, Ill.: InterVarsity Press, 1977), p. 88.
[12]Ramm, *The Christian View of Science and Scripture*, chap. 4.
[13]Vern S. Poythress, "Science as Allegory," *Journal of the American Scientific Affiliation* 35 (June 1983): 65-71.
[14]Donald M. MacKay, *The Clockwork Image*, pp. 36-38.
[15]Bube, *The Human Quest*, chap. 6, p. 125.
[16]Thomas F. Torrance, *Transformation and Convergence* (Grand Rapids: Wm. B. Eerdmans, 1984), chap. 7, "Christian Faith and Physical Science in the Thought of James Clerk Maxwell."
[17]Albert Einstein and Leopold Infeld, *The Evolution of Physics from Early Concepts to Relativity and Quanta* (New York: Clarion, 1938), p. 143.
[18]Kepler, "The Harmonies of the World," trans. Wallis, in *Great Books*, vol. 24, pp. 1080-81. (The translation has been somewhat modernized.)

Epilog: Blaise Pascal: Christian and Scientist

[1]Roger Hazelton, *Blaise Pascal: The Genius of His Thought* (Philadelphia: Westminster Press, 1974), p. 15.
[2]Quoted in Emile Cailliet, *Pascal: Genius in the Light of Scripture* (Philadelphia: Westminster Press, 1945), p. 43.
[3]Rene Taton, "Blaise Pascal," in Gillispie, *Dictionary of Scientific Biography*, vol. 10, pp. 330-34.
[4]Quoted in Hazelton, *Blaise Pascal*, p. 69.
[5]Quoted ibid., p. 62.
[6]Quoted in Cailliet, *Pascal*, p. 69.
[7]Quoted in William B. Ashworth, Jr., "Catholicism and Early Modern Science," in Lindberg and Numbers, *God and Nature*, chap. 5.
[8]Quoted in Cailliet, *Pascal*, p. 273.
[9]Pascal, "Pensées," trans. W. F. Trotter, in Hutchins, *Great Books*, vol. 33, "Pascal," no. 580, p. 276.
[10]Quoted in Cailliet, *Pascal*, p. 290.
[11]Quoted in Emile Cailliet, *Journey into Light* (Grand Rapids: Zondervan, 1968), pp. 95-96.
[12]Quoted in Cailliet, *Pascal*, p. 345.

Author Index

This index can be used as a bibliography. Turn to the page(s) listed below which follow an author's name. On these pages a footnote number will be found. This number refers to a footnote (pp. 277-88) containing the title and all bibliographic data of a book by that author.

Aquinas, Thomas, *103, 104, 151*
Archimedes, *32*
Aristotle, *28, 181*
Ashworth, William B., *272*
Bacon, Francis, *169*
Balme, D. B., *31*
Barbour, Ian G., *168, 187, 228*
Barr, John, *256*
Bellarmine, Robert, *11, 110, 111*
Blackman, H. C., *173*
Blocher, Henri, *202*
Botterweck, G. J., *207*
Bridgman, P. W., *186*
Brown, Colin, *194*
Bruce, F. F., *169*
Bube, Richard H., *219, 262*
Burtt, Edwin Arthur, *63, 76*
Cailliet, Emile, *269, 271-74*
Cajori, Florian, *142*
Calvin, John, *176, 213*
Cantore, Enrico, *157*
Caspar, Max, *74, 79*
Chambers, Robert, *226*
Claggett, Marshall, *32*
Cohen, I. Bernard, *127, 130, 135, 137, 143, 184*
Copernicus, Nicholas, *16,*

44, 46-49
Copleston, Frederick, *24-25, 151*
Cotes, Roger, *145*
Dampier, William C., *155*
Darwin, Charles, *227*
Davis, Edward, *176*
Davis, Percival, *249*
Dawson, J. W., *176*
DeBeer, Gavin, *226*
Diemer, Johann H., *189*
Dillenberger, John, *161*
Dodge, Richard A., *242*
Douglas, J. D., *214*
Drake, Stillman, *83-88, 92, 95, 98, 105-7, 113, 115, 125*
Draper, John, *229*
Dupree, A. Hunter, *228, 231*
Durbarle, Dominique, *99*
Eckelmann, F. Donald, *249*
Einstein, Albert, *185, 263*
Emmel, Thomas C., *246*
Fee, Gordon D., *171*
Foster, M. B., *160*
Frair, Wayne, *249*
Frye, Roland, *232, 253*
Galilei, Galileo, *9-12, 73, 90, 93, 98, 100, 102, 105-7, 113, 115, 120, 124-25*
Geymonat, Ludovico, *116, 125*
Gilkey, Langdon, *218*
Gillispie, Charles C., *225*
Gingerich, Owen, *34, 44, 49, 51, 54, 61, 72, 76, 77, 110, 245*
Gray, Asa, *232, 253*
Greene, John C., *228, 234, 240*
Gregory, Frederick, *230,*

258
Hall, A. Rupert, *99*
Hanson, Norwood R., *155, 182*
Hasel, Gerhard, *207, 209*
Hazelton, Roger, *268*
Heidel, A., *207*
Hellman, Doris, *65*
Hodge, Charles, *231*
Holton, Gerald, *185*
Hooke, Robert, *133, 134*
Hooykaas, R., *32, 161, 174, 189*
Houston, James M., *196*
Hummel, Charles E., *252*
Hutton, James, *225*
Huxley, Julian, *240*
Hyers, Conrad, *205*
Infeld, Leopold, *263*
Jacob, Margaret, *162*
Jaki, Stanley L., *159, 160*
Jeeves, Malcom A., *169, 176*
Jones, R. E., *167*
Kepler, Johannes, *61, 63, 68, 70, 76, 90, 266*
Kerkut, G. A., *239, 247*
Kitchen, K. A., *169*
Knoll, Paul W., *40*
König, Adrio, *203, 251-52*
Koyré, Alexandre, *44, 72, 127, 133, 134, 141, 157*
Kuhn, Thomas S., *16-17, 34, 51, 59, 66, 88, 89, 90, 155-56*
Langford, Jerome J., *11, 94, 96*
Lever, Jan, *225*
Lewis, C. S., *195*
Lloyd, G. E. R., *26*
Lyell, Charles, *225*
McCosh, James, *232*
MacKay, Donald M., *190, 262*

Subject Index